science
YEAR BY YEAR

DK DELHI

Senior Editor Sreshtha Bhattacharya
Project Editor Priyanka Kharbanda
Project Art Editors Pooja Pipil, Neha Sharma
Editors Agnibesh Das, Sonia Yooshing, Deeksha Saikia
Art Editors Tanvi Sahu, Sonali Sharma, Heena Sharma
Assistant Editors Antara Raghavan, Ateendriya Gupta
Assistant Art Editor Priyanka Bansal
Jacket Designer Suhita Dharamjit
Jackets Editorial Coordinator Priyanka Sharma
Senior DTP Designers Harish Aggarwal, Neeraj Bhatia
DTP Designers Jaypal Chauhan, Nityanand Kumar
Senior Picture Researcher Sumedha Chopra
Managing Jackets Editor Saloni Singh
Picture Research Manager Taiyaba Khatoon
Pre-production Manager Balwant Singh
Production Manager Pankaj Sharma
Managing Editor Kingshuk Ghoshal
Managing Art Editor Govind Mittal

DK LONDON

Senior Editor Carron Brown
Senior Art Editor Sheila Collins
Editors Ann Baggaley, Jessica Cawthra, Scarlett O'Hara
Illustrators Jeongeun Park, Dominic Clifford
Jacket Editor Claire Gell
Jacket Designer Mark Cavanagh
Jacket Design Development Manager Sophia MTT
Producers, Pre-production Robert Dunn, David Almond
Producer Gary Batchelor
Managing Editor Francesca Baines
Managing Art Editor Philip Letsu
Publisher Andrew Macintyre
Associate Publishing Director Liz Wheeler
Art Director Karen Self
Design Director Phil Ormerod
Publishing Director Jonathan Metcalf

SMITHSONIAN ENTERPRISES

Product Development Manager Kealy Gordon
Licensing Manager Ellen Nanney
Vice President, Consumer and Education Products Brigid Ferraro
Senior Vice President, Consumer and Education Products Carol LeBlanc
President Chris LeBlanc

Smithsonian Institution Consultant:
Dr James Zimbelman, Planetary Geologist, National Air and Space Museum, Smithsonian

First published in Great Britain in 2017
by Dorling Kindersley Limited,
80 Strand, London WC2R 0RL

A Penguin Random House Company
10 9 8 7 6 5 4 3 2 1
001 – 274832 – 03/2017

A CIP catalogue record for this book is available from the British Library.

ISBN 978-0-2412-1226-4

Printed and bound in China

A WORLD OF IDEAS:
SEE ALL THERE IS TO KNOW
www.dk.com

science
YEAR BY YEAR

Written by
Clive Gifford, Susan Kennedy,
and Philip Parker

Consultant
Jack Challoner

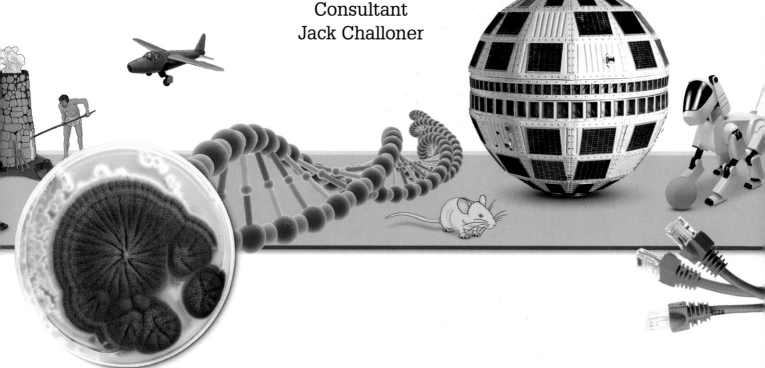

Contents

Travelling through time

The earliest events in this book took place a very long time ago. Some dates may be followed by the letters "MYA", short for "Million Years Ago". Other dates have BCE or CE after them. These are short for "Before the Common Era" and "Common Era". The Common Era began with the birth of Christ. Where the exact date of an event is not known, the letter "c" is used. This is short for the Latin word *circa*, meaning "round", and indicates that the date is approximate.

3 MYA–800 CE
Before science began

The earliest scientific discoveries of our ancestors – such as the use of fire
and the start of farming – happened long before the first civilizations arose
around 4000 BCE. Once people became settled, the pace of change quickened.
The Babylonians made advances in astronomy, the Greeks developed medicine
and mathematics, and the Romans led the way in engineering. After the fall
of the Western Roman Empire in 476 CE, however, much scientific
knowledge was lost for centuries.

3 MYA ▶ 8000 BCE

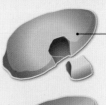 The earliest musical instruments found are flutes more than 40,000 years old, made out of bird bones and mammoth ivory.

400,000 BCE

Hunting with spears
Around this date, early hunters began to use wooden sticks as spears. These tools had sharpened ends and could be thrust or thrown, which meant prey could be targeted from greater distances. By about 200,000 BCE, stone points were added to the spears, making them more effective.

The oldest-known wooden spears were found at Schöningen, Germany.

Early hunter aims his spear

790,000 BCE

First use of fire
Human ancestors may have known how to make and control fire as far back as 1.5 million years ago. The earliest traces of domestic fire are hearths at the site of Gesher Benot Ya'aqov in Israel, dating from 790,000 BCE. With fire, people could cook and eat a wider range of foods.

---

3 MYA | **400,000** | **125,000**

---

c 2.6 MYA–250,000 BCE STONE TOOLS

The first objects known to have been purpose-made by our ancestors were stone tools. The oldest, from Lake Turkana in Kenya, date back 3.3 million years. The toolmakers used one stone to strike small flakes off another stone, creating a sharp cutting edge. Tools made in this way are described as "Oldowan".

Oldowan cutting tool

1: Stone core is prepared

2: Flakes struck off in a pattern

3: Final shape of tool emerges

Handaxes
The Oldowan stone tools were fairly crude. Then, around 1.76 million years ago, a new method of working stone appeared. Known as Acheulean, it involved flaking off two sides of the stone to create a double edge, and shaping the bottom to make it easy to grip. Such tools are called handaxes.

Acheulean handaxe

Levallois technique
Around 325,000 years ago, stoneworkers started using a tool-making technique, now known as Levallois. In this, they cut flake tools in a deliberate pattern from a stone core.

71,000 BCE

Bows and arrows
Small stone arrowheads found in South Africa show that humans had learnt how to make bows and arrows by 71,000 BCE. Such weapons were more efficient than spears. A person could carry many arrows on a hunt and bring down prey at long range.

Early arrowhead

18,000 BCE
Pottery making
People made the first pots with clay, which they shaped and hardened in a fire. These vessels were used for cooking or storing food. The earliest ones found, dated to around 18,000 BCE, come from China. By 14,000 BCE, the Jomon people of Japan were making pottery on a large scale.

Mouflon, an early breed of sheep

Twisting flax fibres made them stronger.

34,000 BCE
Earliest flax fibres
Twisted fibres of flax (a type of plant) found in a cave in Georgia, in the Caucasus region between Europe and Asia, are evidence that humans had learnt how to use plant fibres to make rope or cord by 34,000 BCE. Some of the fibres had been dyed to look colourful.

Jomon pottery vessel from Japan

8500 BCE
Animal domestication
Early farmers began to keep and breed animals, rather than simply hunting them. The first species to be domesticated in this way were sheep and goats, which provided a reliable source of food.

35,000 ▶   **8000** ▶ ▶▶

Narrow needles with pointed end for penetrating animal hide

30,000 BCE
Sewing needles
The use of sharpened bone needles began to spread around this time, suggesting that people had learned to sew. There is some evidence from China, Africa, and parts of Europe that simple bone needles were used as early as 63,000 BCE, although their purpose is uncertain.

10,500 BCE
Domesticating plants
Farming began when villagers at Abu Hureyra, Syria, deliberately sowed seeds of wild rye and einkorn (a type of wheat). People harvested these cereals as an extra source of food that could be gathered without a long foraging trip.

Farming begins
See pages 10–11

8000 BCE
First log boat
Humans must have used boats to reach Australia around 50,000 BCE, but the oldest surviving boat, dating from 8000 BCE, is a canoe found in the Netherlands. Like many early watercraft, it was made by digging out a seating platform from a large log.

❝From the terrace see the planted and fallow fields, the ponds and orchards. ❞

The Epic of Gilgamesh, a poem from Mesopotamia (present-day Iraq) dating from c 2000 BCE

Wood cut away from log to make seating area

The earliest boats closely resembled this Native American dugout canoe.

9

Farming begins

Around 8500 BCE, in southwestern Asia, people began sowing the seeds of cereal plants close to their homes. This spared them long journeys to harvest the plants where they grew. At about the same time, these first farmers domesticated (tamed) wild goats, pigs, sheep, and cattle, selecting the best of them as breeding stock to provide meat, milk, and leather.

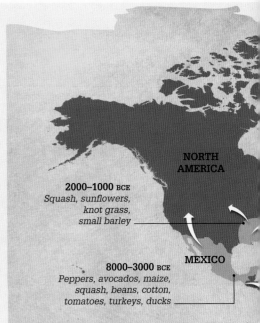

NORTH AMERICA

2000–1000 BCE
Squash, sunflowers, knot grass, small barley

MEXICO

8000–3000 BCE
Peppers, avocados, maize, squash, beans, cotton, tomatoes, turkeys, ducks

Domestication

Bigger and better corn
By about 9000 BCE, villagers in Central America had begun to domesticate the teosinte grass. This plant had small cobs with hard outer shells that shattered when harvested. The early farmers selected plants with larger cobs that did not shatter and so gradually bred modern maize (corn).

Teosinte, a wild corn

Modern maize

Wild boar

Tamer pigs
The first pig farmers were hunters in western Asia. In about 7500 BCE, they began keeping selected wild boar in captivity. Over time, they bred the pig, a smaller and more docile animal.

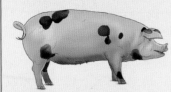

Modern domestic pig

Tastier potatoes
The ancestors of the modern potato were first domesticated in Peru around 8,000 years ago. They were bitter tasting, but cultivation gradually produced improved varieties with better flavours.

Wild potatoes from Peru

Modern potato

Spread of agriculture
Plants and animals were domesticated independently in several different areas: western Asia, eastern Asia, Central and South America, eastern North America, parts of Africa, and the Indian subcontinent. Farming then spread from these regions across the world.

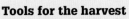

Tools for the harvest
Farmers developed tools, mainly sickles with curved blades to cut the tough stalks of crops. Early blades were made of polished stone but, as metalworking evolved, they were later made of copper, bronze, and iron.

Farm tools with bronze (left) and iron blades

Key events

23,500–22,500 BCE

Hunter-gatherers in the Middle East harvested wild emmer (an early type of wheat), barley, pistachios, and olives. They ground cereals with pestles.

Jomon pot

14,000 BCE

Baked clay pots, essential to future farmers, first appeared in China. But by 14,000 BCE the Jomon people of Japan were the leading producers of high-quality pots.

13,000 BCE

The first domestication of an animal took place when hunters tamed wolves, from which all dogs descend. This probably happened in several areas at the same time.

Wooden model of
an Egyptian sailboat

3000 BCE

First sailing boats

The first boats powered by sails, rather than
oars, appeared in Egypt. Sails meant boats
could be moved fast by the wind, although
they still had oars for rowing against
currents or in calm conditions. Early
sailboats were made of wooden
planks bound together.

Metal-
working
See pages
18–19

3500 BCE

Invention of the wheel

Wheels may have developed
from simple log rollers. Solid
wooden wheels, like the one
shown here, were invented
in Poland, the Balkans, and
Mesopotamia. They were
attached to a wagon with
a wooden axle rod.

3200 BCE

First production of true bronze

Combining two metals creates an
alloy, which is often stronger than
the metals themselves. Craftsmen
in southwest Asia smelted copper
with tin to produce bronze, a much
harder metal than copper, and better
for making armour and weapons.

5000 — **4000** — **3000** ⏩

5000 BCE

Megaliths in Europe

Across western Europe, people
began to build huge stone
structures called megaliths,
most likely for religious
reasons. Megaliths included
circles like Stonehenge
in southern England; rows,
such as at Carnac in France;
and tombs built with stones
inside or around them, such
as at Newgrange in Ireland.

Stone row at Carnac,
Brittany, France

4100 BCE

First cities

In Mesopotamia,
from around this
date, some large
villages and small
towns grew into
important centres of
government and
trade. Remains of
these early cities,
with their massive
palaces and temples,
can be seen at sites
such as Ur and Uruk
in modern-day Iraq.

c 3200 BCE   EARLY WRITING

Writing appeared around 3200 BCE in Egypt and
Mesopotamia. As towns and cities became more
complicated to govern, writing allowed officials to
keep accurate records without relying on memory.

Sumerian cuneiform script
The Sumerians, early people of
Mesopotamia, invented cuneiform,
writing that used pictographs: signs
resembling objects. The wedge-shaped
script was formed by pressing a pointed
reed called a stylus into soft clay.

Egyptian hieroglyphs
Egyptians invented a complicated form
of picture writing called hieroglyphics.
The symbols, or hieroglyphs, could
be carved in stone, cut into clay, or
painted on papyrus (paper made
from reeds).

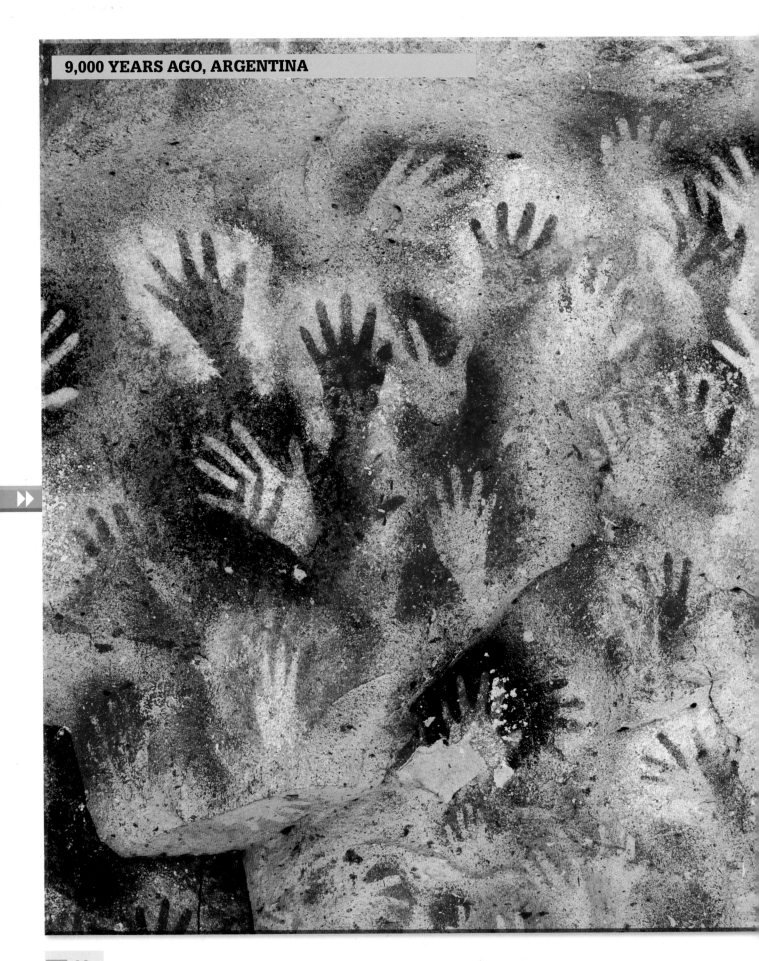

Cave art

People began painting on cave walls at least 35,000–40,000 years ago, during the Stone Age. This 9,000-year-old example is from the Cueva de las Manos (Spanish for the Cave of the Hands) in Argentina. The forest of what appear to be waving hands was created by blowing paint around each hand, like making a stencil. Sometimes figures were engraved on soft cave walls with flint tools. Mineral pigments were used to make paint. Iron oxide gave a red colour, manganese oxide or charcoal provided black, and other minerals added yellow and brown. Cave art techniques included painting with the fingers or using animal-hair or vegetable-fibre brushes.

"Whether in cave paintings or the latest uses of the Internet, human beings have always told their histories and truths through parable and fable. "

Beeban Kidron (born 1961), English film director

Paintings of stencilled hands by children and adults, Cueva de las Manos (Cave of the Hands), Santa Cruz, Argentina

3000 ▸ 2000 BCE

2500 BCE
First town map
The earliest known map was produced in Mesopotamia and shows a plot of land set between two hills. The clay tablet pictured here is the earliest street map. It shows the Sumerian town of Nippur, including the River Euphrates, the city walls, and a temple.

Tablet shows street map of Nippur, c 1500 BCE

3000 BCE
Standardized weights
As cities became larger, trading both locally and with other cities became more complex. Standardized weights were introduced in Mesopotamia (modern Iraq) to ensure that there was no cheating in the marketplace. These were based on grains of wheat or barley, which are all of similar weight.

2500 BCE
Steering oars
Boats in Egypt were steered by an oar or a pair of oars attached to a vertical post. Later, the paired oars were connected by a bar, and the system developed into the rudder and the steering lever called the tiller.

Small model of an early Egyptian boat. The original was found buried near the Great Pyramid of Khufu.

Rack holds the oars in place

High stern curves upwards

Shelter for crew

Paired steering oars

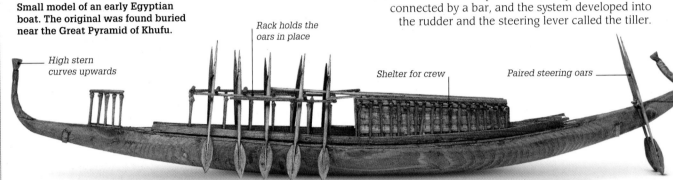

3000 • • • • 2800 • • • • 2600 • • • •

 The Egyptians referred to the material called faience as "tjehnet", which means dazzling.

2625 BCE
Step pyramid of Djoser
Early Egyptian tombs, or "mastabas", were rectangular structures made of mud bricks. The tomb of Pharaoh Djoser (2630–2611 BCE) was constructed from a series of mastabas, one above the other, each smaller than the one below. This stepped structure was the first pyramid built in Egypt.

2500 BCE
Stones to Stonehenge
Neolithic people began to erect the central stone circle at Stonehenge (see pp.22–23) in southern Britain. This was probably a religious site connected with the passing of the seasons. Stonehenge had already been of some importance for several hundred years. Work had first started at the site around 3100 BCE with the erection of timber and stone posts within an earthwork ditch.

c 3000 BCE
Egyptian faience
The Egyptians perfected the technique of creating faience, a paste made of crushed silica and lime. Its attractive blue or turquoise colours are created by the addition of metal oxides to the paste. When heated, faience can be modelled like clay to make statuettes and other objects. It can also be applied on top of other materials as a glaze.

Ancient Egyptian faience bead necklace, 2000 BCE

Tomb of Pharaoh Djoser

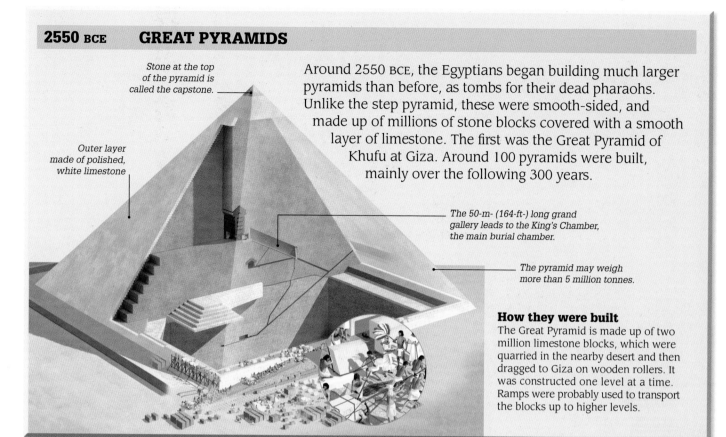

Stone at the top of the pyramid is called the capstone.

Outer layer made of polished, white limestone

Around 2550 BCE, the Egyptians began building much larger pyramids than before, as tombs for their dead pharaohs. Unlike the step pyramid, these were smooth-sided, and made up of millions of stone blocks covered with a smooth layer of limestone. The first was the Great Pyramid of Khufu at Giza. Around 100 pyramids were built, mainly over the following 300 years.

The 50-m- (164-ft-) long grand gallery leads to the King's Chamber, the main burial chamber.

The pyramid may weigh more than 5 million tonnes.

How they were built

The Great Pyramid is made up of two million limestone blocks, which were quarried in the nearby desert and then dragged to Giza on wooden rollers. It was constructed one level at a time. Ramps were probably used to transport the blocks up to higher levels.

2400 • • • • **2200** • • ● • • **2000** ▶▶

2400 BCE

Invention of the shaduf

The shaduf, a device for raising water for irrigation, was invented in Mesopotamia and later also used in Egypt. It had an upright frame with a pole onto which a bucket was attached. A farmer lowered the pole to scoop up a bucketful of water from a channel. The shaduf was then rotated and lowered again to tip the water into another channel, often at a different level.

Wall painting of a peasant drawing water with a shaduf, c 1200 BCE

2100 BCE

Development of the calendar

The earliest-known calendar is the Umma calendar of Shulgi, devised by the Sumerians (people from Sumer, now in southern Iraq). It had 12 months of 29 or 30 days, making 354 days in total. To keep the calendar in line with the real 365.25-day solar year, the Sumerians added a month every few years.

Ziggurat of Ur

2200 BCE

Building of ziggurats

The people of Mesopotamia built the first ziggurats: monumental, pyramid-shaped temples made up of several layers connected by stepped terraces. Ziggurats housed shrines to the gods. Their construction involved huge amounts of material and manpower.

Metalworking

From around 9000 BCE, people began to use naturally occurring metal for making tools instead of stone, bone, or wood. Then, craftsmen discovered how to melt out metal from metal-bearing rocks by using intense heat. First they worked with copper, then bronze (a mix, or alloy, of copper and tin), and finally iron. As technology advanced, tools and weapons became stronger and more durable than before.

Bull-shaped gold ornament from a burial site in Varna, Bulgaria

Bronze axehead with human mask design, Shang Dynasty (12th–11th century BCE), China

Earliest metalworking
Some metals, especially copper and gold, can occur naturally as nuggets. Around 9000 BCE, metalworkers discovered that hammering such metals into thin sheets made them hard enough to fashion into simple objects, such as ornaments.

Heat needed to melt metals

Iron
1540°C (2804°F), but melts at only 1200°C (2192°F) if charcoal is added

Copper
1083°C (1981°F)

Gold
1063°C (1945°F)

Bronze
With 12 per cent tin, it melts at about 1000°C (1830°F)

1500°C (2732°F)

1250°C (2282°F)

1000°C (1830°F)

Smelting copper
By about 5500 BCE, people were extracting copper from its ore (rock in which a metal is embedded) by a process called smelting. This involved heating copper-bearing rocks to high temperatures in a furnace. The molten copper ran off and was moulded or beaten into shape while cooling.

Discovery of bronze
Metalworkers discovered that adding another metal to copper while it was at a high temperature produced bronze. An alloy, bronze is harder than the original metals. At first, from around 4200 BCE, bronze was made by adding arsenic to copper. Then from 3200 BCE, metalworkers used a mixture containing 12 per cent tin.

Egyptian metalworkers heating copper

Crucible contains copper ore that is heated until it melts and releases copper.

Key events

c 9000 BCE
Cold-working of copper and gold, by beating or hammering the pure metals into thin strips or sheets, was developed in the Balkans, in southeastern Europe.

c 5500 BCE
Smelting of copper was discovered in the Balkans and Anatolia. It spread rapidly through the Near East and to Egypt.

4200 BCE
Arsenic was added to copper during smelting to produce a form of bronze.

3200 BCE
Tin was added to copper to produce tin bronze, which is harder than copper, and could be used to make better arms and armour.

c 2500 BCE
Early iron production created a metal that was soft and easily shaped, but did not produce strong objects.

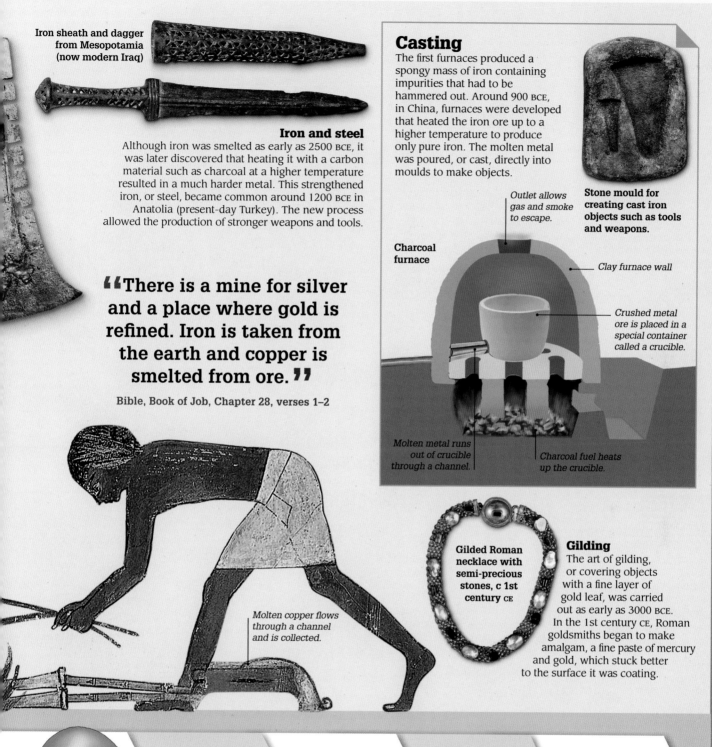

Iron sheath and dagger
from Mesopotamia
(now modern Iraq)

Iron and steel

Although iron was smelted as early as 2500 BCE, it was later discovered that heating it with a carbon material such as charcoal at a higher temperature resulted in a much harder metal. This strengthened iron, or steel, became common around 1200 BCE in Anatolia (present-day Turkey). The new process allowed the production of stronger weapons and tools.

> **"There is a mine for silver and a place where gold is refined. Iron is taken from the earth and copper is smelted from ore. "**
>
> Bible, Book of Job, Chapter 28, verses 1–2

Molten copper flows through a channel and is collected.

Egyptian mirror made of copper

Casting

The first furnaces produced a spongy mass of iron containing impurities that had to be hammered out. Around 900 BCE, in China, furnaces were developed that heated the iron ore up to a higher temperature to produce only pure iron. The molten metal was poured, or cast, directly into moulds to make objects.

Stone mould for creating cast iron objects such as tools and weapons.

Outlet allows gas and smoke to escape.

Charcoal furnace

Clay furnace wall

Crushed metal ore is placed in a special container called a crucible.

Molten metal runs out of crucible through a channel.

Charcoal fuel heats up the crucible.

Gilded Roman necklace with semi-precious stones, c 1st century CE

Gilding

The art of gilding, or covering objects with a fine layer of gold leaf, was carried out as early as 3000 BCE. In the 1st century CE, Roman goldsmiths began to make amalgam, a fine paste of mercury and gold, which stuck better to the surface it was coating.

C 1400 BCE

Pewter, an alloy of copper, antimony, and lead, was first produced in the Near East. It was often used for vessels and tableware.

C 1300 BCE

Metalworkers added carbon to iron when smelting. This produced steel, a much stronger form of iron.

900 BCE

The process of producing cast iron was discovered in China. Using this technique, metal objects were created by pouring molten iron into moulds.

C 100 CE

Roman metalworkers created amalgam, a mix of mercury and gold that that made a more durable material for gilding .than gold leaf.

Archer fires from platform

1800 BCE

Babylonian maths

Scholars in the city of Babylon (in Mesopotamia, now modern Iraq) worked out a complex mathematical system, which they wrote in cuneiform script (see p.13) on clay tablets. The tablet seen here displays a version of Pythagoras's theorem. The text shows the square root of two, correct to six decimal places.

Clay tablet with an earlier working of Pythagoras's theorem, c 2000 BCE

Proto-Sinaitic letter M

Proto-Sinaitic letter H

1800 BCE

Earliest alphabetic script

Turquoise miners in Egypt's Sinai Desert developed the world's earliest alphabetic script. Now known as Proto-Sinaitic, it was based on a version of Egyptian hieroglyphs (see p.13), but with each symbol representing a single sound. Proto-Sinaitic consisted of consonants only.

2000   **1800**   **1600**

1800 BCE

The composite bow

Probably invented in Central Asia, the composite bow was made by bonding layers of horn, wood, and strips of animal sinew. It was not only stronger than bows made with just one material, it also allowed archers to shoot arrows further and with greater force.

1650 BCE

Studying Venus

The Venus cuneiform tablets, compiled in the reign of the Babylonian King Ammisaduqa, are the earliest detailed records of astronomical observations. The text on the clay tablets gives the times of the rising and setting of the planet Venus over a period of 21 years.

Glass production

Around 1500 BCE, Egyptian glassmakers discovered how to use metal rods to dip a core of silica paste into molten glass. When the glass solidified, the core was cut away, creating the earliest glass vessels.

1560 BCE

The Ebers papyrus

One of the oldest medical texts, this papyrus from Egypt contains recipes for medicines and describes ailments such as tumours, depression, and tinnitus (ringing in the ears). It shows early understanding of the heart's role in the body's blood supply.

Fish-shaped glass bottle for ointments, c 1370 BCE

1500 BCE

The halter yoke

As the use of wheeled vehicles spread, it became necessary to find an efficient way of moving them with animal power. The invention of the halter yoke – a set of flat straps stretched across an animal's neck and chest – allowed large weights to be hauled. It also led to the development of light chariots in Egypt, which could be pulled by horses at high speed.

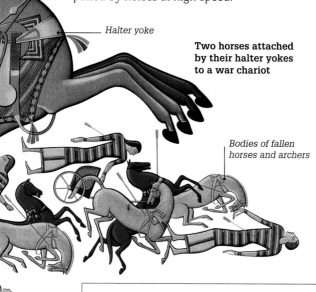

Halter yoke

Two horses attached by their halter yokes to a war chariot

Bodies of fallen horses and archers

Mummified remains of Pharaoh Rameses IV (died 1150 BCE)

1000 BCE

Mummification

The Egyptians invented mummification, a way of preserving a dead body by removing the internal organs and wrapping the dried body in linen. Mummifiers reached the height of their skills by 1000 BCE. The process was used mostly for royalty and the wealthy.

1400 BCE

The wood lathe

The lathe, a tool for shaping wood, was invented in Egypt. In its earliest use, one craftsman rotated the piece to be worked using a cord or rope, while a second worker shaped the piece with a sharp tool or chisel.

1400 ● **1200** ● **1000** ▶▶

1400–1300 BCE   IRON SMELTING

The smelting of iron – extracting iron from iron-bearing ores by heating to a high temperature – was discovered in the Middle East around 1400 BCE, and in India around a century later. The iron produced was much stronger and harder-wearing than bronze, and was used in a variety of tools and weaponry.

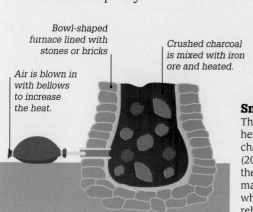

Bowl-shaped furnace lined with stones or bricks

Crushed charcoal is mixed with iron ore and heated.

Air is blown in with bellows to increase the heat.

Iron saw

Iron tongs

Iron dagger

Furnaces develop

The development of taller shaft furnaces in Roman times enabled more ore and charcoal to be fitted in. The waste slag along with pure molten iron was drawn out at the bottom of the furnace. The mixture of ore and charcoal could be topped up periodically.

Vent for waste gas and steam to escape

Tall conical furnace wall of stone or brick

Hole to insert bellows and draw out waste and molten iron

Smelting

The air pushed in by the bellows heated a mixture of iron ore and charcoal up to around 1100°C (2010°F), at which temperature the iron separated out. A spongy mass of iron was left behind, which became hard when reheated and beaten.

"Since Stonehenge, architects have always been
at the cutting edge of technology."

Norman Foster, British architect, born 1935

Stonehenge

The monument at Stonehenge was erected in stages from about 3100 BCE, when the site consisted of earthworks and posts. The building of the central stone circle, begun around 2500 BCE, was a massive feat of engineering for the Neolithic people of Britain. Huge 20-30-tonne sarsen stones (a type of sandstone) were possibly moved on log rollers from the Wiltshire Downs 30 km (18.6 miles) away. It is unclear how the sarsens were pulled upright at Stonehenge. Heavy stone hammers, called mauls, were used to shape the stones and smooth joints with the lintels. At a later stage, bluestones, each weighing about four tonnes, were transported some 200 km (125 miles) from the Preseli Hills of Wales, mostly by manhauling.

This is an aerial view of the central stone circle at Stonehenge in Wiltshire, southern England. Originally, almost all the pairs of standing stones had a third horizontal stone called a lintel on top, but many of these have since fallen down.

1000 BCE ▶ 1 CE

Around 450 BCE, Empedocles of Acragas (a Greek colony in Sicily) had the idea that all matter is made up of four basic elements: earth, air, fire, and water.

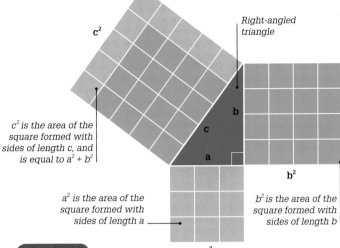

Right-angled triangle

c^2 is the area of the square formed with sides of length c, and is equal to $a^2 + b^2$

a^2 is the area of the square formed with sides of length a

b^2 is the area of the square formed with sides of length b

Cuneiform text

Ocean

Each circle represents a city

Babylon

River Euphrates

600 BCE
Oldest world map
The oldest-known attempt to create a world map was made on a clay tablet in Babylon (now modern Iraq). The tablet portrays the world as a flattened disc, surrounded by an ocean. Babylon is shown as a rectangle in the centre, with eight other cities indicated by circles.

530 BCE
Pythagorean theorem
Greek mathematician Pythagoras was interested in the mystical powers of numbers. A version of the theorem named after him was known to the Egyptians and Babylonians, but Pythagoras was the one who worked it out. It states that the sum of the squares of the two shorter sides of a right-angled triangle is equal to the square of the longer side.

1000 • **800** **600**

700 BCE   ARCHIMEDES SCREW PUMP

The screw pump was probably invented around 700 BCE by the Assyrians (people living in northern Mesopotamia, now in modern Iraq). These people used it to transport water from one level to another in the gardens of King Sennacherib, in their capital of Nineveh. Centuries later, Greek mathematician Archimedes may have seen it working in Egypt. He applied its use to pumping water from the holds of ships. This type of pump came to be named after him.

Central spiral rotates

Water is released at the top

Screw action pulls water upwards

Archimedes of Syracuse
Archimedes (c 287–212 BCE) had a vast range of interests. As well as developing the screw pump, he did important work on geometry, especially in calculating the area of a circle. He is said to have invented a heat ray by focusing light on an array of mirrors.

How the screw works
Water enters an Archimedes screw from the bottom. When the central spiral of the screw is rotated, water is pulled through it and transferred to a higher level, from where it exits the pump.

Paved road in the ruins of the Roman city of Pompeii

 In his book *Elements*, written around 300 BCE, Greek mathematician Euclid established the basis of geometry for the next 2,000 years.

50 BCE

Glassblowing in Syria
Roman glassblowers in the eastern province of Syria discovered that a more even flow of molten glass could be achieved by blowing it through a thin tube. This created higher-quality and stronger glass, so vessels could be made in more complex shapes and lasted longer.

Roman blown-glass containers in the shape of doves, 1st century CE

312 BCE

First Roman road
The Romans built a huge network of roads, beginning with the Via Appia. Its construction started in 312 BCE, and the road connected Rome to the southern Italian city of Capua. The roads were generally built on clay beds filled with loose gravel, and were topped with paving stones or cobbles. The high quality of the Roman roads greatly speeded up communications within the Roman Empire.

420 BCE

Naming atoms
Early Greek philosophers and scientists thought hard about what basic substance made up the Universe. Democritus of Abdera proposed that all matter consisted of tiny particles that could not be divided, which he called atoms, the Greek word for "uncuttable" (see pp.168–169).

400 — **200** — **1** ▸▸

400 BCE

The four humours
Greek physician Hippocrates developed the idea that the body has four basic substances, or "humours": blood, phlegm, black bile, and yellow bile. Hippocrates taught that illness was caused when the humours were out of balance, a theory proved to be incorrect.

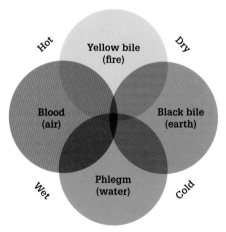

People's health was said to depend on their mix of humours.

Ancient Chinese compass with a magnetized iron spoon as a pointer

200 BCE

Magnetic lodestone
The Chinese were the first to describe lodestone, a naturally occurring magnet. They saw that rubbing lodestone against iron magnetizes the iron. This enabled them to create primitive compasses in which an iron ladle or spoon pointed north.

c 100 BCE

The Antikythera
The Antikythera mechanism is a complicated ancient device with toothed dials. It was discovered in a shipwreck in 1900 and is thought to be around 2,000 years old. The mechanism has more than 30 gears, and was probably used to calculate the positions of astronomical objects and to predict eclipses of the Sun and Moon.

Remains of the Antikythera mechanism

Ancient architecture

Our ancestors made primitive shelters of wood as long ago as 500,000 BCE. From around 9000 BCE, they learnt how to erect larger buildings of stone. By 3000 BCE, architecture and engineering had advanced so far that it was possible to create monumental structures such as pyramids, temples, and palaces.

Stone dwelling at Skara Brae

The outer wall is made of travertine, a type of limestone, while the inner wall is made of concrete.

First buildings
Many early towns, such as Çatalhöyük in Turkey (see p.12), had mud-brick houses. Sometimes towns had protective stone walls, such as those of Jericho in Palestine, built around 8000 BCE. Occasionally, houses were made of stone, as at Skara Brae, a Neolithic village built about 3200 BCE on one of the islands of Orkney, Scotland.

The pyramidal temple of the Inscriptions, Palenque, Mexico

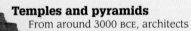

Temples and pyramids
From around 3000 BCE, architects became skilled enough to design very large buildings. They knew how to provide massive support at the base of pyramids, which were common in Egypt and Central America. Another skill was building columns that held up the roof of a large temple while leaving usable space beneath.

Key events

10,000 BCE

Hilltop temple at Göbekli Tepe, Turkey, was constructed. It is the oldest-known large-scale stone building.

C 2575 BCE

The Great Pyramid of Giza, Egypt, was built as a tomb for Pharaoh Khufu. It was the largest building in the ancient world, containing 2.6 million cubic metres (92 million cubic feet) of stone.

438 BCE

Built in Athens, the Parthenon was a temple to the Greek goddess Athena, built mainly in the Doric style (a traditional column design). It was regarded as one of the finest works of Greek architecture.

Parthenon, Greece

The arch

An arch helps spread the weight of the part of a building that lies above it. The true arch was perfected by the Romans after 200 BCE, and allowed larger and lighter buildings, while using less stone or brick.

Corbel arch

The first arches, such as this Gate of the Lions at Mycenae, Greece (c 1250 BCE), were corbelled. This means they were built with layers of stone, each jutting out further until they met at the top. The design did not spread weight evenly and corbel arches needed lintels (horizontal blocks for support) below, or reinforcement at the sides.

Triumphal arch

Having mastered the true arch, the Romans built longer bridges, created aqueducts to carry water, and raised domed buildings by using an extended arch as a roof. They put up triumphal arches to celebrate the victories of their emperors. The Arch of Titus (c 82 CE) in Rome is one of the most splendid.

Concrete

The Romans discovered concrete around 200 BCE when they found that adding lime to pozzolana, a type of sand found near Rome, made it harden quickly. Buildings made with concrete needed less stone, which was expensive. Roman architects used the new material for constructing enormous buildings such as the Colosseum (72–80 CE) and the Pantheon (118–125 CE).

Kerbstones at the side of the ditch give extra support

Finer sand and concrete form the top layer

Layer of larger stones and rubble fills the ditch

Cross-section of a Roman road

Colosseum, Rome

Road construction

The Romans were excellent engineers, and built a large network of high-quality roads to link towns within their empire. To make a road, a ditch was dug and filled with layers of rubble, then smaller stones, and finally fine sand and concrete on top. The most important roads were then surfaced with cobbles.

The 80 concrete arches on each storey strengthened the building and allowed crowds of spectators to enter easily.

C 60 CE

The Pont du Gard is one of the greatest Roman aqueducts, built to carry water into the Roman town of Nemausus (modern Nîmes). More than 275 m (900 ft) long, it originally had 60 concrete arches on three levels.

Pont du Gard, France

C 126 CE

The Pantheon was built in Rome by Emperor Hadrian. Its enormous dome, 43 m (141 ft) high, is still the largest unsupported concrete dome in the world.

683 CE

The Temple of the Inscriptions was completed at Palenque, Mexico. A monument to its Mayan ruler K'inich Janaab' Pakal, it is the largest pyramid structure in Central America.

1▶800 CE

c 25–50 CE

Medical encyclopedia
In the early years of the Roman Empire, great advances were made in the field of medicine. At the beginning of the 1st century CE, a writer called Aulus Cornelius Celsus produced an important encyclopedia entitled *De Medicina*, which gave an up-to-date account of medicine at the time. The work included a description of surgery for kidney stones.

Later Latin edition of Soranus's work

c 100 CE

Papermaking
Around this date, true paper, as we know it today, was invented by Cai Lun, a Chinese court official. (A type of paper had already been in use for some 200 years.) Cai Lun made paper by drying out a pulp of tree bark and old rags on a screen, producing strips that could be written on.

100 CE

Health for women
Soranus, a doctor from the ancient Greek city of Ephesus, produced the first major book on women's health. He wrote about childbirth and the care of babies, including how to make feeding bottles.

127–141 CE

Ptolemy's astronomy
Greek-Roman astronomer Ptolemy devised a model to explain the movement of planets. His scheme took account of the way in which some planets appear to orbit in opposite directions to others. Ptolemy also worked out a system for measuring the latitude and longitude of places in the known world, which made it possible to create a world map.

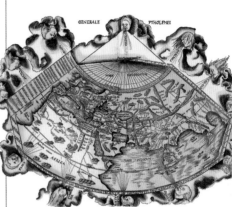

Ptolemy's world map
(14th-century version)

---

1 ⟩   **200** ⟩

---

c 50 CE

Hero's steam engine
Greek inventor Hero devised a large number of machines. His steam engine, which he called an aeolipile, used the force of heated steam to make a metal sphere spin around. It was a clever idea, but never put to practical use.

As steam escapes, the sphere rotates.

Steam rises through tubes

Water is heated in a container to make steam.

132 CE

Earliest earthquake detector
Chinese scholar Zhang Heng built the earliest-known seismoscope, an instrument for detecting earthquakes. When an earth tremor occurred, a pendulum inside the bronze, jar-like machine swung in the direction of one of eight dragon heads attached on the outside. The dragon's mouth released a ball, showing the direction of the earthquake.

Pendulum moves because of an earth tremor, operating a crank that opens the dragons' mouths.

Dragon facing the direction of the earthquake drops a ball into toad's mouth.

Cut-away model of Zhang Heng's seismoscope

c 130–c 210 CE   GALEN

Greek physician Claudius Galen, who came from the city of Pergamum (now in modern Turkey), was one of the ancient world's most influential doctors. He believed in direct observation of patients, including taking their pulses. Galen saw good health as the balanced working of all the body's organs, and was an expert anatomist.

📢 **In 250 CE, Diophantus of Alexandria was the first to use letters and symbols to show algebraic equations in his book *Arithmetica*.**

The dome of Hagia Sophia is 32.5 m (107 ft) in diameter.

532–537 CE

Building of Hagia Sophia

The Byzantine Emperor Justinian asked Greek architects Anthemius and Isidore to build the church of Hagia Sophia in Constantinople (modern Istanbul). They set a round dome over a square base by using curved triangular sections of stone called pendentives, which strengthened the structure. Hagia Sophia remained the world's largest domed building for about a thousand years.

600   **800** ▶▶

475–499 CE

Calculating pi

For hundreds of years, mathematicians had tried to calculate the value of pi (the distance around a circle, or circumference, divided by its diameter, represented by the symbol π). In about 475 CE, Chinese mathematician Zhu Chongzhi calculated pi to seven decimal places and in 499 CE, Indian mathematician Aryabhata estimated it to be 3.1416, which is correct to four decimal places.

circumference (C)

$$\pi = C/d$$

diameter (d)

750 CE

First written work on the astrolabe

The astrolabe, invented around 100 BCE, was a device with movable circles used by ancient astronomers to calculate the positions of the Sun and stars. In the 8th century, it was greatly developed by Islamic astronomers, and one of them, al-Fazari, wrote the first-ever work on the astrolabe.

Most astrolabes are portable.

Face adjusts to show appearance of sky at a given time.

628 CE

Negative numbers

Indian mathematician Brahmagupta was the first to set out rules for using negative numbers in calculations. These included the rule that multiplying two negative numbers gives a positive number.

Medieval Arabic brass astrolabe, dating from around 1100

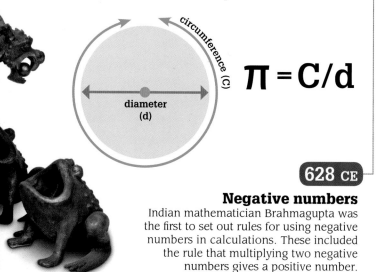

Aristotle

Perhaps the greatest thinker of his time, Greek philosopher and scientist Aristotle (384–322 BCE) had huge influence in the ancient world. Later, in the Middle Ages, his work was very important to Islamic scholars, through whom it then reached Europe. Aristotle's astonishing range of studies included logic, politics, mathematics, biology, and physics.

Alexander's tutor
In 343 BCE, King Philip II of Macedon, Greece, invited Aristotle to tutor his son, later Alexander the Great. Aristotle taught him for many years. Alexander carried with him on his campaigns a copy of the Greek epic poem The Iliad given to him by Aristotle.

> **❝Man is much more a political animal than any kind of bee or herd animal.❞**
>
> Aristotle, *Politics*

Early philosophers

Long before Aristotle's time, Greek philosophers such as Anaximenes of Miletus (who died in 528 BCE) had looked for scientific explanations for what went on in the natural world. For instance, they came up with various theories on what substance made up the Universe (Anaximenes thought it was air).

At the Academy

In his teens, Aristotle went to study at the Academy in the city of Athens, a school founded by the Greek philosopher Plato (427–347 BCE). Plato himself was a former student of Socrates (c 470–399 BCE), another great Greek thinker. Plato had many ideas, still discussed today, about what is real and what exists just in our minds. Aristotle, however, had a more practical outlook and learned to reason things out. He was greatly interested in understanding nature and classifying the differences between animals.

Politics and society

Aristotle was also interested in people and politics. He called people "political animals", best suited to living in a society, ideally a city-state like Athens, rather than alone. He later founded his own school, the Lyceum in Athens, and became famous as a teacher.

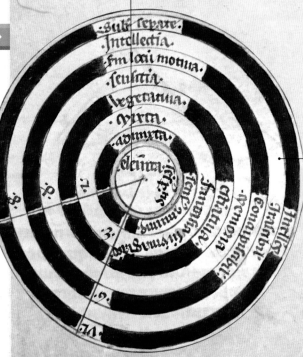

A stationary Earth formed the centre of Aristotle's Universe.

Each planet was thought to sit on a sphere.

Model of Aristotle's Earth-centric Universe

Astronomical theory
Aristotle believed that Earth was situated at the centre of the Universe. He suggested that the other heavenly bodies, such as the Sun and the planets, orbited Earth on concentric spheres.

Aristotle's legacy
Aristotle's works were rediscovered in western Europe in the 12th and 13th centuries. His ideas influenced theologians (people who study God and faith) such as Thomas Aquinas (1225–1274) and his works on politics were widely read. This manuscript is a French translation of Aristotle's work Politics by the scholar Nicholas of Oresme.

Page from Aristotle's *Politics* **illustrating workers in the fields.**

Aristotle with Plato
The School of Athens, a fresco in the Vatican by Italian Renaissance painter Raphael, portrays many famous philosophers of Ancient Greece. Plato (left) and his pupil Aristotle (right) are in deep debate.

> **❝In the sea, there are… objects… which one would be at a loss to determine whether they be animal or vegetable. [Some] are rooted and [may] perish if detached.❞**
>
> Aristotle, *History of Animals*

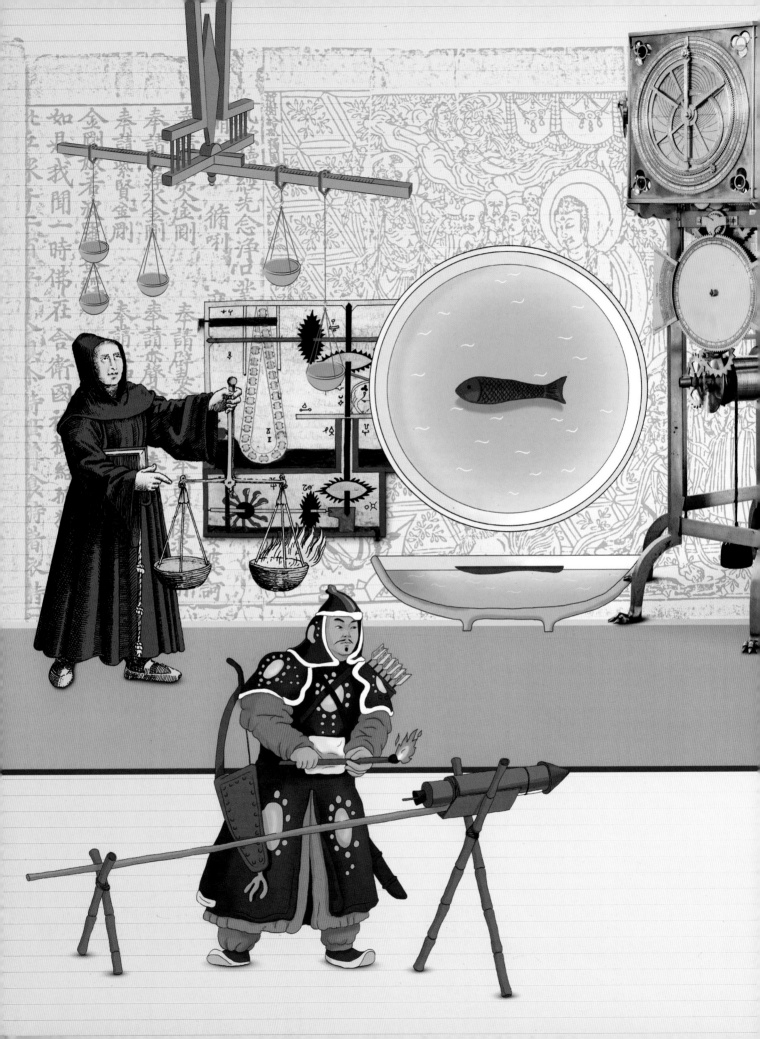

800–1545
New ideas

For much of the Middle Ages, China, India, and the Islamic world led the way in science, with advances in mathematics, medicine, engineering, and navigation. Europe began to catch up when translations of Ancient Greek and Roman works, held in Arabic libraries but long lost elsewhere, arrived in the West. In the 15th century, the rediscovery of this knowledge inspired the Renaissance, a period of new interest in classical arts and thinking. As old ideas were revisited and questioned, science in Europe took great steps forward.

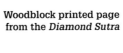

Gathering of scholars at the House of Wisdom, Baghdad

Woodblock printed page from the *Diamond Sutra*

810

The House of Wisdom

The Bayt al-Hikma, or House of Wisdom, was founded in Baghdad (now in Iraq) in the early 9th century. It housed an enormous library and was used by scholars working on translating Greek scientific texts into Arabic.

868

The *Diamond Sutra*

In the 9th century, the Chinese invented the technique of printing books using single carved wooden blocks for each page. The *Diamond Sutra*, a Buddhist religious text discovered in 1907, is the oldest complete example of a book produced in this way. One of the pages bears its date – 11 May 868.

800

845

830

Birth of algebra

The Arabic mathematician al-Khwarizmi published a book describing the type of mathematics now known as algebra. He introduced an important idea for working out equations, although he did not use letters to represent numbers as modern mathematicians do.

In 843, Irish theologian John Scotus Eriugena suggested that the planets Mercury, Venus, Mars, and Jupiter orbit the Sun.

850

al-Kindi's numerals

Abu Yusuf al-Kindi, an Arab mathematician and scholar from Basra (now in Iraq), wrote hundreds of books. Among them was his work on Indian numerals (on which modern numerals are based), which he introduced to the Islamic world. He also devised new techniques in code-breaking, and wrote on the theory of parallel lines.

Ancient Chinese soldier prepares to fire arrows propelled by gunpowder.

855

Discovery of gunpowder

In the mid-9th century, Chinese alchemists were searching for an elixir of life using saltpetre. They found instead that when this chemical was mixed with sulfur and charcoal, it created an explosive substance: gunpowder. Within 50 years it was being used to propel rockets (see p.53).

Statue of al-Khwarizmi in Uzbekistan

c 854–925   AL-RAZI

Born in Rayy (now in Iran), al-Razi was one of the Arabic world's greatest physicians. He was the first to describe hayfever and the symptoms of smallpox. Unlike most doctors of the time, he did not support the theory that an incorrect balance of body fluids known as "humours" affected health.

al-Razi with an assistant in his laboratory

Classifying elements
Interested in alchemy (medieval chemistry), al-Razi devised a system for classifying elements. He divided substances into spirits, metals, and minerals, noting what happened to each when it was heated or subjected to chemical processes.

890

945 ▶▶

876

Development of zero
Although mathematicians had worked out problems involving the use of zero, there was no symbol for it before the 9th century. An inscription dated 876 from Gwalior, India, contains the first known use of a symbol for zero in describing the dimensions of a garden. Its appearance allowed the development of a full decimal system for numbers.

Movable plates adjust the astrolabe's alignment and help the user to calculate the positions of astronomical objects.

> **"We should not be ashamed to acknowledge the truth or to acquire it, wherever it comes from."**
>
> al-Kindi, Arabic mathematician and philosopher, c 800–873

Star pointer shows the position of a particular star.

Mapping the sky
A device called an astrolabe helped ancient astronomers to calculate the positions of stars and other objects in the sky. Around 920, an Arab astronomer, al-Battani, worked out the complicated calculations needed to use the astrolabe.

Ring represents the pathway of the Sun through the sky.

Anatomy

The practice of human dissection – cutting open bodies for examination – dates from around 300 BCE. This was when Ancient Greek physicians began to gain a true understanding of how the human body works. The study of anatomy declined after the collapse of the Roman Empire in the 5th century. It was not until the 15th century that there was renewed interest, leading to the influential work of Flemish-born anatomist Andreas Vesalius in mapping the human body.

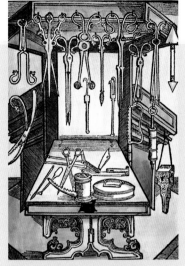

Tools of the trade
By the Middle Ages, anatomists and surgeons possessed a variety of tools. The German surgeon Hieronymous Brunschwig (c 1450–1513) produced a widely read work, *The Book of Surgery*, which gave advice on how to make cuts and included the first account of treating gunshot wounds.

This woodcut is from Brunschwig's *Book of Surgery*, showing his collection of surgical tools, which included scissors, forceps, and saws.

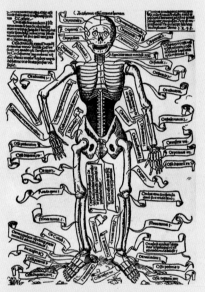

First anatomical prints
The invention of printing allowed wider distribution of anatomical images, such as this 1493 woodcut of a skeleton by French physician Richard Helain. It has inaccuracies, such as an over-large pelvis, and too many teeth.

Leonardo studies the body
Italian artist Leonardo da Vinci (1452–1519) (see pp.58–59) took a keen interest in anatomy and in making accurate drawings of the human body. To gain first-hand knowledge, he attended public dissections. His observations enabled him to produce a series of astonishingly detailed anatomical sketches.

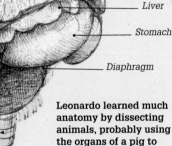

Lungs

Liver

Stomach

Diaphragm

Spine

Leonardo learned much anatomy by dissecting animals, probably using the organs of a pig to make this study.

Key events

See pp.58–59

500 BCE
Greek writer Alcmaeon of Croton stated that the brain is the centre of intelligence. He discovered the optic nerves and performed the first dissections of animals.

300 BCE
Known as the "father of anatomy", Herophilus, a Greek from Chalcedon (now in Istanbul, Turkey) understood the difference between veins and arteries, and performed the first public human dissection.

c 50
Roman doctor Rufus of Ephesus wrote *On the Names of the Parts of the Human Body*, the first work to give a detailed list of anatomical body parts.

c 175
Greek physician Galen (see p.29) described the structure of many body parts, including the brain, nervous system, and heart, and showed that arteries carry blood.

Anatomical theatres

It was the work of Italian doctor Mondino da Luzzi of Bologna University (c 1270–1326) that paved the way for public dissections. He was the first physician since ancient times to teach anatomy to medical students. Eventually, special dissecting rooms, or "theatres", became a feature of European universities. One of the earliest theatres was built at Leiden, in the Netherlands, in 1594.

Skeletons circle a dissection in this fanciful early 17th-century engraving of the anatomy theatre at Leiden University.

Vesalius's drawings

Flemish physician and anatomist Andreas Vesalius (1514–1564) studied medicine at the University of Padua, in Italy, and went on to teach there. Realizing that many of the ideas of ancient anatomists had been wrong, he took a closer look at the human body, and produced many superbly accurate drawings. These were published in his famous book *De Humani Corporis Fabrica* (On the Fabric of the Human Body). The quality of Vesalius's anatomical drawings was higher than anything ever seen before. His work was the beginning of modern anatomy.

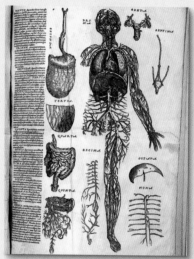

This page from Vesalius's great atlas of the human body describes various aspects of the nervous system.

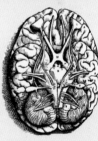

Many details shown in Vesalius's drawings of the brain had been ignored by earlier illustrators.

c 1250

Arabic physician Ibn al-Nafisi discovered the pulmonary circulation (the system by which blood reaching the left side of the heart passes first through the lungs).

c 1525

Jacob Berengar of Carpi, Italy, described two hormone-producing organs: the pineal gland and thymus gland. He also gave an account of the structure of the brain.

1543

Vesalius's *De Humani Corporis Fabrica* was published, the first complete and detailed atlas of human anatomy.

1628

English physician William Harvey gave the first correct description of the heart's role in the circulation of blood around the body.

Heart and blood vessels

945 ▶ 1045

c 980–1037   IBN SINA

The Arab scholar Ibn Sina (also known as Avicenna) lived in Central Asia. He wrote more than 400 books on such subjects as philosophy, medicine, psychology, geology, mathematics, and logic. From direct observation, he deduced that Venus is closer to Earth than the Sun. He also developed a theory of earthquakes and their role in the formation of mountains.

Canon of Medicine
Ibn Sina's *Canon of Medicine* was one of the most important medical books in Europe and Asia during the Middle Ages. In it, he showed how Aristotle's view that there were four causes of disease could be made to agree with the theory that four humours (fluids) make up the human body.

979
Zhang Sixun's mechanical clock
Zhang Sixun, a Chinese astronomer, created an advanced mechanical clock powered by a waterwheel, which completed a full revolution every 24 hours. Every two hours, mechanical jacks emerged from inside the mechanism carrying tables that showed the time.

982
Sheng Hui Fang
Chinese physicians compiled many manuals for drug recipes during the early part of the Song Dynasty (962–1279). One of the most important of these was the *Sheng Hui Fang*, put together under government orders and containing 16,834 medicinal recipes.

945 • • • **965** • • • ● ● ● **985** •

 Decimal numbers first appeared in Europe in the manuscript *Codex Vigilanus*, written by Spanish monks in 976. Knowledge of decimals had spread from the Arab world.

984
Ibn Sahl's work on refraction
Persian mathematician Ibn Sahl was interested in the refraction of light (its change in direction when it passes from one material to another). In his work *On Burning Mirrors and Lenses*, written in 984, he concluded that the amount of light that is refracted is different for each material.

Abacus in Europe
The French scholar monk Gerbert of Aurillac introduced the abacus to Europe in about 990. As a rapid way of making calculations, it was useful to astronomers, mathematicians, and merchants.

This modern abacus is very similar in design and function to the devices used 1,000 years ago.

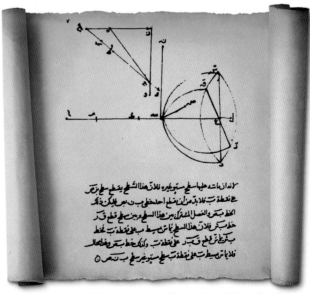

Page from Ibn Sahl's manuscript illustrating light refraction

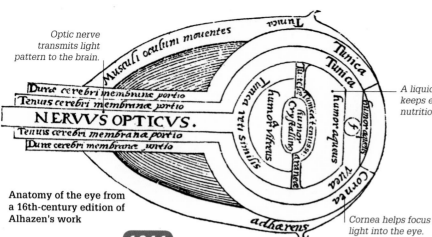

Optic nerve transmits light pattern to the brain.

A liquid called aqueous humour keeps eye's shape and provides nutrition for the cornea.

NERVVS OPTICVS.

Cornea helps focus light into the eye.

Anatomy of the eye from a 16th-century edition of Alhazen's work

Top view

Rim of bowl

Magnetized "fish" needle

S   N

Side view

Water on which needle floats

1011

Alhazen's optics
Arab scholar Ibn al-Haytham (or Alhazen) wrote a seven-volume book, *Kitab-al-Manazir* – an important work on optics. In it, he suggested that vision occurs when light is emitted from objects into the eye (and not by rays coming from the eye, as was believed previously).

1044

Early Chinese compass
Although the Chinese had long understood that lodestone (an iron ore) could magnetize objects, the first use of a compass, with a magnetized needle that pointed to the south, came in 1044. Early compasses consisted of a thin piece of metal floating in water, like the "south-pointing fish" seen here.

1005   **1025**   **1045** ▶▶

---

c 1040   MOVABLE TYPE

Around 1044, Bi Sheng, an otherwise obscure Chinese alchemist, invented a method of printing that employed movable clay blocks bearing impressions of letters. Previously, books had been printed using carved wooden blocks for each page, which could not be altered. The new method meant the blocks could be rearranged to create new pages, making printing much quicker.

Setting type
Bi Sheng baked his clay letters until they were hard and durable and then placed them on an iron frame, with the lines divided by iron strips. The letters were fixed in place by a paste of pine resin and wax, and then dipped in ink before the whole frame was pressed against paper.

Clay blocks
Each block of Bi Sheng's clay type had one Chinese character. Metal type, far longer lasting than clay or wood, appeared in Korea in around 1224.

❝For printing hundreds or thousands of copies, it was marvellously quick. ❞

Shen Kuo on Bi Sheng's movable type,
Dream Pool Essays, 1088

"Preparing Medicine from Honey", an illustration from a 13th-century Arabic translation of *De Materia Medica*, a book by Greek physician Dioscorides (c 40–90 CE) describing hundreds of drug remedies.

Medieval medicine

A great deal of medical knowledge was lost when the Roman Empire fell in the 5th century CE. Remnants survived mostly in areas that became part of the Islamic empires after the 7th century. Islamic scholars translated classical medical texts into Arabic and introduced new ideas. From about 1050, word about Arabic medical writing filtered into Europe through various centres of learning, including Salerno in Italy and Toledo in Spain. Techniques such as the washing of wounds and the use of early anaesthetics spread. In 1316, Italian physician Mondino da Luzzi wrote the first anatomy textbook in Europe since Roman times.

❝Nor may a subdeacon, deacon, or priest practise the art of surgery, which involves cauterizing [treating damaged tissues by burning] and making incisions.❞

Decision of the Fourth Lateran Council prohibiting Christian clerics from carrying out surgery, 1215. (Many medieval clergymen practised medicine, but they were forbidden to shed blood. The rule was originally intended to stop them fighting in war.)

1045 ▶ 1145

1066
Halley's comet
The appearance of Halley's comet just before the Norman defeat of the English at the Battle of Hastings was later explained as the cause of the disaster. Having no real explanation for comets, people generally believed they were evil omens.

In the Bayeux Tapestry (c 1080) people point at the comet

Constantine the African lectures at the school of Salerno, Italy

1085
Medical writings spread
Around this date, Constantine the African, a North African Muslim who converted to Christianity, collected Arabic medical manuscripts such as Haly Abbas's *Complete Art of Medicine*. He translated these at the medical school at Salerno in Italy and helped spread Arabic medical knowledge to Europe.

In 1121, philosopher Abu' l-Barakat of Baghdad proposed that the more force applied to an object, the greater its acceleration.

1045 • • • • • **1070** • • • **1085** • **1095** • •

1054
Sighting of Crab Nebula
On 4 July, Chinese astronomers noticed a new star so bright it could be seen in daylight. They called it the "guest star". What they saw was a supernova (exploding star), whose collapse, caused by extreme gravity, formed the cloud of debris in outer space that we now call the Crab Nebula.

1085
Translation of Ptolemy's *Almagest*
When Christian Spanish king Alfonso VI captured Toledo, which had been under Islamic rule, the city became a centre for the translation of Arabic scientific works into Latin. One of the most important was Ptolemy's great work on ancient astronomy, the *Almagest*.

Jia Xian's version of the mathematical pattern called Pascal's triangle

1050
Pascal's triangle
The Chinese mathematician Jia Xian created a version of the number pattern that today we know as Pascal's triangle, in which each number is the sum of the two numbers above it. This found later use in calculations involving probability.

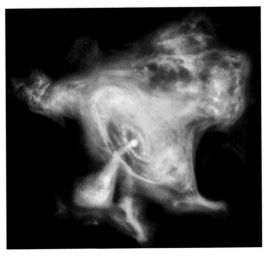

An image of the fast-rotating Crab Nebula from NASA's Chandra X-ray observatory.

1088
Magnetic compass described
Spoon-shaped, lodestone compasses had been used in China since around 200 BCE. In 1088 CE, the Chinese scholar Shen Kuo gave the first description of a compass with a magnetized needle. He included it in his work *Dream Pool Essays*, which also contained a discussion of fossils. By the early 12th century, Chinese ships were navigating by compass.

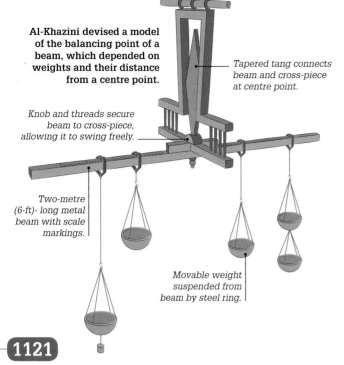

Al-Khazini devised a model of the balancing point of a beam, which depended on weights and their distance from a centre point.

Tapered tang connects beam and cross-piece at centre point.

Knob and threads secure beam to cross-piece, allowing it to swing freely.

Two-metre (6-ft)- long metal beam with scale markings.

Movable weight suspended from beam by steel ring.

1121

Theories of balance and gravity

The Arab scholar al-Khazini published a work on balance and equilibrium. In it he put forward a version of the theory of gravity, stating that the weight of a heavenly body depended on its distance from the centre of the Universe.

1120 ▸ • • • • 1145 ▸

1126

Key translation

English philosopher Adelard of Bath travelled widely in Italy, Sicily, and the Middle East, becoming familiar with the works of Arab scholars. He translated the famous mathematician al-Khwarizmi's *Astronomical Tables of Sindhind*, spreading knowledge of them to western Europe.

1121

Chinese grid map

A map carved on a stone tablet in Sichuan, China, made the first known use of grid squares to show scale. Known as the *Jiu You Shouling tu*, it has around 1,400 place names and is a sign of how sophisticated Chinese map-making had become.

Travelling the world See pages 92–93

"Seeing the abundance of books in Arabic... he learned... Arabic... in order to translate them."

Life of Gerard of Cremona (an Italian scholar), c 12th century

c 1048–1131   OMAR KHAYYAM

Persian poet and philosopher Omar Khayyam was also a talented mathematician and astronomer. By the age of 25 he had written an important work on music and one on algebra. Later, translations of his poetry made him famous in the West, but in the Islamic world of his time he was famed as a scientist. In 1073, the ruler of Persia, Malik Shah, invited him to set up an observatory in Isfahan. There Omar Khayyam made many important observations and compiled a set of astronomical tables.

Length of a year

While at Isfahan, Omar Khayyam calculated the length of the year to be 365.24219858156 days. This is correct to five decimal places and shows remarkably precise measurement, considering the astronomical instruments available to him.

Book on algebra

In his book on algebra, Omar Khayyam used geometrical methods to solve cubic and quadratic equations. He turned the numbers in the equations into curves and found the solution where they intersected. This technique was very advanced for its time.

Astronomy

Many ancient peoples, such as the Maya of Central America, the Chinese, Indians, and Babylonians, tried to make sense of the motions of stars and planets. From the 4th century BCE, the Greeks developed models to explain why planets changed position in the sky. Not until the 16th century did astronomers realize that the Sun, not Earth, is the centre of the Solar System.

Ruins of the ancient El Caracol ("Snail") observatory, Mexico

Ancient observatories

The Maya, whose culture was at its peak from 250–900 CE, built observatories, such as El Caracol ("Snail", named for its shape) at Chichén Itzá, in Mexico. They accurately calculated the length of the year and recorded the movements of the planet Venus.

Eclipses

In the 13th century, English monk Johannes of Sacrobosco reproduced calculations made by the astronomer Ptolemy of Alexandria in the 2nd century CE. These showed how the movement of the Moon in front of the Sun causes an eclipse.

Solar and lunar eclipses, from Sacrobosco's book *De sphaera mundi* (Sphere of the World)

Astronomers using astrolabes, in the *The Travels of Sir John Mandeville*, 1356

Key events

c 500 BCE

Babylonian astronomers created the zodiac, dividing the sky into 12 equal zones through which the Sun and the planets appeared to travel.

c 350 BCE

Eudoxus of Cnidus, a Greek mathematician, devised the first model of the Solar System based on concentric spheres. He used 27 spheres, several for each planet, to explain irregular orbits.

c 280 BCE

Aristarchus of Samos suggested that Earth orbits around the Sun. Fellow Greek astronomers and scholars criticized his ideas, which were not accepted.

c 240 BCE

Eratosthenes of Cyrene (now in Libya) accurately measured the circumference of Earth by comparing shadows cast by the Sun in two different locations.

Ideas from the East

Medieval astronomers in India developed highly sophisticated mathematical tools for making astronomical calculations. Around 525 CE, the Indian mathematician Aryabhata put forward the idea that Earth rotates on its axis, correctly explaining the apparent movement of the stars. Much of this knowledge passed to astronomers in the Islamic world, who improved on existing theories and refined calculations of how the planets moved within spheres. They also perfected the use of devices called astrolabes, which allowed them to measure the positions of the Sun and stars.

Brass armillary sphere, made in Italy, 1554

The Ptolemaic system

Early Greek astronomers explained the movements of planets by suggesting they orbited within concentric spheres around Earth. This theory was worked out in detail by Ptolemy of Alexandria (c 100–170 CE). To explain oddities in planetary motion, he used a system of epicycles (small circles) within which planets revolved, while at the same time orbiting in larger spheres around Earth. Complicated models, called armillary spheres, were made to illustrate Ptolemy's system.

Planets orbit the Sun   *Sky divided into 12 zodiacal zones*

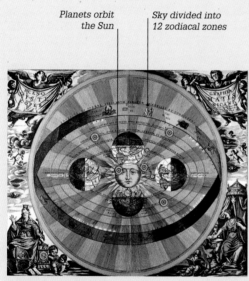

The Copernican Universe, Dutch engraving, 17th century

The Copernican Universe

Polish astronomer Nicolaus Copernicus (1473–1543) disagreed with Ptolemy's views on the Universe. He devised a model, known as a heliocentric system, in which Earth and the planets moved in orbits, with the Sun (rather than Earth) at the centre of the Solar System.

Refracting telescope

In 1609, the Italian astronomer Galileo Galilei built a telescope. He was not its inventor, but he was the first person to use a telescope for astronomical purposes. Its greatly increased magnification meant Galileo was able to discover four new satellites of Jupiter and to study sunspots for the first time.

Galileo with his telescope, c 1620

Objective lens bends light rays   *Focal point*   *Eyepiece lens magnifies image*

Light ray

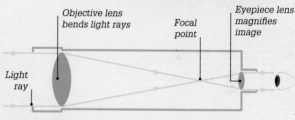

How it works

Galileo used a refracting telescope, with lenses to gather light and to produce a magnified image. Most modern refracting telescopes are designed as shown above (and work slightly differently from Galileo's). These have an objective lens at one end that gathers light from far objects and refracts (bends) it to a focal point, producing an image. The light then passes through an eyepiece that magnifies the image.

---

c 130 BCE

Hipparchus, a Greek from Nicaea (now Iznik, Turkey), devised the first accurate star map. He used Ptolemy's model to predict lunar and solar eclipses.

Moon

c 975

Llobet of Barcelona wrote a work introducing the astrolabe to Europe. This device, well known in the Islamic world, calculated the position of the Sun and stars.

1259

An astronomical observatory was built at Maragha, Iran. It allowed Islamic astronomers to make highly accurate measurements of the planets and stars from which to compile charts and tables.

1543

Copernicus published *On the Revolutions of the Celestial Spheres*, setting out his model of a Solar System with Earth orbiting the Sun.

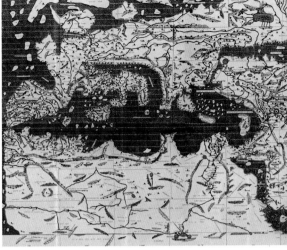

Modern copy of *Tabula Rogeriana*, al-Idrisi's ancient world map

1154
Striking clocks
Arab engineer Muhammad al-Sa'ati constructed the first striking clock in Damascus, Syria. Like many early clocks, it was powered by water. In 1203, his son Ridwan gave a detailed description of the clock's mechanism.

1154
Al-Idrisi's world map
Arab scholar Muhammad al-Idrisi was commissioned by King Roger II of Sicily to compile a world map. It took 15 years to complete and was inscribed on a 2-m- (6.5-ft-) wide silver disc. The most accurate map of its time, it was accompanied by a book detailing all the lands it portrayed.

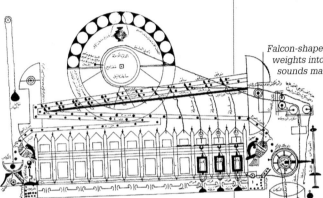

Falcon-shaped figures released weights into a metal vessel, the sounds marking the hours.

Water power turned the ropes and pulleys that set al-Sa'ati's clock in motion.

1180
Vertical windmills
The first windmills with sails mounted on a vertical tower were introduced in Europe. The spinning of the sails caused a shaft to rotate, which operated hammers used to grind grain. Earlier windmills, developed in Persia (now Iran), had been horizontal, with rectangular sails rotating around an upright shaft.

1145 · ● ● **1165** ● ● ● **1185** ·

1160
The first printed map
The earliest printed map in the world, the *Shiwu Guofeng dili zhi tu* (Geographic Map of Fifteen States), appeared around this date. It was printed from woodblocks and showed parts of western China. It was published in the *Liu jing tu*, a Chinese encyclopedia. The map listed place names, including rivers and 15 provinces.

📣 **In 1150, Indian mathematician Bhaskara II proved that numbers have two square roots, one positive and one negative.**

c 1170–1250   FIBONACCI
Leonardo Bonacci, nicknamed Fibonacci, was a merchant from Pisa, Italy, who learned much about Arabic mathematics while trading in North Africa. His book *Liber Abaci* introduced Arabic numerals and decimal notation to Europe. He also did important work in solving certain algebraic equations and in number sequences.

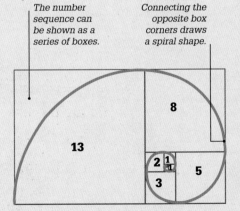

The number sequence can be shown as a series of boxes.

Connecting the opposite box corners draws a spiral shape.

Fibonacci's sequence
Fibonacci described a sequence, later named after him, in which each number is the sum of the two numbers before it (0, 1, 1, 2, 3, 5, 8, 13, and so on). Scientists found mapping a series of squares whose area corresponds to the numbers, and then connecting them, draws a spiral shape often seen in nature – such as a snail's shell.

> **"He had engraved on it a map of the seven climates, and their lands and regions."**
>
> Muhammad al-Idrisi, *Nuzhat al-Mushtaq fi Ikhtiraq al-Afaq* (Book of Pleasant Journeys into Faraway Lands), 1154

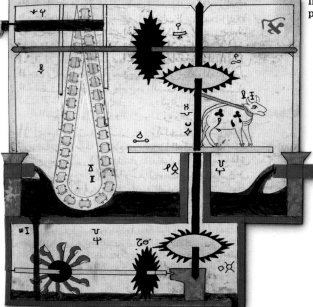

Illustration of a water pump designed by al-Jazari

1206

Mechanical devices

In *The Book of Knowledge of Ingenious and Mechanical Devices*, Arab engineer al-Jazari described more than 50 machines and gave instructions for building them. Among them were the first crankshaft (to convert circular motion into back-and-forward motion) and a 2-m- (6.5-ft-) high water clock in the shape of an elephant.

1237

Major medical book for women

Chinese physician Chen Ziming wrote *The Great Treatise of Beneficial Formulae for Women*, the first major Chinese medical work on treating women. It described 360 female medical conditions, as well as problems linked to pregnancy and childbirth.

1205 — **1225** — **1245** ⏩

Healing people
See pages 76–77

1214

Use of antiseptics in Italy

Hugh of Lucca, an Italian surgeon, described how wine could be used as an antiseptic to clean wounds and prevent infection. Traditionally, doctors had thought, wrongly, that letting pus form in a wound helped injuries to heal.

 Robert Grosseteste was the first chancellor of the University of Oxford, in England, from 1214.

1232

Gunpowder rockets

The first military use of rockets propelled by gunpowder was made by the Chinese against the Mongols during their siege of the town of Kaifeng in north-eastern China. These "flying-fire arrows" consisted of bamboo tubes filled with gunpowder attached to a stick. They were very inaccurate, but still caused the Mongols to abandon the siege and flee.

1225

A bishop's theories

Robert Grosseteste, Bishop of Lincoln in England, tried to show how the philosophy and science of the Ancient Greek Aristotle (see pp.30–31) agreed with Christian ideas. Grosseteste held the belief that light fills the Universe and shapes its form. He thought scientific theories were best examined through experiments and that ideas not supported by observation should be rejected.

13th-century portrait of Bishop Grosseteste

Roger Bacon

The 13th-century English friar Roger Bacon (c 1214–1292) was nicknamed "Doctor Mirabilis" (Wonder Doctor) for his wide-ranging scientific interests. At a time when universities taught very few subjects in an unchanging curriculum, Bacon wanted to introduce a different type of education.

Bacon the monk

Bacon studied at the University of Oxford in the 1230s, before moving to Paris as a lecturer. He returned to Oxford in 1247, where he began his scientific research. In 1257 he became a Franciscan monk. Living in a strict religious community, he found it hard to continue his experimental work.

Reform of universities

Medieval university students learned mainly theology (study of religious belief) and were also introduced to grammar, logic, and rhetoric (the art of speaking and writing effectively). Classical Greek and Latin authors such as Aristotle were used as models. In his important book *Opus Maius* (Latin for "Greater Work"), Bacon argued for a much wider range of subjects, including optics, geography, mechanics, and alchemy (medieval chemistry).

Optics

Bacon had new ideas about vision. While Greek scientists believed sight was caused by a ray that came from the eye, Bacon thought all objects gave out a wave that rippled outwards. When this wave reached the eye, the object was seen.

Later years

In 1268, Bacon lost a protector when Pope Clement IV, who supported Bacon's work, died. Many Franciscans thought Bacon's ideas went against the teachings of the Catholic Church. He may even have been imprisoned for a while in Italy. Bacon eventually returned to England where he wrote new works, including one on mathematics. He died in 1292.

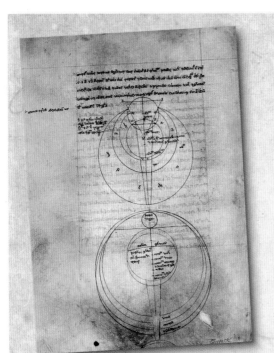

Opus Maius
This drawing of an eye is taken from Bacon's book Opus Maius. Bacon was not allowed to publish without the consent of the Franciscans, but in 1266 Pope Clement IV asked him to produce a summary of all the things he believed should be taught in universities. By the time Bacon had completed his work in 1268, Clement had died.

Bacon holds scales to measure the weight of substances.

Scale pan containing the element fire in balance with left-hand pan

Scale pan containing the element water

The alchemist
Like many scholars of the time, Bacon practised alchemy. Alchemists believed that everything was made of four "elements": earth, air, fire, and water. They also thought they could transmute (transform) metals such as lead into gold.

Lecturer in Paris
Bacon is seen here presenting one of his works to the Chancellor of Paris University. Bacon taught there for 10 years from around 1240. He met other scholars, such as Peter Peregrinus, who wrote a work on magnetism and inspired Bacon's love of experimenting.

Astronomical observer
An avid astronomer, Bacon argued that the Universe must be spherical. He calculated the distance from Earth to the stars as 130 million miles (209 million km). We now know the distance is many millions of times greater.

"The things of this world cannot be made without a knowledge of mathematics."

Roger Bacon, *Opus Maius*,
1267–1268

📢 In 1267, English monk Roger Bacon described the eye's structure, the use of magnifying lenses, and also an early type of telescope.

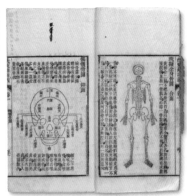

The earliest manuscript of Song Ci's *The Washing Away of Wrongs* is from 1408. This example is from the 19th century.

1286

Eyeglasses

In the 13th century, scientists began experiments with magnifying objects using glass lenses. In 1286, Italian friar Giordano da Pisa gave the first description of lenses used as spectacles. Early eyeglasses corrected long-sightedness, a particular problem for monks and friars who often had to read and write manuscripts in dim light.

French clergyman wears eyeglasses for close work.

1247

Work on forensic medicine

Song Ci, a Chinese lawyer, wrote *The Washing Away of Wrongs* – the world's first work on forensic medicine (the use of scientific knowledge in crime investigation). His aim was to improve the evidence presented in legal cases, particularly of murder. He collected information about past cases and was critical about the unreliable tests traditionally conducted by court officers.

1245 ▸ **1275** ▸

1260

Using anaesthetics

In his groundbreaking medical writings, Italian surgeon Teodorico Borgognoni discussed many aspects of surgery and the care of wounds. Using an early form of anaesthesia, he sedated his patients before operations with sponges soaked in opium or other sleep-inducing herbs.

Seeds from poppy head

Mandrake root

Healing people
See pages 76–77

A solution made with ingredients such as opium poppy seeds or mandrake root was soaked on a sponge and given to patients to make them sleep.

1269

Magnetic force

French scholar Pierre de Marincourt described the lines of magnetic force surrounding a magnet. He showed that a compass has two poles, and that oppositely charged magnetic poles attract each other, while similarly charged poles repel (push apart) each other.

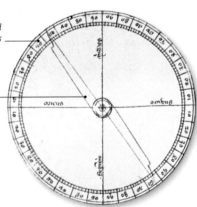

Dial marked in degrees

Magnetized needle

Diagram of a needle compass, from de Marincourt's *Epistola de Magnete* (Letter on the Magnet)

"Then the stone that you hold in your hand will appear to flee the floating stone."

Pierre de Marincourt on magnetic repulsion, *Epistola de Magnete*, 1269

1300

Rainbow theory

German monk Theodoric of Freiburg used small, water-filled glass bottles to show that light passing through them was both reflected and refracted (sent in different directions). He concluded that beams of sunlight hitting water drops in a cloud bend in the same way, causing a rainbow.

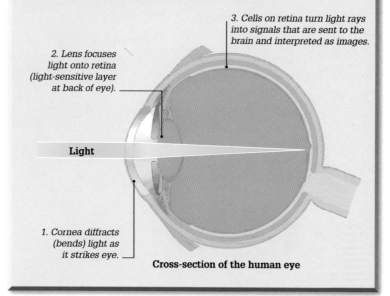
1305

1315

1323

1345

First public dissection

Italian physician Mondino da Luzzi performed the first public dissection of a body at Bologna, Italy. This gave medical students and doctors a greatly improved understanding of human anatomy.

Ockham's razor

In his book *Summa Logicae* (The Sum of Logic), English friar William of Ockham reasoned that seeking an explanation for something should be simplified by cutting out any unnecessary information or arguments. The principle became known as Ockham's razor.

c 1200–1280   ALBERTUS MAGNUS

German Dominican friar Albertus Magnus was inspired by the work of the Ancient Greek philosopher Aristotle (see pp.30–31) to compile an encyclopedia of philosophical and scientific knowledge. Albertus believed in discovering the causes of things through science, and he is regarded as the founder of natural science as a field of study. His work ranged across many subjects, including theology (study of religion), logic, zoology, and alchemy (medieval chemistry). He was an excellent teacher and among his pupils was the famous Christian theologian Thomas Aquinas.

Page from Magnus's treatise on natural history

French crusaders use cannons in an attempt to breach the walls of the North African city of Mahdia in 1390.

History of gunpowder

The Chinese understood the explosive properties of gunpowder – a mixture of saltpetre, sulphur, and charcoal – as early as the 9th century CE. They adapted its use to military purposes, producing "fire-arrows", rockets, and flamethrowers. Around 1250, they made the first cannons. Knowledge of gunpowder weaponry spread westwards, reaching Europe about 1300. Cannons soon appeared in battles there. Within a hundred years, handheld guns were developed, but it was early artillery – the big guns – that proved most effective in sieges, where they could demolish fortifications once thought indestructible. There was no such success for the French at the so-called Mahdia Crusade pictured here, as their firepower was not sufficient to breach city walls.

> **❝It made such a noise in the going, as though all the devils of hell had been on the way. ❞**
>
> Jean Froissart, *Chronicles*, giving an account of the use of cannons at the siege of Oudenaarde, in Flanders, 1382

1345 ▶ 1445

 In 1357, French philosopher Jean Buridan developed the theory of impetus, the force that makes an object move.

Anatomy
See pages 36–37

1368
Guild of Surgeons
The foundation of a Guild of Surgeons in England, in 1368, was the first attempt to provide rules and regulations for the profession. Before this, anyone – commonly barbers – had been able to practise surgery.

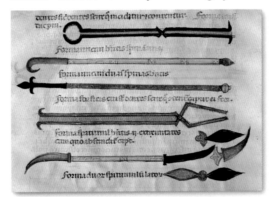

An array of surgical instruments illustrated in the manuscript *De Chirurgia* (On Surgery) by the great Arab physician Albucasis.

1349
Motion and forces
French mathematician Nicolas d'Oresme worked out a new way of drawing graphs to represent the motion of moving objects. The graphs helped to explain the relationship between the speed, time, and distance travelled.

1380
Rocket warfare reaches Europe
The first recorded use in Europe of rockets in warfare came at the battle of Chioggia, a naval conflict between the Italian cities of Venice and Genoa. Rockets are difficult to make and their military use showed how a greater understanding of gunpowder weaponry was developing.

1345 **1385**

1364
Astronomical clock
Italian clockmaker Giovanni de Dondi completed his astrarium – a complex clock with dials showing the movements of the Sun, Moon, and planets. It had more than 100 gear wheels. As well as allowing astronomers to calculate the position of heavenly bodies, it provided a calendar of Church holy days.

The astrarium had seven dials and its central weight swung around 30 times a minute.

1377
A rotating Earth
In his *Livre du ciel et du monde* (Book of Heaven and Earth), Nicolas d'Oresme disproved all the popular ideas that Earth was stationary at the centre of the Solar System. He also suggested that Earth rotated on its axis. However, he could not go as far as believing that Earth moved around the Sun.

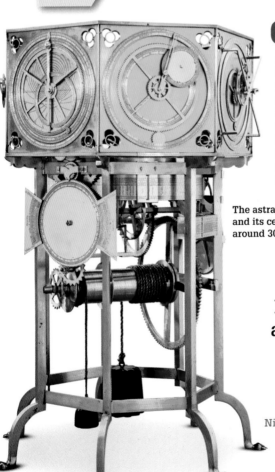

❝One could by this believe that the earth and not the heavens is so moved, and there is no evidence to the contrary.❞

Nicolas d'Oresme on the rotation of Earth, *Livre du ciel et du monde*, 1377

Nicolas d'Oresme seated by an armillary sphere, a model of the Solar System

c 1400–1600   RENAISSANCE ARCHITECTURE

During the Renaissance, a cultural movement that began in Italy in the mid-14th century, artists and architects rediscovered the classical past. Architects based their buildings on Greek and Roman models, using columns, arches, and domes. Architect Filippo Brunelleschi of Florence spent 16 years building the remarkable dome of Florence Cathedral. This dome, at 45 m (147 ft) wide and 114 m (374 ft) high, was the largest unsupported dome yet built.

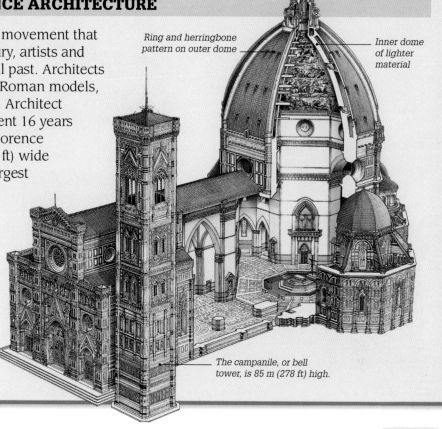

Ring and herringbone pattern on outer dome

Inner dome of lighter material

The dome of Florence Cathedral
Building such a huge dome was believed to be impossible. Brunelleschi designed an inner dome of lightweight material and an outer one of heavier stone. Oak timbers set in rings connected the two domes and supported them. Constructing the outer dome was made easier because the builder could balance on the already finished inner dome.

The campanile, or bell tower, is 85 m (278 ft) high.

 1405 ● ○ ● ● **1445** ▸▸

1421

First recorded patent
The first patent – a licence giving an inventor sole rights to an invention – was granted by the city of Florence to the Italian architect Filippo Brunelleschi. It was for a barge and hoist used to transport heavy marble slabs up the River Arno. The patent forbade anyone else from copying the idea for three years.

1436

Perspective in painting
Roman artists knew how to use perspective (a mathematical system for creating the appearance of distance on a flat surface). Knowledge of the technique was later lost, but rediscovered during the Italian Renaissance. In 1436, Leon Battista Alberti, an architect and scholar, gave a full account of it in his work *On Painting*.

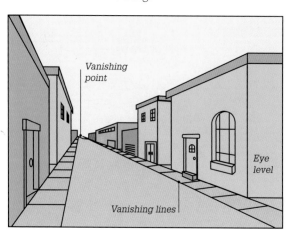

Vanishing point

Eye level

Vanishing lines

Perspective gives the illusion of depth. The artist draws objects smaller and closer together until eventually they form a single point known as the vanishing point.

NICOLAVS CVSANVS

Nicholas of Cusa
German theologian Nicholas of Cusa (1401–1464) believed that all things in the Universe are in motion. From this he concluded that Earth is not fixed and must move around the Sun.

Nicholas of Cusa, portrayed here in a woodcut, had theories on the Universe that would influence scientists in later centuries.

In 1490, Leonardo da Vinci described capillary action: when water moves up inside a thin tube, in a direction opposed to the force of gravity.

Wooden plate for holding paper

Lever tightens plates together, pressing inked type onto paper.

Solid wooden frame holds plates steady to prevent slippage.

Replica of Gutenberg's original press

1450

Gutenberg's press
Johannes Gutenberg set up the first European printing press in Mainz, Germany. This used movable type that could be rearranged and reused to make up different pages of text. Producing books was made much easier and the technique spread rapidly throughout Europe.

1464

Trigonometry text
German mathematician Johannes Müller (known by his Latin name, Regiomontanus) wrote *On Triangles*, the first textbook on trigonometry (the study of the relationship between angles and lengths in triangles).

1489

First use of + and − signs
Johannes Widman, a German mathematician, was the first to use the modern signs for plus (+) and minus (−). Previously, mathematicians had used a variety of signs, including "p" and "m". The sign "=" to mean "equals" came into use later, in 1557.

Page from Regiomontanus's *On Triangles*

1445 • • **1465** • • **1485** • •

1472

A comet observed
An interest in astronomy led Regiomontanus (Johannes Müller) to make the first detailed observations and descriptions of a comet. Using trigonometrical techniques, he worked out methods for calculating the size of a comet and its distance from Earth.

1492

Christopher Columbus discovers America
When Genoese mariner Christopher Columbus sailed westward from Spain, he was hoping to reach China. Instead he discovered the Americas, landing somewhere in the Bahamas. His voyage led to European colonization and an exchange of food crops – and diseases – between Europe and the Americas.

Tent canvas on a wooden frame

Model of the parachute Leonardo designed in his sketchbooks

Da Vinci's parachute
In his notebooks, Leonardo da Vinci (see pp.58–59) sketched out many ideas for machines centuries before their final invention. In 1481, he drew and described a parachute made of tent canvas.

Woodcut of a comet, from the *Nuremberg Chronicle*, 1493

Model of *Santa Maria*, Columbus's flagship on his first expedition

1473–1543   NICOLAUS COPERNICUS

Born in Poland, Copernicus studied astronomy, mathematics, law, and medicine in Italy. When asked to take part in a reform of the calendar, Copernicus began to study Greek astronomer Ptolemy's 1,500-year-old system of celestial spheres, in which he found flaws.

First surviving globe

The first surviving globe of the world was produced in 1492 by cartographer Martin Behaim, who made it for his home city of Nuremberg in Germany. It shows a world map and has many decorative illustrations.

The Copernican cosmos

Copernicus did not disagree with Ptolemy's idea that the planets rotated in concentric spheres, but he made corrections to some of Ptolemy's other notions. In his amended version, he placed the Sun at the centre of the Universe, not Earth, as Ptolemy had done.

Painting by Andreas Cellarius depicting Copernicus's Sun-centred Universe, 1660

1505 • **1525** ● • ● **1545** ▶▶

1527

Classifying chemicals

German chemist Theophrastus von Hohenheim (better known as Paracelsus) worked out a new classification for chemical substances. This was based on a division of substances into salts, sulfurs, and mercuries, according to their properties.

1543

Illustrated anatomy

Flemish physician Andreas Vesalius published *De Humani Corporis Fabrica* (On the Structure of the Human Body), which remained a standard textbook for centuries. New printing techniques produced full-colour plates illustrating human anatomy in the clearest detail seen so far.

 By 1500, printing presses had been set up in 282 cities and had printed around 28,000 editions of books.

Diagram of muscles from *De Humani Corporis Fabrica*

57

GREAT SCIENTISTS

Leonardo da Vinci

The Italian artist Leonardo da Vinci (1452–1519) was also an extremely clever scientist. As well as painting the *Mona Lisa*, one of the most famous works of art of all time, he studied anatomy, geology, geography, and optics. He was a brilliant engineer and drew designs for submarines, parachutes, and airships centuries before the technology existed to build them.

Renaissance Florence

In 14th-century Italy, people began to take a fresh interest in Greek and Roman learning that had been lost for centuries. By the late 15th century, the city of Florence, Leonardo's birthplace, was at the heart of what is called the Renaissance (rebirth), a time of cultural renewal. From art to medicine and from architecture to engineering, scholars relearnt old techniques and discovered new ones.

The engineer

Leonardo's desire to understand how things worked, combined with his skill at technical drawing, sparked in him an interest in machines and engineering. He designed complex levers, pulleys, and springs for use in construction. Leonardo was also a talented military engineer, and in 1500, he advised the Venetians on how to defend themselves from attacks by the Turks. One of his suggestions was to use a form of submarine to sink enemy ships. In his lifetime, Leonardo's inventions attracted little public interest. Today, we recognize his importance to science.

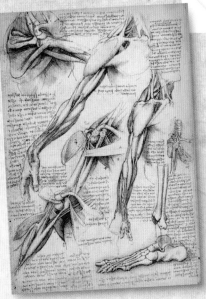

The anatomist
From the 1490s, Leonardo studied anatomy. He dissected animals and attended post-mortems of human corpses so that he could see the internal structure of the body. As a result, he was able to produce a series of highly detailed anatomical sketches.

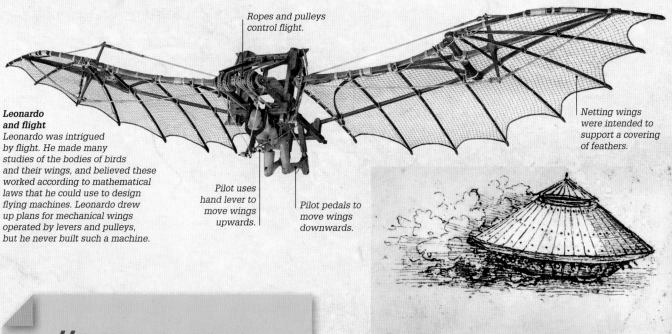

Ropes and pulleys control flight.

Netting wings were intended to support a covering of feathers.

Leonardo and flight
Leonardo was intrigued by flight. He made many studies of the bodies of birds and their wings, and believed these worked according to mathematical laws that he could use to design flying machines. Leonardo drew up plans for mechanical wings operated by levers and pulleys, but he never built such a machine.

Pilot uses hand lever to move wings upwards.

Pilot pedals to move wings downwards.

Leonardo's inventions
This wooden tank-like vehicle for storming fortifications was just one among many ingenious machines that Leonardo devised. Others included a parachute, a dredging machine, and a robotic knight that could grasp objects and open and close its jaw.

> **"No human investigation can be called real science if it cannot be demonstrated mathematically."**
>
> Leonardo da Vinci, *Trattato della Pittura* (Treatise on Painting)

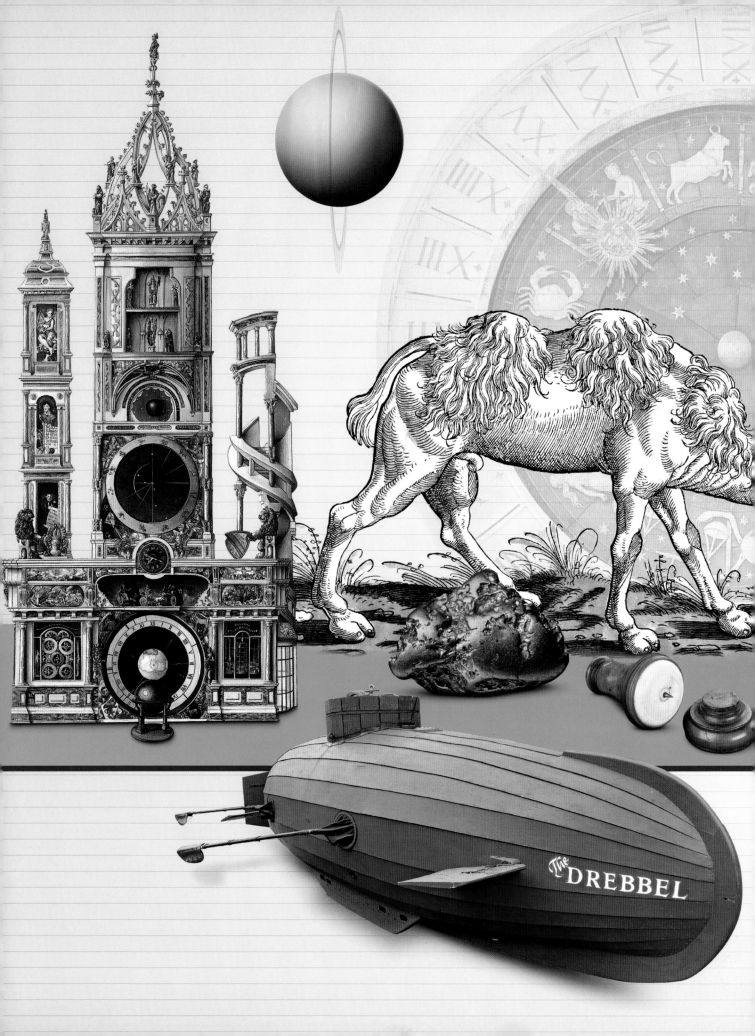

The DREBBEL

1545–1790
The age of discovery

In the 16th century, new scientific knowledge replaced old ways of thinking. The invention of the microscope and the telescope stimulated the study of anatomy and astronomy. Long-distance travel at sea led to more accurate ways of measuring distance and time. These advances created a need for complex calculations, which brought about advances in mathematics. Instead of relying on traditional teaching, scientists (then known as natural philosophers) began to test ideas and theories through observation, investigation, and experimentation. Their discoveries laid the foundations of modern science.

1545 ▶ 1570

 All the platinum ever mined would fit in an average-sized living room.

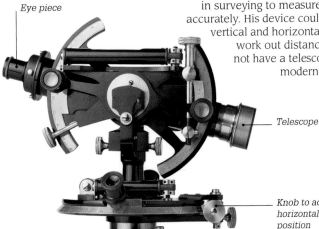

Eye piece

Telescope

Knob to adjust horizontal position

Modern example of a theodolite

1551
Measuring distances
English surveyor Leonard Digges invented an early theodolite, an instrument used in surveying to measure distances accurately. His device could measure vertical and horizontal angles to work out distances, but did not have a telescope, unlike modern examples.

Platinum nugget

1551
Prolific inventor
Islamic scientist Taqi al-Din wrote a book describing how a steam turbine worked. He also invented the first weight-driven astronomical clock, clocks that measured minutes and seconds, and an early telescope.

1557
Rare metal
Italian scholar Julius Caesar Scaliger wrote that Spanish explorers in Mexico had found a substance that did not melt at high temperatures and did not rust. It is the first known reference in European writings to platinum, one of Earth's rarest metals.

1545 • • • • **1550** ● • • • **1555** •

1551
Animal magic
Swiss naturalist Konrad von Gesner set out to catalogue all the world's animals in his five-volume *Historiae Animalium* (History of Animals), one of the first works of zoology. Although his colourful drawings are noted for their accuracy, he included some fictional beasts such as unicorns.

Gesner's illustration of a two-humped (Bactrian) camel and driver

1557
Maths symbols
Welsh mathematician Robert Recorde wrote *The Whetstone of Witte*, the first book on algebra in English. He popularized the use of + (plus) and – (minus) signs, and is credited with inventing the = (equals) sign.

Travelling the world
See pages 92–93

1560

First scientific society

Giambattista della Porta was an Italian playwright and polymath (someone who knows a lot about many subjects). He founded what is believed to be the world's first scientific society in Naples, Italy. Membership of the society, called the *Academia Secretorum Naturae* (Academy of the Mysteries of Nature) was open to anyone who had made a new scientific discovery.

1561

Anatomical discovery

Gabriello Falloppio, an Italian anatomist and professor of surgery at Padua University, in Italy, published a description of the human reproductive organs. He gave his name to the Fallopian tubes, the pair of channels in female mammals through which eggs pass from the ovaries to the uterus.

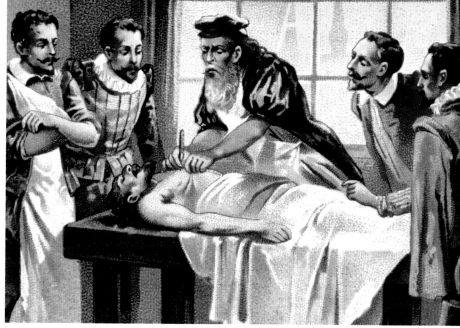

Ambroise Paré operates on a patient in this 19th-century print

1564

Compassionate surgery

French surgeon Ambroise Paré wrote a manual of modern surgery based on his experience of carrying out amputations on the battlefield. Ahead of his time, Paré stated that pain relief, healing, and good patient care were essential to successful surgery.

1560 • • • • **1565** • • • • **1570** ▸▸

1550–1570   MAPMAKING SKILLS

Advances in navigation and exploration in the 1500s led to improvements in mapmaking. The centre of mapmaking was Antwerp (in modern-day Belgium), then a busy centre of international trade. Printed collections of maps familiarized Europeans with the new lands discovered in America and Asia.

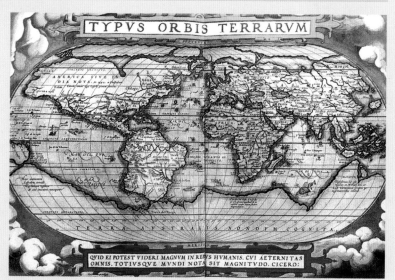

TYPVS ORBIS TERRARVM

Gerard Mercator

In 1569, Flemish mapmaker Gerard Mercator published a new world map. His representation, or projection, of the globe on a flat surface used a grid of straight lines to show direction. This proved an aid to sailors.

The first atlas

Abraham Ortelius, a Flemish cartographer, published the first modern world atlas in 1570. It contained 70 separate maps on 53 sheets, showing all the countries and continents known at that time.

Measuring things

In ancient times, parts of the human body were used to measure length (some systems today still use "feet"). The first weights were often based on fixed quantities of grain. These traditional units served well for thousands of years, until the rise of scientific experimentation brought the need for far more accurate methods of measuring things.

Early weights and measures

Today, we measure length, weight, and volume using international standard units. In the past, these units were local – each city or country set their own. For example, in medieval England, an inch was equivalent to three grains of barley laid length to length.

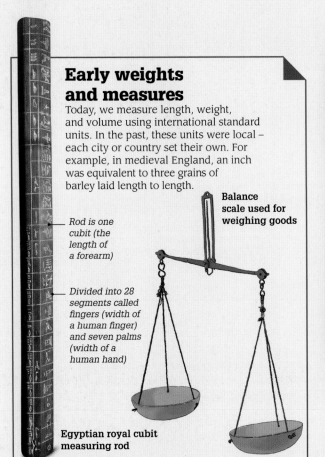

Rod is one cubit (the length of a forearm)

Divided into 28 segments called fingers (width of a human finger) and seven palms (width of a human hand)

Egyptian royal cubit measuring rod

Balance scale used for weighing goods

Thermometer with Fahrenheit scale, 1720s

Degrees of temperature

Two scales for accurately measuring temperature were invented in the 1700s – the Fahrenheit scale in 1724 and the Celsius (or centigrade) scale in 1742. Today, the Celsius scale is used in nearly every country in the world. The USA still uses the Fahrenheit scale.

Measuring small distances

Engineers and others who need to measure small distances use a two-armed instrument called a caliper. The simplest form of caliper is a pair of compasses or dividers. This much more elaborate gunner's caliper was used to measure the bore (internal dimension) of a cannon as well as the external width of a cannonball.

Arc marked with a scale gives diameter.

Compass for navigation also has a sundial.

Curved arm with scale

Points are used to measure internal and external distances.

Key events

Egyptian royal cubit

Cubit

Palm

c 3000 BCE

The royal cubit was a standard measurement of length in Ancient Egypt. It was based on the length of the forearm, from the middle fingertip to the elbow.

1631

French mathematician Paul Vernier invented a sliding scale for taking accurate measurements that are smaller than the smallest on an instrument's main scale. The Vernier scale is still used today.

1724

Dutch physicist Gabriel Fahrenheit devised the temperature scale named after him. It has 32° as the freezing point of water, and 212° as its boiling point.

Caliper using vernier scale

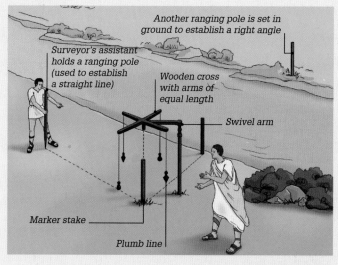

Another ranging pole is set in ground to establish a right angle

Surveyor's assistant holds a ranging pole (used to establish a straight line)

Wooden cross with arms of equal length

Swivel arm

Marker stake

Plumb line

Surveyor's tool
The Romans, who were skilled builders and surveyors, used a device called a groma to measure right angles. It consisted of a horizontal wooden cross and a weighted cord (plumb line), which hung from each of the four arms. The surveyor would look down each pair of plumb lines in turn to establish a right angle.

Metric and imperial systems
The metric system, first introduced in France, is the official system of measurement in most countries today. The imperial system was once used throughout the British Empire. The USA is the only major country that still uses it officially – it is known there as the customary measurement system. Whilst both systems are still in use, the values are not directly equivalent.

Metric	Imperial
Centimetre (cm)	Inch (in)
Metre (m)	Foot (ft)
Kilometre (km)	Mile (m)
Kilometre per hour (km/h)	Mile per hour (mph)
Gram (g)	Ounce (oz)
Kilogram (kg)	Pound (lb)
Litre (l)	Gallon (gal)
Celsius (°C)	Fahrenheit (°F)

Scale marked in degrees

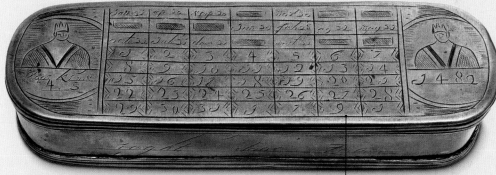

Dual-purpose device
The lid of this small tobacco box, which belonged to an 18th-century seaman, was engraved with a perpetual calendar (meaning it is valid for numerous years) so he always knew what day of the week it was. Mathematical tables on the bottom, used with the ship's log float (see p.93), also enabled him to calculate the ship's speed.

Sailor's tobacco box

Perpetual calendar engraved on lid

Gunner's caliper from Venice, Italy, 16th century

1875
The Treaty of the Metre, signed in Paris by representatives of 17 nations, agreed to international standard units of measurement based on the metre and the kilogram.

1960
The International System of Units (SI), the modern form of the metric system, was officially adopted. It is the most widely used system of measurement.

Leica DISTO D3 is an LDM

1993
The handheld Laser Distance Meter (LDM) came into use. It shoots a laser pulse at a distant object and measures the time taken for the pulse to be reflected back.

1570 ▶ 1590

The light passes through a lens (or small opening).

Darkened room

The image of the building appears upside down on the opposite wall.

Building

Telling the time
See pages 80–81

19th-century replica of the Strasbourg astronomical clock

Moving figures

1570

Camera obscura

Italian scholar Giambattista della Porta refined the camera obscura – an optical device that projects an image of an object through a pinhole (small opening) onto a flat surface. Instead of using a pinhole to focus the image, della Porta used a convex lens (see p.137). This innovation imitated the shape of the lens in the human eye.

1574

Complex timepiece

An astronomical clock, nearly 18 m (59 ft) high, was built in the Cathedral of Notre-Dame in Strasbourg (now in France). It included a celestial globe, an astrolabe, a calendar dial, and automata (moving figures), representing the latest ideas in mathematics, astronomy, and clockmaking.

 1570 **1575**

1577

Taqi al-Din's observatory

Islamic scientist Taqi al-Din built an observatory in Istanbul (in modern-day Turkey) equipped with the latest instruments for measuring the positions of the planets and other heavenly bodies. Unfortunately, he also incorrectly predicted that the Sultan would win a war against the Persians. When he lost, the Sultan ordered the observatory to be pulled down.

Typhoid fever

In 1576, Italian physician Gerolamo Cardano wrote the first clinical description of the symptoms of typhoid fever. This highly infectious disease killed many people.

Astronomers at work in Taqi al-Din's observatory in Istanbul

Seed

Roots — Botanical illustration of a dandelion

1546–1601   TYCHO BRAHE

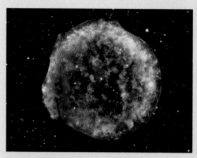

Danish nobleman Tycho Brahe was one of the leading astronomers of his day. Under the patronage of King Frederick II of Denmark, he built a huge observatory on the island of Ven (in Sweden), where he studied the stars and planets. He made all his observations with the naked eye, before the invention of the telescope. As a student, he lost part of his nose in a duel and wore a false metal one for the rest of his life.

Brahe's new star
In 1572, Brahe observed a bright new star in the constellation of Cassiopeia (at the top, labelled "I" on his map). Modern telescopes have revealed that this was an exploding star, or supernova.

Brahe's map of Cassiopeia showing his new star

Modern-day image of SN 1572, believed to be Brahe's supernova

1583

Plant studies
Italian botanist Andrea Cesalpino developed a method of grouping flowering plants by their fruits, seeds, and roots in his book *De Plantis Libris XVI* (The Book of Plants XVI).

1585   **1590**

1582

New calendar
Pope Gregory XIII introduced a new calendar to modify the Julian calendar, which had been used in Europe since Roman times. Known as the Gregorian calendar, this calendar calculated the date of the holy festival of Easter more accurately. At first recognized only by Catholic countries, the Gregorian calendar is now used by many countries around the world.

1589

First knitting machine
English inventor William Lee designed a machine called a stocking frame for knitting woollen and silk stockings. He demonstrated it to Queen Elizabeth I, who feared his invention might put hand-knitters out of work. He was unable to patent his invention in England, so he moved to France.

Spring maintains tension

Knitted stocking

Foot treadle for operating machine

Wool or silk yarn

Replica of William Lee's knitting machine

Great Britain did not switch to the Gregorian calendar until 1752.

Pope Gregory XIII presides over the discussion to reform the calendar in Rome

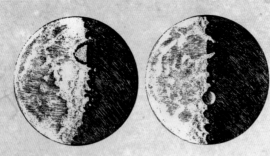

Surface of the Moon
Galileo was one of the first people to point a telescope at the sky and he made many important observations. He wrote about his discoveries in a book called The Starry Messenger. *Until then, people had thought the Moon was a flat, silvery disc. Galileo's drawings, based on his observations, revealed that it is a sphere with an uneven surface ridged with mountains and craters. The book brought him instant fame.*

> **❝It is a beautiful and delightful sight to behold the body of the Moon. ❞**

Galileo Galilei,
The Starry Messenger, 1610

Lever (pawl) attached to pendulum stops and releases pinwheel with each swing back and forth.

Pendulum clock
Galileo studied pendulums throughout his life. Just before his death, he designed a clock that used the regular sweeps of a pendulum to keep time. By now he was totally blind, but he described the mechanism to his son Vincenzio, who made a drawing of it. Vincenzio began building the clock but it was never completed. This model is based on Vincenzio's drawing.

Weighted pendulum swings to other extreme.

Galileo Galilei

Italian scientist Galileo Galilei, who is always known by his first name, was born in 1564 near the town of Pisa, Italy. He originally studied to become a doctor but was much more interested in mathematics. While still a medical student, he noticed a lamp in Pisa Cathedral swaying to and fro. Using his pulse to time the intervals, he worked out that the lamp took the same time to complete each swing, regardless of the length of the arc followed during the swings.

Professor of mathematics
Galileo never became a doctor. He was made Professor of Mathematics at Pisa University at the age of 25 and began to study the physics of motion, as well as engineering. He moved to Padua University and turned his attention to astronomy after building his first telescope in 1609.

Support for Copernicus
In 1614, Galileo publicly stated his support for the Copernican theory that the planets, including Earth, orbit the Sun. This went against the Church's teaching that Earth was at the centre of the Universe and Galileo was told to stop spreading such ideas. He was a devout Catholic and agreed to remain silent, though he was convinced that Copernicus was right.

Final years
Galileo continued with his scientific experiments, but was arrested and put on trial in 1633 for denying the Church's teachings. He spent the rest of his life under house arrest in the village of Arcetri, near Florence. Here he wrote *Dialogues Concerning Two New Sciences*, his last great work on physics, which included his law of falling bodies. He died in 1642.

The trial of Galileo
Galileo's trial took place before a crowded Church court in Rome. Charged with heresy and facing a punishment of torture or death, Galileo publicly denied that Earth moves around the Sun. He is said to have muttered defiantly under his breath "And yet, it moves."

Galileo in old age
This portrait of Galileo was painted in 1636, when he was living at Arcetri. He holds a telescope in his right hand, though by this time he was going blind.

❝Mathematics is the language with which God has written the Universe. ❞

Galileo Galilei

1590 ▶ 1610

Looking closely
See pages
84–85

*Compass needle held
at different positions
always points north*

North Pole

*Model of Earth
made from
magnetic rock*

**Illustration of Earth
as a magnetic rock**

South Pole

1600

Giant magnet
English scientist William Gilbert believed that Earth must have a huge magnet inside because navigators' compasses always pointed north. He made models of Earth from magnetic rock and found that compass needles held close to the rock pointed towards the model's North Pole, behaving just like real compass needles on Earth.

1590

Inventing the microscope
Dutch spectacles-maker Zacharias Janssen is credited with inventing the compound microscope. He inserted two lenses into a tube and looked through one end. Small objects at the other end appeared nine times larger.

Replica of Janssen's original microscope

1600

Burned at the stake
Giordano Bruno, an Italian friar and mathematician, was burned at the stake as a heretic by the Catholic Church. Influenced by Copernicus's ideas of Earth revolving around the Sun, Bruno had argued that the Sun was not the centre of the Universe because the Universe was infinite, and that Earth was unlikely to be the only inhabited world.

◢◢ **1590** • • • • **1595** ● • • • •

Water cistern

1596

Flush toilet
Sir John Harington, a member of Queen Elizabeth's court, invented a flush toilet, called the Ajax. It worked much like a modern toilet except that the water swept the contents of the pan straight into a pit below. Sadly, his invention did not catch on. Hygienic, flushing toilets did not come into use for another three centuries.

1596

Puzzle of continents
After noting that their coastlines seemed to fit together like pieces of a jigsaw puzzle, Flemish mapmaker Abraham Ortelius suggested that the continents of Africa and the Americas were once joined together. This idea would be confirmed by the theory of continental drift developed by German geophysicist Alfred Wegener in 1915 (see p.170).

*Handle releases
water into toilet*

Toilet seat

**Illustration
of Harington's
water closet, 1596**

Exit pipe

> ❝It would make unsavoury Places sweet… and filthy Places cleanly.❞
>
> Sir John Harington,
> describing his flush toilet

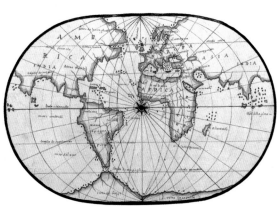

**World maps, such as
this one from 1590, could have
inspired Ortelius's theory.**

1608   THE TELESCOPE

Hans Lippershey was a German lens-maker working in the Netherlands, then the centre of the optical industry. He is believed to have invented the refracting telescope in 1608, though Zacharias Janssen may also have had a hand in its development. A refracting telescope uses two lenses to gather and focus light, making distant objects appear closer than they are. Lippershey's invention could make objects seem three times larger. It is likely that he intended his telescope for use at sea or on the battlefield.

Lippershey experiments with lenses

Gold patterning

Galileo's telescope
Based on reports of Lippershey's telescope, Galileo built his own telescope in 1609. It could make distant objects appear eight times larger. He later built a telescope that could magnify objects 30 times.

The tube is made of strips of wood covered with leather.

1605   **1610**

1604

Falling objects
Galileo worked out a law that describes how objects fall under the influence of gravity. At the time, most scientists believed Greek philosopher Aristotle's idea, that the heavier an object is, the faster it falls. Galileo had already realised that all objects should fall at the same rate and land together, but that air resistance affects the falls of some objects more than others. He supposedly tested his idea by dropping cannonballs of various weights from the Leaning Tower of Pisa, Italy, although historians dispute the story.

1609

Planetary motion
German astronomer Johannes Kepler published a work confirming Copernicus's belief in a Sun-centred cosmos. He also used mathematics to prove that the planets travel in elliptical orbits around the Sun, and that their speed is not constant, they speed up when they come closest to the Sun.

Elliptical orbit

Sun is not at the centre of the orbit.

Planet travels more slowly when it's farther from the Sun.

Faster firing
The flintlock was first used in France in 1608. The spring-operated mechanism increased the firing rate and safety of handheld muskets and pistols. It remained in use for more than 200 years.

Metal balls of different weights

Galileo dropping balls from the Leaning Tower of Pisa

English flintlock pistol, c 1650

The falling flint strikes a spark to ignite the gunpowder.

71

Circular orbits

Nicolaus Copernicus was the first European astronomer to argue that the Sun was at the centre of the Universe. He believed that Earth and the other planets travelled around it in circular orbits. He published his revolutionary ideas just before his death in 1543.

Copernicus's drawing of the Sun (at the centre) and planets

Paths in the sky

Astronomers had no idea what keeps planets in their orbits, until English scientist Isaac Newton realized that it is a force called gravity. This force, which makes objects fall down on Earth, is the same force that keeps the planets from flying off in straight lines. The planets are actually falling towards the Sun – but they are also moving sideways in their orbits. If they stopped moving, they would crash into the Sun.

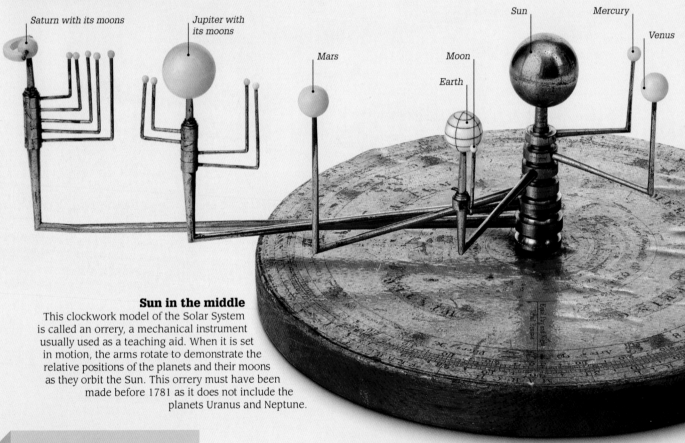

Saturn with its moons

Jupiter with its moons

Mars

Moon

Earth

Sun

Mercury

Venus

Sun in the middle

This clockwork model of the Solar System is called an orrery, a mechanical instrument usually used as a teaching aid. When it is set in motion, the arms rotate to demonstrate the relative positions of the planets and their moons as they orbit the Sun. This orrery must have been made before 1781 as it does not include the planets Uranus and Neptune.

Key events

140 CE

Greek mathematician Ptolemy stated that Earth is the fixed centre of the Universe. His views were not challenged for the next 1,500 years.

1543

Nicolaus Copernicus published a book in which he proposed that Earth and the other planets travel around the Sun in circular orbits.

1609

In his three laws of planetary motion, Johannes Kepler proved mathematically that the planets travel in elliptical paths.

1610

Using a telescope, Italian scientist Galileo observed four moons in orbit around Jupiter, proving that not everything in space orbits Earth.

Europa, a moon of Jupiter

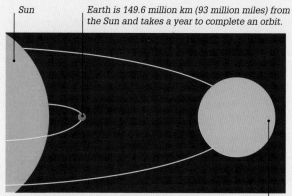

Sun

Earth is 149.6 million km (93 million miles) from the Sun and takes a year to complete an orbit.

Orbital times

Jupiter is 5.2 times farther away from the Sun than Earth. It takes 11.9 Earth years to complete an orbit.

Kepler's discoveries

Johannes Kepler, a German astronomer, set out to prove that Copernicus's theory of a Sun-centered Universe was correct. Rather than orbit the Sun in circles, Kepler found that the planets travel around it in ellipses (oval paths). He also discovered that the farther a planet is from the Sun, the longer it takes to complete its orbit.

Artist's impression of Kepler-444 star system

Planets beyond our Solar System

We now know of thousands of planets orbiting parent stars beyond our Solar System. They are known as exoplanets. NASA's Kepler space telescope, launched in 2009, is able to detect orbits of exoplanets by measuring how far a star's light dims when a planet passes in front of it. The Kepler-444 star system, discovered by this telescope, contains five planets that orbit their star in less than 10 days.

Newton's law of gravity

Astronomers could not explain why the planets follow elliptical orbits until Isaac Newton, the great English physicist, supplied the answer (see p.88). Gravity, which makes an apple fall to the ground on Earth, also keeps the planets in orbit around the Sun. All matter exerts gravity, pulling other matter towards it. The strength of gravity depends on the mass of the object, and weakens with distance.

Elliptical orbits

Newton's law of gravitation predicts mathematically what the gravitational force on an object will be – the force between any two objects depends upon their masses and how far apart they are. Newton worked out the forces on planets – and his equation predicted that orbits would be elliptical, just as Johannes Kepler had observed.

Planet's elliptical orbit

Gravity pulls the Sun towards the planet.

Sun

Planet

Gravity pulls the planet towards the Sun.

The planet revolves around the Sun in this direction due to gravity.

The planet would move in a straight line in the absence of gravity.

Mercury's orbit changes over time.

Mercury's wobbly orbit

Over time, the planet Mercury's orbit shifts slightly. Newton's law of gravity could not explain this puzzling fact. In 1915, physicist Albert Einstein solved the mystery in outlining his theory of relativity (see p.173). The wobbly orbit is due to Mercury having to travel through an area of space that is curved due to the Sun's mass.

Sun

> **" We revolve around the Sun like any other planet. "**
>
> Nicolaus Copernicus

1687

Isaac Newton formulated the universal law of gravitation and explained that it is the force of gravity that holds the planets in elliptical orbits around the Sun.

1781

William Herschel, a British astronomer, discovered the planet Uranus in orbit beyond Saturn. It was the first planet to be discovered since ancient times.

1846

Mathematical calculations correctly predicted the existence of a new planet, later given the name of Neptune, before it was observed by telescope.

2009

NASA launched Kepler, a space observatory, to discover habitable, Earth-sized planets orbiting other stars. By 2016, it had discovered 21 Earth-like planets.

1610 ▶ 1630

Calculating machines
See pages 124–125

Set of movable rods inscribed with digits for multiplying and dividing

Fixed column divided into numbers from 1 to 9

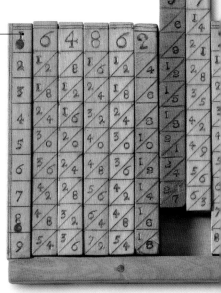

Napier's bones

1610

Moons of Jupiter

Observing the night skies through the telescope he had built himself, Galileo Galilei (see pp.68–69) noticed three small stars near the planet Jupiter that changed position over a period of time. He realized they were moons, or satellites (objects that orbit a planet or star), circulating the planet, and later identified a fourth. These four were the brightest of Jupiter's moons, often called the Galilean moons. Galileo's observation contradicted the Church's teaching that everything in the Universe rotated around Earth.

Io

Europa

Ganymede

Callisto

1614

Multiplying numbers

Scottish mathematician John Napier introduced logarithms, which are used to multiply and divide very large numbers – especially useful in astronomy. In 1617, he introduced another aid to calculation – a set of rods divided into sections and marked with digits, which became known as Napier's bones.

| 1610 | • | • | • | ⬤ | 1615 | • | • | • | • | 1620 | • | • |

1620

First submarine

Cornelis Drebbel, a Dutch inventor living in England, built a submarine made of a wooden frame covered with leather. It was powered by oars. The submarine stayed underwater for three hours when given a trial run in the River Thames, but it is unclear how the oarsmen sitting inside were able to breathe.

Slide rule

Another handy aid to calculation was the slide rule, invented by English mathematician William Oughtred in 1622. Slide rules remained in use until the late 20th century, when they were replaced by pocket calculators.

Replica of Drebbel's submarine

The DREBBEL

Illustration of Santorio's clinical thermometer

1578–1657 WILLIAM HARVEY

English physician William Harvey proved that the heart pumps blood around the body. He found that the body has a fixed amount of blood that is always circulating. Before this discovery, doctors believed that blood was continuously being made in the liver.

Royal physician
Harvey studied at the universities of Cambridge, England, and Padua, Italy. On returning to England, he became physician to King James I, and tended to victims of the English Civil War (1642–1651).

One-way flow
Arteries carry blood away from the heart and veins return it to the heart. This key discovery of the circulatory system was outlined in Harvey's book *De Motu Cordis* (The Motion of the Heart), where he shows how a one-way valve in a forearm vein prevents the blood from flowing back to the hand.

1626
Body temperature
Italian physiologist Santorio Santorio was the first person to use a thermometer to measure the temperature of the human body. Santorio was an early pioneer of the study of metabolism – the chemical processes in the body essential for life.

1625 ● ○ ○ ● **1630**

1629
Fanciful steam engine
Italian inventor Giovanni Branca published a design for a steam engine known as an aeolipile. He suggested it could be used to power pestles and mortars to grind medicinal drugs. It was never built and it is doubtful it would have been of any practical use.

1626
Death by freezing
Sir Francis Bacon, a major English figure in the history of science, is said to have died of pneumonia after trying to see if he could preserve meat by stuffing a chicken carcass with snow. Bacon famously maintained that scientists should prove the truth of their ideas through experimentation.

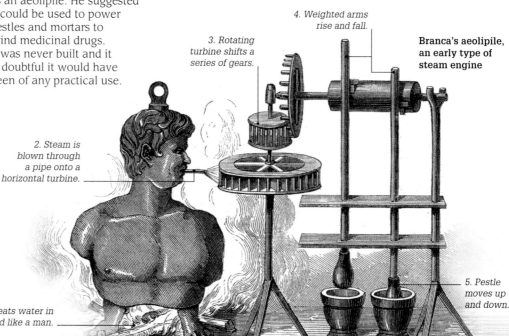

4. Weighted arms rise and fall.

3. Rotating turbine shifts a series of gears.

Branca's aeolipile, an early type of steam engine

2. Steam is blown through a pipe onto a horizontal turbine.

5. Pestle moves up and down.

1. Fire heats water in boiler shaped like a man.

Healing people

In the past, the practice of healing the sick was based on traditional knowledge of herb-based remedies. The Ancient Greeks were the first to study the causes of sickness, and passed their knowledge on to Roman and Islamic physicians. The scientific study of medicine emerged again in western Europe in the 1600s, leading to ever more effective ways of diagnosing, preventing, and treating disease.

Islamic medicine
In the Middle Ages, translations of *The Canon of Medicine*, a book by Persian scholar Ibn-Sina (Avicenna), brought Greek and Arabic knowledge of medicine to the West. This illustrated page from an edition dated 1440 shows a pharmacist's shop alongside various medical practices of the time.

"The physician is only nature's assistant."

Galen, Roman physician and surgeon

Alternative medicine
Alternative medicine refers to any form of healing that falls outside the "western" scientific tradition of medicine. Some forms are very old and are followed by millions of people around the world.

+ Ayurveda
Originating in ancient India, ayurveda aims for balance between mind, body, and spirit. It uses dietary adjustments, herbal remedies, and massage treatments.

+ Acupuncture
In this Chinese form of healing, fine needles are inserted into certain sites in the skin to treat a variety of conditions.

+ Homeopathy
Based on the idea of "like cures like", homeopathy treats ailments with tiny doses of natural drugs.

Bloodletting
The process of removing blood from a patient, or bloodletting, was practiced in medicine for thousands of years. It was thought to balance the body's fluids and was believed to be a cure for most ailments. One way of taking blood was to attach leeches (blood-sucking parasitic worms) to the skin. Leeches are sometimes used today to clean wounds.

Leeches were kept in water.

A woman attaches leeches to her arm in a woodcut from 1638.

The gauge displays the pressure.

Sphygmomanometer for measuring blood pressure, c 1883

Key events

460 BCE
Hippocrates, the Ancient Greek physician, was born. The first person to study the causes of disease, he is called the father of modern medicine.

1543
Flemish physician Andreas Vesalius published *De humani corporis fabrica* (On the Fabric of the Human Body), a work that revolutionized the understanding of human anatomy.

1628
English physician William Harvey described the circulation of blood in animals, showing that the heart pumps blood in one direction around the body.

1816
René Laennec, a French hospital doctor, invented the stethoscope – an instrument to listen to the chest of patients as an aid to their diagnosis.

Laennec's stethoscope

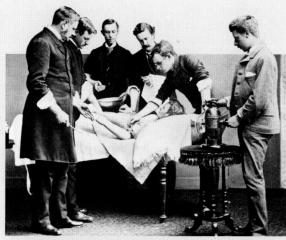
An antiseptic spray is used during an operation, c 1870

Hospital care

In the past, hospitals were dirty, over-crowded places. Two of the people who helped to change all that were British surgeon Joseph Lister (see p.144), who introduced antiseptics, making surgery safer, and British nursing pioneer Florence Nightingale, who demonstrated that clean hospitals prevented infection and helped sick people get better faster.

Deadly diseases

In most parts of the world, people live far longer than they did 500 years ago, when average life expectancy was about 40 years. With vaccines and antibiotics, medical workers can now prevent or cure many infectious diseases that would previously have killed thousands.

+ Smallpox
Once a feared killer, smallpox has now been wiped out thanks to a global immunization campaign.

+ Polio
This highly infectious viral disease targets children. Vaccines are helping to end it worldwide.

+ Plague
Bubonic plague (the Black Death) killed millions of people in Europe in the 1300s. Outbreaks still occur today, but the disease is treatable with antibiotics.

> **" The very first requirement in a hospital is that it should do the sick no harm. "**
>
> Florence Nightingale, *Notes on Nursing*, 1860

Medical aids

Tools such as tweezers and scalpels (sharp-bladed knives), similar to those doctors use today, date back to ancient times. Over the centuries, as medical knowledge advanced, the need arose for more complicated instruments, such as endoscopes and blood pressure monitors to identify and treat patients' symptoms.

Wood and pewter syringe, late 1700s

The tube ends in a rubber bulb, which is placed on the skin and inflated.

Candle

The funnel directs light from the candle.

Viewing lens

Nozzle

Otoscope for looking inside the ear, 1890s

Engraving of a doctor wearing a beak-shaped mask for protection against plague, 1656

1865
Joseph Lister introduced life-saving standards of cleanliness and hygiene into operating theatres and hospitals.

1895
German physicist Wilhelm C Röntgen produced the first X-ray photograph. X-rays, which can penetrate skin and tissue to reveal bone, have become a key tool in medicine.

1928
Sir Alexander Fleming, a Scottish biologist, discovered penicillin, heralding the era of antibiotics. Penicillin was first used as an effective drug in the 1940s.

1977
The first MRI (magnetic resonance imaging) scan was carried out. MRI creates multiple images of the body without exposing it to damaging radiation.

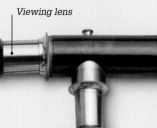
First MRI machine

1630 ▶ 1650

> **"It is not enough to have a good mind. The main thing is to use it well."**
>
> René Descartes,
> *Discourse on the Method*

Descartes's discourse

1637

French philosopher René Descartes published *Discourse on the Method*, one of the most important books written in the history of philosophy and science. In it, he said that in order to arrive at the truth you should start by doubting everything.

Mathematical puzzle

1637

French mathematician Pierre de Fermat scribbled a theorem (a mathematical statement) in the margin of an old textbook. He claimed he had proof that his theorem was true, but had no room to write out the answer. Fermat's theorem was not solved until 1995.

Descartes's Discourse on the Method

Pierre de Fermat

1631

Wonder drug

Agostino Salumbrino, an Italian missionary living in Peru, noticed that the Quechua people used the powdered bark of the local cinchona tree to treat fever. A small sample was sent to Rome, where it was used successfully to treat malaria, then a common disease in marshy parts of Europe. We now know that cinchona bark contains a drug called quinine.

Cinchona leaves and bark

1630 | ● | ○ | ● | **1634** | ○ | ○ | ● | **1638** | ●

1633

The trial of Galileo

Italian astronomer Galileo Galilei was put on trial in Rome on charges of heresy. He had published a book in which he attacked the Church's view that the Earth was at the centre of the Universe and supported Polish astronomer Nicolaus Copernicus's theory of a Sun-centred Universe. Fearing torture or death, Galileo denied his beliefs in court.

Galileo Galilei
See pages 68–69

1639

Transit of Venus

English astronomer Jeremiah Horrocks correctly predicted that the shadow of the planet Venus would pass in front of the Sun, a rare event known as the transit of Venus. To observe the occurrence, Horrocks projected the Sun's image through a telescope onto a sheet of paper.

Title page of *Somnium*

1634

First sci-fi novel

Johannes Kepler, a German astronomer, wrote a story about a young Icelandic boy who was taken by demons to the Moon. The novel was published a year after Kepler's death in 1633. Written in Latin, it was titled *Somnium* (The Dream), and has been described as the first work of science fiction.

Roundel from a stained glass window celebrates Horrocks's observation of the transit of Venus

1643

The first barometer

When Italian physicist Evangelista Torricelli placed a glass tube filled with mercury in a bowl of mercury, the mercury in the tube fell, leaving a vacuum at the top. He realized this was due to atmospheric pressure (weight of air). Torricelli's discovery led to the invention of the barometer, an instrument that measures air pressure to forecast the weather.

Replica of Torricelli's barometer

How a barometer works

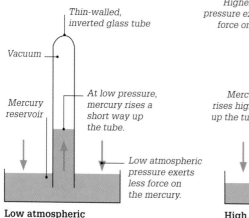

Thin-walled, inverted glass tube

Higher atmospheric pressure exerts stronger force on the mercury.

Vacuum

Mercury reservoir

At low pressure, mercury rises a short way up the tube.

Mercury rises higher up the tube.

Low atmospheric pressure exerts less force on the mercury.

Low atmospheric pressure

High atmospheric pressure

One of Hevelius's maps of the Moon

1647

Atlas of the Moon

Polish astronomer Johannes Hevelius published the first atlas of the Moon's surface. Hevelius, who was a brewer by trade, built his own observatory. His detailed maps showing the Moon's mountains and craters were the result of four years of observation.

1642

1646

1650

1642

Calculating machine

At the age of 19, Blaise Pascal invented a mechanical calculating machine to help his father, a French government tax collector. The machine could add, subtract, divide, and multiply. Pascal went on to become a leading mathematician and philosopher of the age.

Calculating machines
See pages 124–125

 French scientist Blaise Pascal built about 20 calculators in his lifetime.

Display windows show answers

Pascal's first calculator

Dials for inputting numbers

Telling the time

The earliest people who tried to keep track of time used simple devices such as sundials to track the movement of the Sun through the sky. It was many centuries later, about 700 years ago, that mechanical clocks were introduced in Europe. Faster communications in the 19th century led to timekeeping becoming standardized across the world.

Hour hand indicates the hour of the day

Gilded sun marks the position of the Sun in the Zodiac

Originally, the phases of the Moon were indicated.

Early timekeeping

Sundials
Sundials measure time by using a shadow cast by an upright rod (gnomon) to track the position of the Sun in the sky.

Water clocks
In water clocks, a jar is filled with water, which drains away at an even rate to indicate how much time has passed.

Hourglasses
A specific quantity of sand flows from one glass bulb into another through a narrow opening. The sand flows through at a fixed rate, usually taking an hour.

Incense clocks
In China and Japan, incense sticks that burn at an even rate were used to measure time.

Candle clocks
Slow-burning wax candles had evenly spaced lines marked on them, which were numbered to mark the hours.

Sundial (9th century) in Northern Ireland

When the sand has run through to the bottom, the hourglass can be turned upside down.

Hourglasses from 17th century

The clock tower and detail of clock face (above) in St Mark's Square, Venice.

Astronomical clocks
Early mechanical clocks in Europe used a falling weight on a chain and a pendulum to turn a series of gears (see box opposite). They often combined 24-hour clock faces with information about the Sun, Moon, and stars. Their elaborate designs often included moving figures (automata) that danced or rang bells at certain times of the day.

Key events

1500 BCE
Sundials were first used in Egypt and Mesopotamia (now Iraq) thousands of years ago. They are only able to tell the time when the Sun is shining.

1088
In China, Su Song built a water-driven mechanical clock to track the cycles of the stars and planets.

Su Song's water clock

1656
Dutch inventor Christiaan Huygens built the first pendulum clock. Driven by the regular sweeps of a weighted pendulum, it was accurate to within a few seconds a day.

1759
English clockmaker John Harrison built the marine chronometer – a spring-driven timepiece that was accurate over a long time, allowing sailors at sea to calculate longitude (see p.93).

Inner dial shows the signs of the Zodiac.

How pendulum clocks work

A pendulum clock can keep excellent time because the rate at which the pendulum swings can be precisely controlled. Inside the clock, the pendulum regulates the rate at which a drum turns, via a catch on the escape wheel. A weight unwinds the cord from around the drum and turns the gears, which are connected to the minute and hour hands. The weight takes eight days to unwind the cord and then the cord must be rewound with a key.

This catch swings back and forth with the pendulum, alternately catching and releasing the cogs on the escape wheel.

The drum rotates the main wheel that connects through gears to the minute and hour hands.

Each swing of the pendulum takes one second.

Escape wheel

Gears connect the escape wheel to the second hand, moving it forward every second.

Hour hand

Another set of gears from the main wheel moves the minute and hour hands forward at the correct intervals.

Drum

The falling weight unwinds a cord to turn the drum.

Minute hand

Workings inside a pendulum clock

Outer dial shows the 24 hours of the day in Roman numerals.

Atomic clocks

Atomic clocks are the most accurate way of keeping time yet known. They keep time by counting the high-frequency waves emitted by energized atoms in elements such as caesium. A caesium clock will not gain a second in 1 million years.

World's first caesium atomic clock, 1955

Time zones run along lines of longitude

Greenwich Mean Time

International date line

Time zones

Since 1884, to standardize the time around the world, the globe has been divided into 24 time zones. Times are measured from Greenwich Mean Time, or GMT, with each zone either hours ahead or behind GMT. For example, New York City is five hours behind GMT and Tokyo is nine hours ahead.

New York City

Areas that have adopted a time between two zones

Tokyo

Modern watches

Wristwatches have been popular since the early 1900s. Today's watches use quartz crystals to keep time and are powered by a battery, or even by solar power. They display the time in analogue (the way it appears on a traditional clock face) or in digital form, according to the wearer's preference.

Early digital watch, 1970s

1884

Greenwich Mean Time became the global time standard after an international conference adopted the Greenwich meridian in the UK as the Prime Meridian (line of 0° longitude).

Marker for the Prime Meridian Line at Greenwich, UK

1927

The first quartz clock, driven by the natural electricity generated by a rapidly vibrating quartz crystal, was built at the Bell Telephone Laboratories, New York City, USA.

1949

The first atomic clock was built in Washington DC, USA. In 1967, a second was redefined as the time that elapses during 9,192,631,770 cycles of radiation from a caesium-133 atom.

1970s

Watches and clocks began to show the time in digital form using light-emitting diode (LED) or liquid-crystal display (LCD) instead of a traditional (analogue) clock face.

Von Guericke made an early friction machine for producing static electricity.

Display of power

To demonstrate his understanding of vacuums, German inventor Otto von Guericke made two copper hemispheres, sealed them together, and emptied them of air using a vacuum pump he had invented earlier. Then he got two teams of eight horses to try and pull the hemispheres apart. They failed to do so because the external air pressure that kept the hemispheres pressed together so tightly was too strong.

Von Guericke carries out his experiment at Magdeburg, Germany

1650 • • • • **1655** • • • •

1629–1695 **CHRISTIAAN HUYGENS**

Christiaan Huygens was a Dutch physicist, astronomer, mathematician, and instrument maker. Best known for proposing that light is made of waves, he made important discoveries in many areas of science. He also travelled widely in Europe and met with many of the leading scientists of the day.

KEY DATES

1654 Huygens began making improvements to telescopes with his brother Constantijn.

1656 He produced his design for a pendulum clock.

1678 He proposed that light is made up of waves.

1689 He met Isaac Newton on a visit to England.

Astronomical discoveries

Huygens taught himself to grind the lenses for the telescopes he built. It was with his 3.7-m- (12-ft-) long telescope, which could magnify objects 50 times, that he first observed the rings around Saturn (see p.87), and discovered its largest moon, later named Titan.

Pendulum clock

Huygens designed a clock with a weighted pendulum that kept time accurately to within a few seconds a day – a vast improvement on existing clocks.

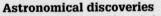

Swinging pendulum keeps regular time.

1662

Boyle's law

Anglo-Irish scientist Robert Boyle published a law to show that the volume of a gas decreases with increasing pressure, and vice versa. Boyle carried out many experiments using an air pump he had made. Often called the father of modern chemistry, he introduced the idea of an element as a substance that cannot be broken down.

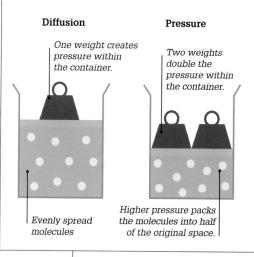

Diffusion

One weight creates pressure within the container.

Pressure

Two weights double the pressure within the container.

Evenly spread molecules

Higher pressure packs the molecules into half of the original space.

Artist's impression of a dodo

Dead as a dodo
The dodo, a large flightless bird, had become extinct by 1662. It lived only on the island of Mauritius in the Indian Ocean, where it was hunted for food by visiting European sailors.

Lower transfuses blood from a lamb to a man

1666

Blood transfusion

Richard Lower, an English doctor, carried out a successful blood transfusion between two dogs. A year later, he injected a small quantity of lamb's blood into the vein of a human patient, who appears to have survived despite the risk of a massive allergic reaction.

1665

1670

1669

Fossils in rock

Danish geologist Nicolas Steno explained that sediment formed horizontal layers of rock (called strata) over time. As new strata formed on top, animal remains within each layer turned gradually into fossils. So the oldest fossils are always at the bottom, with the newer ones above them.

1669

A new element

In his search for the "philosopher's stone", to turn base metal into gold, German alchemist Hennig Brand boiled up concentrated human urine and accidentally discovered the element phosphorus, which gives off a greenish glow.

Network of capillaries covering exterior of lung

Malpighi's drawing of a frog's lungs

Cross-section shows tiny sacs called alveoli

1661

Microscopic discoveries

Italian biologist Marcello Malpighi used a microscope to study the structure of the lung. He discovered capillaries, the minute blood vessels that connect the veins and arteries. William Harvey had suggested 30 years earlier that these blood vessels existed (see p.75).

Hennig Brand is said to have used 5,670 litres (1,250 gallons) of human urine in his experiments.

Hennig Brand in his laboratory

Looking closely

The invention of the microscope revealed a whole new world. For the first time, scientists could observe objects too small to be seen with the naked eye. Researchers began to understand the building blocks of life as they studied the structure of cells and discovered the existence of micro-organisms. Today, microscopes can even identify individual atoms.

Eyepiece lens

Scientific bestseller

Micrographia, published by Robert Hooke in 1665, introduced the public to the world of the microscope. It included wonderfully detailed drawings of the objects observed through his microscope, including fleas, hairs, and even a fly's eye. The book became an instant bestseller.

Hooke's illustration of a flea

Wooden barrel

Water-filled sphere focuses light from oil lamp.

Discovering cells

Robert Hooke, a noted English scientist, was the curator of experiments at the Royal Society in London, England. He designed a compound microscope that used a water-filled sphere to focus light from an oil lamp onto the specimen. Hooke noticed the spaces between long empty cell walls in a piece of cork he was examining and first coined the word "cell" to describe them.

Lens concentrates light onto specimen.

19th-century poster celebrates the 300th anniversary of Janssen's microscope

Specimen mounted on pin

The first microscope

By the 1590s, Dutch spectacle-makers were making microscopes by fixing two lenses in a tube. They found that light, refracted by the two lenses, made objects larger than a single lens did on its own. One of these spectacle-makers, Zacharias Janssen, may have made the first microscope.

Hooke's compound microscope

Key events

1590	1661	1665	1674	1860
Zacharias Janssen is usually credited with the invention of the first compound microscope.	Italian biologist Marcello Malpighi saw red blood cells, which he called particles, through a microscope.	Robert Hooke published *Micrographia*. It contained illustrations of the tiny objects he had observed through a microscope.	Antoni van Leeuwenhoek designed a single-lens microscope that was able to magnify objects up to 270 times.	French chemist Louis Pasteur used a microscope to carry out research into disease-carrying microbes.

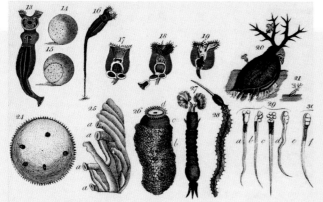

Leeuwenhoek's drawings of microscopic life

Single-lens microscope

Dutch scientist Antoni van Leeuwenhoek was able to achieve greater magnifications with his single-lens microscopes than Robert Hooke did with his compound microscope. Leeuwenhoek ground all his lenses himself, some of them no bigger than a pinhead.

Oil lamp

How a compound microscope works

Compound light microscopes use at least two lenses. Light from below is reflected up through the object being viewed – the specimen – into the objective lens, which produces the first magnification. The eyepiece lens then magnifies the image again.

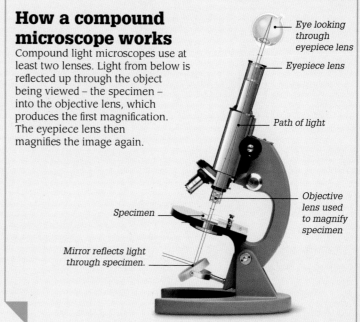

Eye looking through eyepiece lens

Eyepiece lens

Path of light

Objective lens used to magnify specimen

Specimen

Mirror reflects light through specimen.

The world magnified

Today, there are three kinds of microscope. Researchers use light, or optical, microscopes to view biological specimens such as cells and tissue. Electron microscopes, including the scanning tunnelling microscope, which use a beam of electrons to reveal an image, can look at much smaller things in very great detail.

2,000 times

This 19th-century light microscope can magnify objects up to 2,000 times. Its achromatic lenses create a sharper image by focusing different colour wavelengths together.

10 million times

Electron microscopes fire a beam of electrons at a specimen contained in a vacuum. This example, dating from around 1946, was one of the first to be mass-produced. Modern versions can magnify up to 10 million times.

1 billion times

The scanning tunnelling microscope (STM) uses a sharp metal probe to scan the surface of an object at an atomic level, allowing scientists to "see" individual atoms. The atomic force microscope works in a similar way.

1880s

Working for German instrument-maker Carl Zeiss, German optical scientist Ernst Abbe made radical improvements to microscope design.

1882

German microbiologist Robert Koch developed ways of staining bacteria with violet dye to make them more visible under a microscope.

1903

German chemist Richard Zsigmondy built the ultramicroscope, which let him view objects that could not be seen with a light microscope.

1931

German physicist Ernst Ruska invented the first scanning electron microscope (SEM) that used electron beams to create images.

1981

The scanning tunnelling microscope was the first that allowed scientists to see at an extremely small scale, down to a nanometre (a billionth of a metre).

Zsigmondy's ultramicroscope

1670 ▸ 1690

1672
Rainbow colours
English physicist Isaac Newton (see pp.88–89) published a paper on light. He described an experiment he had carried out using two prisms to show that white light is made up of the seven colours of the rainbow.

Newton's sketch of his experiment with prisms

Calculating machines
See pages 124–125

1672
Calculating questions
Gottfried Leibniz, a German mathematician, created a calculating machine called the step reckoner. In 1674, he invented calculus, the mathematics of infinitesimal (very small) changes. Isaac Newton (see pp.88–89) also devised a version of calculus, and the two men fell out over who had done so first.

1678
Hooke's law
English scientist Robert Hooke observed that the force needed to stretch a spring is proportional to the distance it stretches. If the force is doubled, the distance is doubled. There is a point beyond which the spring does not stretch, but snaps.

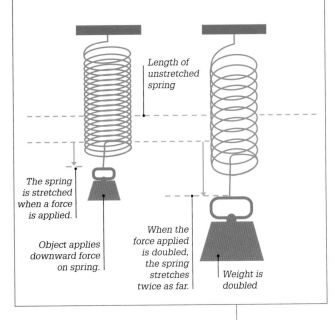

Length of unstretched spring

The spring is stretched when a force is applied.

Object applies downward force on spring.

When the force applied is doubled, the spring stretches twice as far.

Weight is doubled

1670   ## 1675

1675
Astronomer to the king
England's King Charles II appointed John Flamsteed the first Astronomer Royal to head a new observatory in Greenwich, London. This observatory marked what would later become the prime meridian (0° longitude) between east and west.

Royal Observatory, Greenwich, UK

1679
Steam digester
French inventor Denis Papin demonstrated a cooking device that used high-pressure steam to extract fat from bones. A forerunner of the modern pressure cooker, Papin's digester was fitted with a steam release valve and a piston, leading in time to the development of the steam engine.

Lens for viewing microscopic samples

Screw adjusts position of specimen.

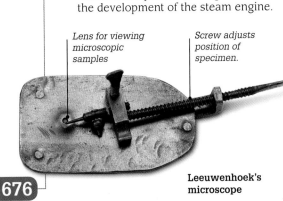

Leeuwenhoek's microscope

1676
Life in miniature
Antoni van Leeuwenhoek, a Dutch merchant, made his own microscopes. He used them to observe tiny living creatures swimming in a drop of water, which he called "animalcules". These were, in fact, single-celled protozoans called amoeba.

1625–1712 GIOVANNI CASSINI

Born in Italy, astronomer Giovanni Cassini moved to France in 1669, where he was put in charge of the Paris Observatory. Among his contributions to astronomy, Cassini calculated the distance from Earth to Mars, and from Mars to the Sun. His figures were close to current estimates. He discovered four of Saturn's moons – Iapetus, Rhea, Tethys, and Dione – and also shares credit with English scientist Robert Hooke for the discovery of a storm on Jupiter known as the Great Red Spot.

The large gap between Saturn's rings is known as the "Cassini Division".

Rings around Saturn
In 1675, Cassini identified a gap that appeared to divide Saturn's rings into two. He also correctly suggested that the rings were made up of thousands of tiny particles.

Isaac Newton was born in 1642, the year that Galileo died.

Dental hygiene
One of the first books on dentistry was published in 1685. It recommended brushing teeth only once a week. Not surprisingly, most people had rotten teeth, which had to be extracted by force.

1685 • **1690** ▶▶

1686

New term
In *Historia Plantarum*, a three-volume history of plants, English naturalist John Ray used the word "species" to describe a group of plants or animals sharing the same characteristics and able to breed with one another. It was the first biological use of the term, and established "species" as the basic unit of taxonomy (the classification of living things). His book described 18,600 species.

Title page of John Ray's *Historia Plantarum*

> **"One species never springs from the seed of another nor vice versa."**
>
> John Ray, *Historia Plantarum*, 1686

Newton's universal law of gravitation

Gravitation exerts an identical force on two objects, pulling them together.

Doubling the mass of both objects increases the forces to four times their original strength.

Doubling the distance between them reduces the forces by a quarter.

Isaac Newton See pages 88–89

1687

Breakthrough science
Isaac Newton published a book called *Principia Mathematica* in which he described his three laws of motion and the universal law of gravitation. According to the latter, the force of gravity between two objects is stronger as their masses increase, and weaker when the distance between them is bigger. These four laws together form the basis of mechanics – the science of forces and how things move.

3. Observer sees reflected image from small mirror through eyepiece.

2. Concave mirror reflects image back up tube onto angled small mirror.

1. Light enters telescope tube.

Replica of Newton's reflecting telescope, c 1672

Reflecting telescope
While he was studying optics, Newton built the first reflecting telescope, using two mirrors to reflect and focus the image. It gave a better result than the traditional refracting telescope (see p.71).

❝If I have seen further it is by standing on the shoulders of giants.❞

Isaac Newton, in a letter to Robert Hooke, 1675, supposedly acknowledging earlier work by other scientists

Principia Mathematica

Newton's most famous book was published with the help of fellow scientist Edmond Halley. In this book, Newton described the universal law of gravitation (see p.87) and the three laws of motion (below).

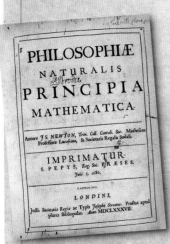

The laws of motion
1. An object remains at rest or continues moving in a straight line unless a force acts upon it.

2. The greater the mass of an object, the more force it will take to accelerate it.

3. For every action, there is an equal and opposite reaction.

Title page of Principia Mathematica

Isaac Newton

British scientist Isaac Newton was born in the village of Woolsthorpe, England, in 1642. One of the leading minds of the 17th-century scientific revolution, he is best known for outlining the law of universal gravitation to explain what holds the Universe together.

Schoolboy and student
Newton's interest in science and mechanics became apparent at an early age. An uncle recognized his ability and encouraged him to continue his studies at university. In 1661, he became a student at Trinity College, Cambridge, England.

Escape from the plague
When the plague broke out in Cambridge in 1665, Newton withdrew to Woolsthorpe. He is said to have developed his theory of gravity after seeing an apple fall from a tree in the orchard there. This is probably just a story, but it was during his time at Woolsthorpe that he developed his ideas on gravitation and made his first experiments with light.

Cambridge professor
Returning to Cambridge, Newton was appointed Lucasian Professor of Mathematics at the age of 26. In 1687, he published *Philosophiae Naturalis Principia Mathematica* (usually called the *Principia Mathematica*), one of the most important works in the history of science, and where he described his three laws of motion.

Later years
In 1689, Newton became a Member of Parliament and moved to London. Appointed Master of the Royal Mint in 1699, he reformed the coinage and took severe measures against forgers. He was elected President of the Royal Society in 1703 and made a knight in 1705. He died in 1727 and was buried in Westminster Abbey.

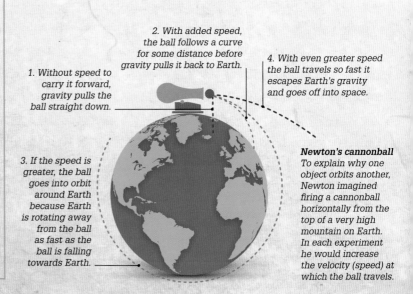

2. With added speed, the ball follows a curve for some distance before gravity pulls it back to Earth.

1. Without speed to carry it forward, gravity pulls the ball straight down.

4. With even greater speed the ball travels so fast it escapes Earth's gravity and goes off into space.

3. If the speed is greater, the ball goes into orbit around Earth because Earth is rotating away from the ball as fast as the ball is falling towards Earth.

Newton's cannonball
To explain why one object orbits another, Newton imagined firing a cannonball horizontally from the top of a very high mountain on Earth. In each experiment he would increase the velocity (speed) at which the ball travels.

Studying light
Newton made many studies of light. In his book Opticks, published in 1704, he described light as a stream of tiny particles travelling at speed and showed that white light contains all the colours of the rainbow.

"To myself I seem to have been only like a boy playing on the seashore... while the great ocean of truth lay all undiscovered before me. "
Isaac Newton

In 1699, Welsh naturalist and museum keeper Edward Lhyud published the first illustrated catalogue of British fossils.

1694

Secrets of flowers

German botanist Rudolf Camerarius provided scientific proof that flowering plants reproduce sexually. He showed that pollen, a powdery dust produced on the male stamens, is necessary for fertilization of the female germ cells (called ovules). When he removed the stamens, the flowers failed to seed.

Fruit

Flower

Castor oil plant, studied by Camerarius

Comparing brain sizes

Macaque monkey brain

Chimpanzee brain

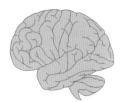

Human brain

1699

Chimpanzee study

Edward Tyson was an English physician and anatomist. He dissected the body of a chimpanzee, which he called an orang-outang, or "man of the woods". The creature had been brought to London on a ship from Africa and died shortly afterwards. Tyson concluded that its anatomy, particularly its brain, was closer to that of a man than a monkey.

1690 ● ● ● ● **1695** ● ● ● ●

1697

Mistaken theory

Georg Stahl, a German chemist, argued that a substance or "essence" called phlogiston is released into the air whenever something is burned, leaving the calx (or ash). His theory was widely believed until disproved by Antoine Lavoisier (see p.107).

World traveller

William Dampier, an English adventurer, sailed three times round the world, making one of the earliest scientific expeditions to the coast of New Holland (now Australia). He wrote a best-selling account of his voyages.

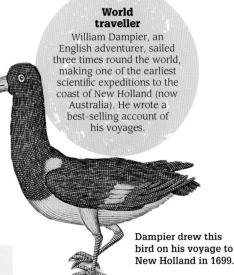

Dampier drew this bird on his voyage to New Holland in 1699.

1698

Steam pump

English inventor Thomas Savery designed a steam pump to extract floodwater from mines. It worked by condensing steam to create a vacuum. As air rushed in to fill it, atmospheric pressure forced up water from the mine. The entire process was controlled by a system of taps.

3. Tank showers water on vessel to condense steam.

2. Steam enters vessel beneath cold water tank.

1. Water in boiler is heated to produce steam.

Model of Savery's steam pump

4. Water from below is forced up pipe.

Crowds turn out to admire Halley's Comet on its appearance in 1835.

Mercury thermometer by Fahrenheit, c 1718

"... I dare venture to foretell, That it [the comet] will return again in the Year 1758."

Edmond Halley, *A Synopsis of the Astronomy of Comets*, 1705

1709

Handy thermometer

Gabriel Fahrenheit, a Polish physicist working in the Netherlands, made the first compact, modern-style thermometer. It had a series of scaled markings and was filled with coloured alcohol, which expanded as the temperature rose. Later versions used mercury. Fahrenheit devised the temperature scale named after him in 1724.

1705

Halley's prediction

English astronomer Edmond Halley predicted that a comet he had observed in 1682 would be seen again from Earth in 1758. His prediction proved correct. The comet, which is visible roughly every 75 years, is now known as Halley's Comet.

1705 · · · · · · **1710** ▶▶

1701

Agricultural pioneer

Jethro Tull, an English farmer, invented the mechanical seed drill – a device that planted seeds in neat, evenly spaced rows. His drill wasted much less seed than the traditional method of scattering it by hand. Although Tull's invention did not catch on at first, it would have a key role in modernizing farming.

 Sheep and cattle were improved by selective breeding in order to produce more meat.

1708

Porcelain discovery

Porcelain, a bluish-white ceramic imported from China, was extremely popular in Europe, but no one knew how to make it. After 20 years of experimentation, Ehrenfried von Tschirnhaus, a German scientist, found the secret: a paste made of kaolin (a fine white clay) mixed with alabaster.

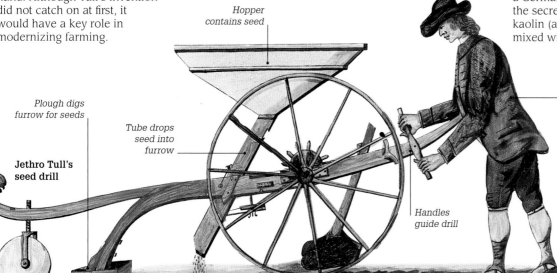

Hopper contains seed

Plough digs furrow for seeds

Tube drops seed into furrow

Jethro Tull's seed drill

Handles guide drill

The farmer's yield is increased because the seeds have more space to grow.

Travelling the world

The word "navigation" originally meant finding your way at sea. For centuries, sailors would keep close to the coast, using landmarks and local knowledge of currents and weather conditions to navigate by. Later, they used compasses to indicate the direction in which to sail and they developed navigational aids to calculate their position at sea. Now we use the term navigation to mean finding your way anywhere.

Celestial navigation

The sextant was a highly accurate instrument used to determine latitude (position north or south of the Equator) by measuring the angle between the horizon and the Sun during the day, or the Moon, planets, and stars at night. Invented in the 18th century, it remained the ultimate navigational tool until the arrival of satellite navigation (sat nav).

Top mirror

2. Lower mirror reflects light to the telescope and is fixed on the horizon.

Early mariners' compass, c 1500–1700s

Arc measures one-sixth (sextant) of circle.

1. Movable arm adjusts top mirror to reflect light from Sun onto lower mirror.

Portolan chart of the Gulf of Mexico, 1547

Early navigational chart

This portolan is drawn "upside-down" with south at the top. Places along the coast are carefully named and located, while inland areas contain fanciful scenes. Compass "roses" give direction. The captain plotted a course by following the lines that criss-cross the chart from the roses.

Key events

1000

The Vikings used a device called a sun compass (a wooden disc with directional markings) to help them navigate by the Sun.

Viking sun compass

1300

Knowledge of the magnetic compass reached Europe from China, where it had been in use for at least 1,000 years.

1400

European sailors began using coastal charts called portolans in combination with a compass to plot a course from port to port.

1569

Mercator's map projection, on which lines of latitude and longitude intersect at right angles, made it easier to navigate at sea.

Log float with gauge, c 1861

Measuring speed

Speed at sea is measured in knots because sailors used to throw a rope (also called a log) tied with knots behind their ship. They allowed it to roll out for a specific amount of time, then counted the number of knots to calculate how fast the ship was moving. Later, a log float with a mechanical gauge was thrown from the ship.

The marine chronometer

In the 1700s, ships were frequently lost at sea because captains had no way of keeping track of longitude (how far the ship has travelled east or west). To do this required an accurate clock that would always show the right time back at home port. Sailors worked out their longitude by comparing that time with "local" time. This was difficult to achieve on board a rolling ship. After working on the problem for many years, John Harrison built the first accurate marine chronometer (timepiece) in 1759.

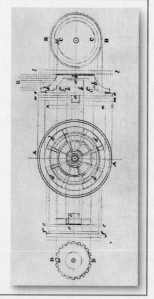

The original designs for Harrison's chronometer. It was about the size of a large pocket watch.

3. Telescope focuses light from mirrors so you see the Sun on the horizon.

4. Angle between horizon and the Sun is read off the scale.

Sextant, 18th century

Early lighthouses were often built on rocky outcrops.

Lighthouses

The Romans built the first lighthouses at the entrance to harbours. Modern lighthouses date from the early 1800s. They were designed to prevent shipwrecks by shining a powerful beam of light to warn approaching ships of dangerous hazards such as rocky reefs.

Satellite navigation

Sat nav systems such as GPS (Global Positioning System) use a series of global satellites to work out where a receiver is located. The receiver, which could be a smartphone, picks up signals from at least four satellites to instantly calculate its position and speed (see p.232).

1750

Sextants, navigational instruments used to measure the altitude of the planets and stars, had come into use. Sailors used them to determine latitude at night as well as day.

1759

John Harrison built an accurate marine chronometer to calculate longitude at sea.

1935

Radar, which locates unseen objects by bouncing radio waves off them, was invented. It is used on ships to reveal coastlines and other ships.

1990

GPS, the first sat nav system, came into use. It quickly replaced most other navigation aids.

Radar screen

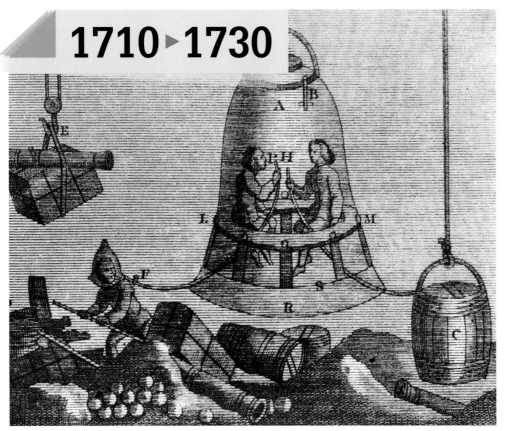

Illustration of Halley's diving bell, from a 19th-century encyclopedia

> **"The whole cavity of the bell was kept entirely free from water, so that I sat on a bench... with all my clothes on."**
>
> Edmond Halley, on going underwater in the diving bell, 1715

1715

Halley's diving bell

English scientist Edmond Halley designed a practical diving bell. An air-filled, weighted barrel was suspended next to the bell and kept it constantly fed with air through a hose. Halley dived to a depth of 18 m (60 ft) inside his bell and remained submerged for 90 minutes. Diving bells were used to recover goods from sunken ships.

1710   **1715**

1712

Practical steam engine

Thomas Newcomen, an English engineer, built the world's first practical steam engine, designed to pump water out of mines. A growing demand for coal meant that mines were being dug deeper, and flooding was a serious problem.

4. The up-and-down action of the pump expels water from the mine.

2. The rocking beam falls, pushing the pump down.

3. Cold water sprays into the cylinder to condense the steam. This creates a vacuum that forces the piston down and the pump up.

1. Steam from the boiler enters the cylinder, pushing the piston up.

Fire

Diagram of Newcomen's steam engine

1716   MALARIA

Italian physician Giovanni Lancisi argued that mosquitoes, which breed in swamps, are responsible for spreading malaria. Few people believed him at the time, but he was proved right in 1894.

Female *Anopheles* mosquito

Malaria lifecycle

Malaria is transmitted to humans in the bite of infected female *Anopheles* mosquitoes. Tiny parasites from the mosquito's saliva enter the victim's bloodstream and multiply in the liver, causing fever.

6. It bites another person, who also becomes ill with malaria.

1. An infected mosquito lands on a human host.

2. Its bite infects the host with parasites carrying malaria.

3. The parasites multiply in the liver.

5. A second mosquito is infected after feeding on the host's blood.

4. More red blood cells are infected.

Sweet tooth

Pierre Fauchard, a French doctor, was the first person to link the eating of sugar to tooth decay. In his book *The Surgeon Dentist*, he urged people to give up eating sugar.

Illustration from *The Surgeon Dentist*, published in 1728

1729

Electrifying experiments

Stephen Gray, a self-taught English scientist, was an early pioneer of electricity, which he produced by friction. He was able to conduct an electric charge hundreds of metres along a thread, which was draped through the house and out into the garden. He later put on public displays of electricity, including a spectacle called the Flying Boy.

1721

Smallpox protection

Variolation was a way of protecting healthy people from getting smallpox by scratching them with infected material from a smallpox scab. It became fashionable after members of the British royal family underwent the procedure.

2. The charged rod is passed over the boy's body to give him an electrostatic charge.

3. Silk cords act as insulators.

4. The static charge from the boy's face and hands attracts pieces of paper.

Instrument used to puncture the skin in variolation

1. A glass rod is rubbed to generate static electricity.

5. A small ivory ball is also attracted.

Gray's Flying Boy

1725

1730

1725

Speedy weaving

Basile Bouchon, a French silk maker, invented the first semi-automated weaving machine. He came up with a way to speed up weaving by using a perforated paper tape to control the raising of the warp threads on the loom. His invention was the forerunner of other programmable machines, such as the computer.

Samrat Yantra sundial

Telling the time
See pages 80–81

1727

Indian observatory

Jai Singh II, Maharaja of the kingdom of Jaipur, India, began constructing the Jantar Mantar astronomical observatory at Jaipur. It contained a collection of massive astronomical instruments built of brick and stone – including the world's largest sundial, Samrat Yantra.

This triangular wall is the gnomon (the part of a sundial that casts a shadow from the Sun). The shadow travels at a rate of about 1 mm (0.04 in) per second.

This wall is a scale that registers the position of the shadow cast by the gnomon.

 Samrat Yantra, the sundial at Jantar Mantar, has a height of 27 m (88 ft).

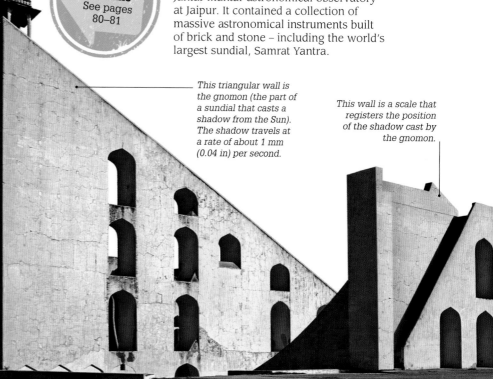

Celestial atlas

This atlas of the heavens (*Atlas Coelestis*) was published in 1729 – ten years after the death of its author John Flamsteed, Astronomer Royal of Great Britain. It is based on his detailed observations of 2,935 stars visible with a telescope from the Royal Observatory at Greenwich. *Atlas Coelestis* was one of the first major atlases to be based on observations through a telescope, and was considered much more accurate than previous star atlases.

The constellations of the northern and southern hemispheres from the *Atlas Coelestis*

"You are to apply the most exact care and diligence to rectifying... the places of the fixed stars."

King Charles II's instructions to John Flamsteed on making him Astronomer Royal, 1675

1730 ▶ 1750

Seismic waves
See page 164

Laura Bassi

Page from Linnaeus's *Systema Naturae*

Stretchy stuff
While in the Amazon rainforest, French explorer Charles de la Condamine came across the substance rubber, which is obtained from a rainforest tree called *Hevea brasiliensis*. He sent samples back to Europe.

Incision made in the tree's bark

Rubber latex fluid collected from tree

1731
Earthshaking discovery
Inventor Nicholas Cirillo used a pendulum to measure earthquakes in Naples, Italy. The amplitude of the pendulum's sways (the extent of their to-and-fro movement) indicated where the earth tremors were most intense. His device was the first seismograph.

1731
Female pioneer
Italian academic Laura Bassi was the first woman to hold a university post in science when she was appointed Professor of Anatomy at the University of Bologna, Italy. A year later, she was also made Professor of Philosophy.

1735
Classifying life
Swedish botanist Carl Linnaeus divided the natural world into three kingdoms – animal, plant, and mineral. In his book *Systema Naturae,* he introduced the binomial (two-name) system that classified plants and animals by genus and species. This system is still used today.

1730

1734

1738

1733
The flying shuttle
Invented by Englishman John Kay, the flying shuttle was a simple device that revolutionized the textile industry. On a loom, the shuttle drew the weft (yarn) through the warp (lengthwise threads). The weaver then passed Kay's flying shuttle, which was in a box attached to a cord, at high speed back and forth across the warp.

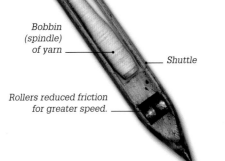

Bobbin (spindle) of yarn

Shuttle

Rollers reduced friction for greater speed.

Bornite, an ore containing cobalt

1735
Goblin ore
Georg Brandt, a Swedish mineralogist, identified the element cobalt, which is present in Earth's crust in combination with other minerals. The name cobalt comes from the German word *kobold,* meaning "goblin ore".

1738
Bernoulli's principle
Swiss mathematician Daniel Bernoulli stated that as the speed of a moving fluid (liquid or gas) increases, the pressure within it decreases. His principle explains how an aircraft gains lift because air flows faster over the top of its wings and slower underneath.

Bernoulli published his principle in a book, *Hydrodynamica*

 Pitot tubes, invented in 1732 to measure how fast rivers flow, are still used to measure airspeed on aircraft.

1745   STORING ELECTRICITY

The Leyden jar was the first device able to store a static electric charge built up by a friction generator, while also being capable of releasing it later. It was not a battery as it did not produce a charge itself, but it was a handy way of storing electricity. Benjamin Franklin used Leyden jars in his experiments with electricity (see p.100).

Inventing the Leyden jar

Scientist Ewald Georg von Kleist created the first Leyden jar in Germany. Pieter van Musschenbroek and Andreas Cunaeus from the Dutch city of Leiden (the English spelling is Leyden) developed it further.

Cunaeus (left) and Van Musschenbroek (right) at work

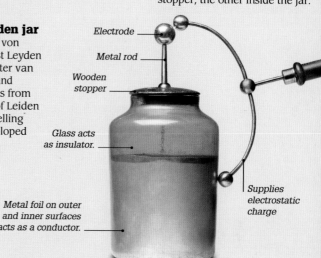

Leyden jar

The glass jar had a foil lining on the inside and around the outside. It stored a static charge between two electrodes, one at the external end of a brass rod passing through the stopper, the other inside the jar.

Electrode

Metal rod

Wooden stopper

Glass acts as insulator.

Metal foil on outer and inner surfaces acts as a conductor.

Supplies electrostatic charge

1742   **1746**   **1750**

1741

Arctic voyage

Danish explorer Vitus Bering died when his ship was wrecked off the coast of Alaska. The naturalist on this expedition, Georg Steller, survived and discovered six new animal species. Among them was Steller's sea cow, a large sea mammal that was extinct by 1767.

Steller's sea cow (top) with eared seals and a sea otter (bottom right)

1742

Celsius scale

Anders Celsius, a Swedish astronomer and mathematician, devised a temperature scale in which the boiling point and freezing point of water were set 100 degrees apart. It developed into the modern Celsius scale. On Celsius's original scale, 100° signified the freezing point and 0° the boiling point, instead of the other way round, as used today.

1749

Animal studies

French naturalist Georges Buffon began publishing *Natural History*, a work that eventually stretched to 44 volumes. Buffon was one of the first people to realize that our planet is very ancient and that many species have disappeared since it was formed.

Woodpecker from Buffon's *Natural History*

1750 ▶ 1770

❝The heat which disappears in the conversion of water into vapour is not lost.❞

Joseph Black, on latent heat

1753
Citrus cure
Scurvy was a dreadful disease that killed thousands of sailors on long voyages. James Lind, a British naval surgeon, was able to show that it could be prevented by drinking lemon or lime juice. We now know that scurvy is caused by a lack of Vitamin C, which is found in all citrus fruits.

Sum of all knowledge
In 1751, French philosophers Denis Diderot and Jean d'Alembert began publishing the *Encyclopedia* (*Encyclopédie* in French), a vast work that aimed to include all the world's knowledge. They completed it in 20 years.

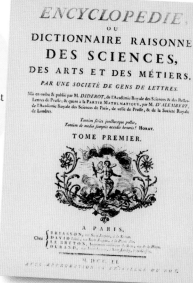

 The 28-volume *Encyclopedia* contained 71,808 articles and 3,129 illustrations.

Title page of Volume 1 of the *Encyclopedia*

1750 • • • **1754** • • • **1758** •

1752
Bright spark
Future American statesman, Benjamin Franklin, risked death to prove that lightning is caused by electricity. He took his son to fly a kite in a thunderstorm, tying an iron key to the kite string. When lightning hit the kite, the key gave off a stream of sparks.

1754
Dense gas
Scottish chemist Joseph Black discovered a gas that is denser than air, and called it "fixed air". We now know it as carbon dioxide. Black later discovered latent heat (the energy absorbed or released when a substance changes from a solid to a liquid state, or vice versa).

Marine chronometer
English clockmaker John Harrison built a chronometer, to be used at sea to measure longitude accurately. It proved a great aid to navigation (see pp.92–93).

Harrison's No. 4 chronometer, 1759

1760–1870 THE INDUSTRIAL REVOLUTION

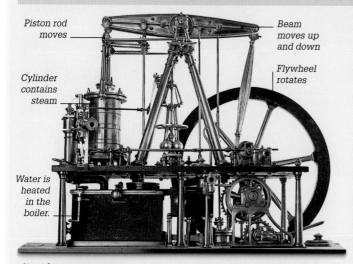

Piston rod moves

Beam moves up and down

Flywheel rotates

Cylinder contains steam

Water is heated in the boiler.

The development of new technologies led to a period of social and economic change called the Industrial Revolution, when the growth of factories, mines, canals, and later, railways, changed the landscape forever. Increasing numbers of men and women moved from the countryside to find work in the new industrial towns.

Getting up steam

In 1775, Scottish engineer James Watt designed a steam engine (see pp.130–131) that was smoother and more efficient than previous engines. His improvements meant that steam engines were no longer restricted to pumping water from mines, but could also be used to drive machinery in mills and factories, and to power steamships and railway locomotives.

Textile mills

The invention of new technologies for spinning and weaving textiles led to the mass manufacture of cloth. Conditions were hard for the thousands of women and children who worked long hours in the new textile mills.

Women and girls at work in a cotton mill

1762   **1766**   **1770**

Metrosideros collina, one of the plants collected by Joseph Banks during his voyage

1769

Scientific voyage

Captain James Cook voyaged to the Pacific in HMS *Endeavour* to observe the transit of Venus (when Venus passes in front of the Sun) from the island of Tahiti. He went on to discover the east coast of Australia in 1770. On board was botanist Joseph Banks, who collected thousands of plants in Botany Bay in Sydney, Australia. On their return, Banks's record of the voyage sparked interest across Europe.

1769

Steam car

French engineer Nicolas-Joseph Cugnot designed a steam-driven, self-propelled vehicle for carrying heavy weapons. It had three wheels and a large copper boiler that hung over the front wheel. The vehicle was so heavy that it proved impossible to steer.

In 1765, British physicist Henry Cavendish discovered that hydrogen, which he called "inflammable air", is a separate element.

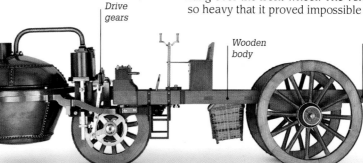

Boiler

Drive gears

Wooden body

Frame for carrying heavy weapons

Studying weather

The science of weather and climate is called meteorology, a Greek word that originally meant the study of things in the sky. People have always tried to understand and predict the weather. The invention of instruments that measure air pressure, temperature, and humidity allow us to forecast weather more accurately.

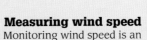

Spinning cups rotate a vertical rod

Hollow cup catches the wind

Measuring wind speed

Monitoring wind speed is an important part of weather forecasting. Meteorologists use an instrument called an anemometer (*anemos* is the Greek word for wind). The most common type of anemometer, invented in 1846, has three or four cups attached to horizontal arms that spin with the wind.

Rod turns at a rate proportional to wind speed

Dial records wind speed

Spinning-cup anemometer, c 1846

Early weather watcher

About 2,400 years ago, the ancient Greek philosopher Aristotle wrote a book called *Meteorologica* (Meteorology). In it he discussed many kinds of weather events, including whirlwinds and monsoons. Some of his theories were right, and others were wrong.

Latin version of Aristotle's *Meteorologica*, 1560

Turning in the wind

Fixed on the top of church steeples or other high buildings, weathercocks have been used for hundreds of years to show the direction of the wind – vital information for farmers, fishermen, and sailors.

Arrow indicates the direction the wind is blowing from

Key events

1450

Leon Battista Alberti, an Italian architect, gave the first written description of a mechanical anemometer, an instrument used to measure the speed of wind.

1643

Italian physicist Evangelista Torricelli's experiments with vacuums and air pressure led to the development of the barometer, which measures changes in atmospheric pressure.

1686

English scientist Edmond Halley published a map charting the directions of ocean winds and monsoons. It is generally regarded as the first meteorological map.

1806

Francis Beaufort, an officer in the British Royal Navy, devised a scale for measuring wind speeds, which is still used today.

Torricelli makes the first mercury barometer

Scale registers contraction or expansion of hair

Hair hygrometer

Amazingly, a human hair can measure changes in air humidity (the amount of moisture in the air). In 1783, Swiss physicist Horace Bénédict de Saussure observed that hair lengthens on damp days and shrinks when it's dry. He put this fact to good use in making an instrument to measure humidity called a hair hygrometer.

Strand of hair

Hollow glass sphere

Barometers

A barometer measures atmospheric pressure (the weight of air in the atmosphere). Until recently there were two kinds: mercury barometers (see p.79), invented in 1643 by Evangelista Torricelli (above), and aneroid barometers, invented in 1844. Today they are mostly electronic.

Naming clouds

We owe the names used today for different types of cloud to Luke Howard, a London pharmacist. He had a passion for meteorology and, in 1802, published a list of cloud types, giving them Latin names based on their characteristics.

Cluster thermometer

A thermometer is used to measure temperature. This 18th-century Italian thermometer is based on an invention of Galileo's. The six alcohol-filled tubes contain a number of small, hollow glass spheres. When the temperature rises, the alcohol expands, so its density decreases and the spheres sink.

Cirrus (curl)
High, thin, wispy clouds composed of ice crystals that may indicate a change of weather.

Stratus (layer)
A low-level, flat blanket of cloud that produces overcast weather or light rain.

Cumulus (heap)
Puffy, cauliflower-like clouds that grow upwards and may cause thunderstorms.

Hurricane approach

Today, satellites collect and monitor weather data. Here, data from a NASA weather satellite was used to create this image of a hurricane moving to strike the coast of Florida, USA. Meteorologists use satellites and computer modelling to give early warning of hurricanes.

Satellite image of Hurricane Andrew, 1992

TIROS-1

1849
The Smithsonian Institution established a weather observation network across the USA. Hundreds of volunteers submitted reports by telegraph on a monthly basis.

1929
The first radiosonde – a box of instruments attached to an air balloon that collects meteorological information at high altitudes – was launched.

1953
The US National Hurricane Service began the system of assigning personal names to tropical storms originating in the Atlantic Ocean.

1960
NASA launched TIROS-1, the first successful weather satellite to provide accurate weather forecasts based on observations made from space.

❝The Little Ice Age... was an irregular seesaw of rapid climatic shifts, driven by complex and still little understood interactions between the atmosphere and the ocean. ❞

Brian Fagan, *The Little Ice Age: How Climate Made History* (2001)

This painting depicts a frost fair on the frozen River Thames held in the winter of 1683–1684.

The Little Ice Age

Between 1300 and 1850, Earth underwent a period of widespread cooling when glaciers advanced in many places around the world. Today, climatologists refer to this as the Little Ice Age, but the idea of an Ice Age was not understood until the 19th century. Until then it was thought that each area of the world had a fixed climate. We now know that climate change occurs in cycles, and may be affected by factors such as increased volcanic activity, changes in ocean circulation, and a fall in solar energy reaching Earth. The winter of 1683–1684 was particularly harsh in northern Europe and the River Thames in London froze over for two months. When the ice was at its thickest, a frost fair was held on the river.

1770 ▶ 1790

1771

Spinning tales
The water frame, a machine for spinning yarn from cotton fibre, was invented by English inventor Richard Arkwright. Powered by a water wheel, his machine could spin 128 threads at a time – the beginning of mass production.

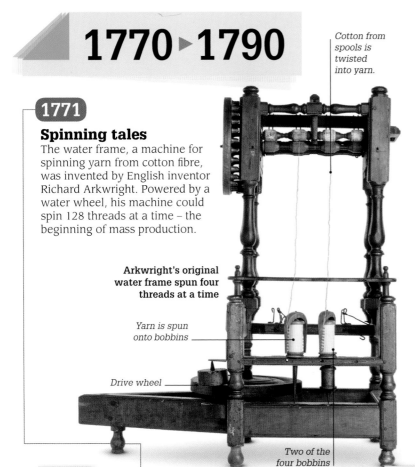

Cotton from spools is twisted into yarn.

Arkwright's original water frame spun four threads at a time

Yarn is spun onto bobbins

Drive wheel

Two of the four bobbins

The Montgolfier balloon is readied for take-off

1775

1772

Discovery of oxygen
Swedish chemist Carl Scheele produced a gas, which he called "fire air", when he heated various chemical compounds together. We now know the gas as oxygen. English scientist Joseph Priestley independently discovered the same gas in 1774. He showed that candles do not burn without oxygen.

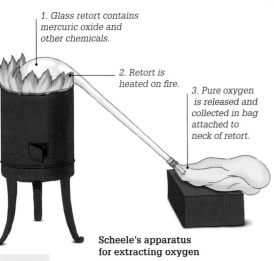

1. Glass retort contains mercuric oxide and other chemicals.

2. Retort is heated on fire.

3. Pure oxygen is released and collected in bag attached to neck of retort.

Scheele's apparatus for extracting oxygen

1776

Sub attack!
In North America, inventor David Bushnell designed a submarine called the *Turtle*. He planned to use it to attach bombs to the hulls of British ships during the American War of Independence (1776–1783), but it was not a great success.

1778

How plants make food
Dutch biologist Jan Ingenhousz discovered that plants need sunlight to make food and that they give off oxygen as a waste product. This process is now known as photosynthesis.

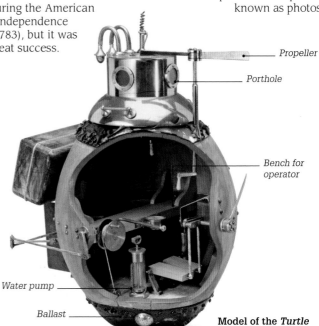

Propeller

Porthole

Bench for operator

Water pump

Ballast

Model of the *Turtle*

1783
Balloon ascent
The Montgolfier brothers designed a hot-air balloon made of paper. Crowds in Paris were amazed when it ascended 900 m (3,000 ft) into the air. The brothers realized that when hot air is trapped inside a bag, it will float upwards because hot air is less dense than cold air.

1743–1794   ANTOINE LAVOISIER

Antoine Lavoisier is regarded as the father of modern chemistry. Born into a wealthy family in Paris, France, he set up his own laboratory to carry out experiments, helped by his wife and several assistants. Known for his precise experiments and careful measurements, Lavoisier discovered the role oxygen played in rusting, combustion (burning), and respiration (breathing).

Experimental scientist
As well as his work in understanding oxygen, Lavoisier also showed that matter is neither created nor destroyed during chemical changes. He was executed during the French Revolution because he had previously worked as a tax inspector for the king.

Elements of Chemistry
Lavoisier published the *Elements of Chemistry*, a book that laid the foundations of chemistry as a science. It contained a list of 33 elements (substances that could not be broken down any further) and introduced modern chemical names, including oxygen and hydrogen.

The Elements of Chemistry *was published in 1789, the year of the French Revolution.*

1785   **1790**

1781
Seventh planet
William Herschel, a German-born astronomer living in England, identified a new planet with a telescope he had built in his back garden. It was given the name Uranus (the Latin form of Ouranos, the Greek god of the sky). Eight years later, a newly discovered element was called uranium after the planet.

Uranus lies at an angle of more than 90° to the rest of the Solar System.

1785
Changing landscapes
Scottish geologist James Hutton wrote that the landscape is continually being shaped by slow-moving natural processes, such as erosion. According to this view, Earth must be millions of years old. His ideas proved correct, though opposed at the time by Christians, who believed that Earth was only 6,000 years old.

> **" ... little causes... are considered as bringing about the greatest changes of the Earth. "**
>
> James Hutton, 1795

1781
Leap frog
When Italian scientist Luigi Galvani connected the exposed nerves of a dead frog to a metal wire during a thunderstorm, its legs twitched with every flash of lightning. His macabre experiments were a key step in understanding electricity, and inspired the novel *Frankenstein*.

Iron plate | Frog's leg | Brass rod

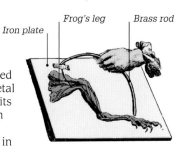

Tin foil | Spinal cord

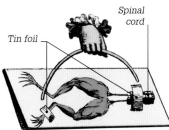

Brass hook

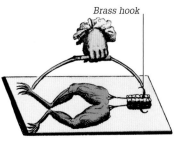

Galvani experimented on frogs' legs by lying them on metal plates and touching them with different metals.

1790–1895
Revolutions

In the 19th century, the world was transformed by the development of steam-driven machines, leading to rapid industrialization. The world began to feel like a smaller place due to both faster communication, with the invention of the telegraph, the telephone, and radio, and faster travel, with the introduction of the railways. Electricity lit homes and cities. A better understanding of disease improved the health of people in the western world, while scientists led the quest for technological innovations to change lives. Most revolutionary of all was the realization that life on Earth had emerged through an extremely long process of evolution.

1790 ▶ 1805

> **"I shall endeavour to find out how nature's forces act upon one another"**
>
> Alexander von Humboldt, 1799

1792

All lit up

Scottish inventor William Murdoch invented gas lighting. He heated coal to produce a flammable gas and used it to light his home in Cornwall, England. Gaslights were much brighter than oil lamps, and the new form of lighting was soon being used to illuminate factories and streets.

Gas lamps reached London streets in 1809.

Nature travels
See pages 112–113

Scientific journey

German naturalist Alexander van Humboldt, who is regarded as the founder of ecology – the study of how organisms interact with the environment and each other – spent five years exploring South America from 1799 to 1804.

Humboldt's woolly monkey is among the creatures he discovered.

1790 • • • **1795**

1793

Cotton gin

In the USA, inventor Eli Whitney invented the cotton gin, a mechanical device for removing the seeds from cotton fibre prior to spinning it, a job previously done by hand. The cotton gin led to a huge increase in the production of raw cotton.

Cleaned cotton

Cotton fibres containing seeds

1796   FIRST VACCINATION

English doctor Edward Jenner made a medical breakthrough with the first vaccination. He infected a healthy boy with cowpox, a disease similar to but milder than smallpox. When Jenner injected him with smallpox germs, the boy did not become ill – the dose of cowpox had built up his immunity. However, many people remained nervous about the process.

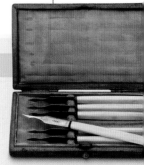

Blades used for vaccination

This cartoon of the time shows people sprouting cow's heads after vaccination.

Glass supporting rod

Contact between zinc and copper discs (the electrodes) produces small electric current.

Saltwater solution is an electrolyte or conductor for electric current.

Voltaic pile

📢 **In 1801, Jean-Baptiste Lamarck came up with the term "invertebrates" to describe animals without backbones.**

1804
First railway journey
Richard Trevithick, a Cornish engineer, built a high-pressure steam engine and mounted it on wheels. His locomotive pulled five wagons carrying 70 passengers and 10 tons of coal a distance of 14 km (9 miles). It travelled at a speed of 8 kph (5 mph).

1800
First electric battery
Italian inventor Alessandro Volta found he could create an electric current by stacking discs of zinc, copper, and cardboard soaked in saltwater in alternating layers. His device, known as a "voltaic pile", was the first "wet cell" electric battery. Adding more discs increased the amount of electricity generated.

Gay-Lussac and Biot make their ascent

1804
Up in the air
French scientists Joseph Louis Gay-Lussac and Jean-Baptiste Biot ascended to a record height of 7,016 m (23,108 ft) in a hot-air balloon to study the composition of Earth's atmosphere at altitude.

1800 — **1805** ▶▶

1801
Jacquard loom
Joseph-Marie Jacquard, a French inventor, designed a power loom to manufacture elaborate textiles such as brocades using a series of punched cards to control the pattern. The Jacquard loom inspired Charles Babbage to employ punched cards in his design for a prototype computer, the Analytical Engine (see p.124).

Drive shaft from power source operates the machinery.

Rods attached to hooks lift the threads through the holes.

The holes indicate where the threads will be.

Chain of cards punched with holes circulates on rotating drum.

1803
Atomic theory
In a lecture to an audience in Manchester, English chemist John Dalton suggested that all matter is composed of atoms, and that atoms of the same element are identical. He compiled a table of elements based on their atomic weights.

ELEMENTS

Hydrogen 1	Strontian 46
Azote 5	Barytes 68
Carbon 5	Iron 50
Oxygen 7	Zinc 56
Phosphorus 9	Copper 56
Sulphur 13	Lead 90
Magnesia 20	Silver 190
Lime 24	Gold 190
Soda 28	Platina 190
Potash 42	Mercury 167

Dalton's table of elements

"Nature offers unceasingly the most novel and fascinating objects for learning."
Alexander von Humboldt

This illustration from one of Humboldt's books shows a raft on a river in Guayaquil, Ecuador. Humboldt spent 20 years writing up his travels.

Nature travels

In 1799, German naturalist Alexander von Humboldt set out to explore the rivers and mountains of South America, from Venezuela to Ecuador and Peru. He travelled more than 9,600 km (6,000 miles), collected thousands of natural specimens, climbed a volcano, and even described a fight with an electric eel. He studied the interactions between geology, climate, and the distribution of plants and animals, and is regarded as the founder of ecology, the study of the relationship between living organisms and their environment.

1807

River steamboat

American engineer Robert Fulton built a steamboat, the *Clermont*, to carry passengers from New York City to Albany, USA, along the Hudson River. The boat had two paddle wheels and completed the 240 km (150 mile) journey in just over 30 hours.

The *Clermont* steamboat

 Meriwether Lewis and William Clark arrived on the Pacific Coast of the USA in 1806. On their journey across North America they discovered new plants and animals.

1810

First tin can

Peter Durand, a British merchant, patented a method for preserving meat by sealing it in an iron container coated with tin to prevent rusting. By 1818, the British Royal Navy was consuming 24,000 large tins of meat a year. Today, food cans are made of 100 per cent steel, though in other ways the process has changed very little.

1805 ● ● **1810** ●

1809

First electric light

British chemist Humphry Davy connected two sticks of charcoal to a large battery. The continuous flow of electricity between them created an incredibly bright light. Davy's arc lamp, as it was called, was the world's first electric light. Davy made other contributions to science, including the discovery of the elements chlorine and iodine.

Chimney ____

1809

How the giraffe got its neck

French biologist Jean-Baptiste Lamarck came up with one of the first theories about the evolution of life. He believed that species change over time by passing on characteristics acquired during their lifetime. For example, giraffes gained their long necks because generations of giraffes reached up to feed from higher and higher branches on trees.

Platform for driver

Understanding evolution
See pages 120–121

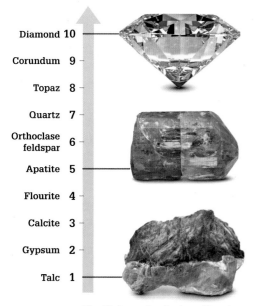

Diamond	10
Corundum	9
Topaz	8
Quartz	7
Orthoclase feldspar	6
Apatite	5
Flourite	4
Calcite	3
Gypsum	2
Talc	1

The Mohs scale of mineral hardness

1812

Mohs scale

German geologist Friedrich Mohs created a scale for classifying minerals based on their hardness. On this scale, consisting of ten standard minerals, diamond is the hardest mineral and talc the softest. Geologists still use the Mohs scale today.

1815

1813

Getting up steam

Locomotives – steam engines that moved as opposed to those that were fixed – were now being used to pull heavy loads in mines and quarries. *Puffing Billy*, the oldest surviving steam locomotive in the world, was built in 1813 to pull coal trucks at a mine in northern England. It remained in service until 1865, and is now preserved in London's Science Museum.

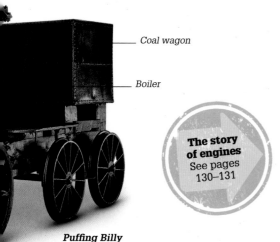

Coal wagon

Boiler

The story of engines See pages 130–131

Puffing Billy

1799–1847   MARY ANNING

The daughter of a carpenter, Mary Anning lived in Lyme Regis, a town on southern England's "Jurassic coast", an area rich in fossils. She was only 11 when she found and dug out the complete skeleton of an ichthyosaur, a reptile that swam in the sea in the age of the dinosaurs.

KEY DATES

1823 Anning found her first plesiosaur fossil, which brought her international fame.

1828 She discovered the skeleton of a pterosaur, a flying reptile.

1838 She was awarded an annual grant by the British Association for the Advancement of Science.

Fossil hunter
Anning had no formal education, as women were barred from academic life, but had an impressive understanding of her subject. The idea of extinct creatures was groundbreaking and she made a living as a fossil hunter, selling fossils she had found to both private collectors and museums. However, the work could be dangerous as the cliffs where she searched for fossils were unstable and liable to collapse.

Flipper for swimming   Long neck

Amazing finds
Despite having no formal training, Anning was recognized as one of the leading fossil experts of the day. She made many significant discoveries. Her most famous find was the almost complete skeleton of a plesiosaur, thought to be a sort of "sea dragon". It was actually a large marine reptile with a broad, flat body, long neck, and four flippers.

Plesiosaur fossil discovered by Mary Anning

❝The carpenter's daughter has won a name for herself, and has deserved to win it. ❞

Writer Charles Dickens in an article about Mary Anning, 1865

Studying fossils

Fossils are the remains of plants or animals that once lived on Earth and have been preserved in rocks for millions of years. It was in the 1600s that scientists first began to wonder how fossils had been formed. By the 19th century, palaeontology (the study of fossils) had become a recognized science. Today, palaeontologists are able to study the DNA (see pp.198–199) of some fossils to give us a clearer picture of life on Earth.

How fossils form

Usually when an organism dies, its remains rot and disappear. For the remains to become a fossil, the conditions have to be just right. It helps if the plant or animal is living in a watery environment and is quickly buried in mud or sand after death.

More layers of sediment build up

1. The body of a dead fish falls to the bottom of the sea. It quickly sinks into the mud or sand.

2. The soft parts of the body rot, leaving the hard bones behind. More sediment falls through the ocean and covers the bones.

3. The fish's skeleton dissolves and is replaced by minerals that harden, while the sediment around it turns to rock.

Types of fossil

There are two types of fossil. A body fossil is formed from the hard parts of a plant or animal's structure – woody trunks, shells, teeth, or bones. A trace fossil is something left behind by an animal, such as its footprints, eggs, or dung.

Insect in amber

Trapped in amber

Millions of years ago this spider was trapped in resin, a sticky liquid that oozes out of some trees. The resin fossilized into amber, preserving the body of the spider intact.

Ammonite fossil

Turned to stone

Most body fossils are copies, or moulds, of the original organism. As the bones, or shell in the case of this ammonite, dissolved, minerals seeped in to fill the space left behind in the mud or sand. Gradually, the minerals hardened into stone.

Dinosaur footprint

Dinosaur print

This dinosaur's footprint, made in soft sand about 140 million years ago, was covered by new layers of sand, which protected its outline. Trace fossils like these give palaeontologists clues about how dinosaurs behaved.

Strong legs to support heavy body

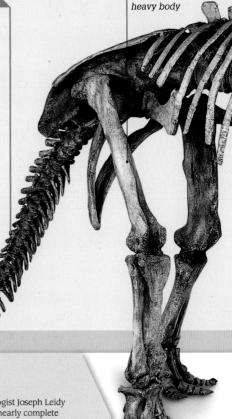

Key events

1669

Danish naturalist Nicolas Steno suggested that fossils are the remains of once-living creatures deposited in layers of sedimentary rock that formed slowly over time.

1796

French zoologist Georges Cuvier showed that a giant fossil skeleton from Argentina was related to the modern land sloth. He named the creature *Megatherium* (giant beast).

1858

American zoologist Joseph Leidy uncovered the nearly complete skeleton of a dinosaur in New Jersey, USA. Named *Hadrosaurus*, it was the first dinosaur species found in North America.

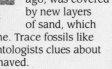

Megatherium

Dinosaur eggs

In 1925, a fossil-hunting expedition led by American naturalist Roy Chapman Andrews found a clutch of dinosaur eggs in Mongolia, Asia. This was proof that dinosaurs were egg-laying reptiles. Andrews is said to have inspired the movie character *Indiana Jones*.

Roy Chapman Andrews (right) inspects the dinosaur eggs.

Palaeontology

Palaeontology isn't just about dinosaurs. Scientists study the fossilized remains of extinct organisms, including fungi, bacteria, and other tiny single-celled organisms. From these they can learn about life on Earth thousands of millions of years ago, and discover why mass extinctions took place.

Working on the rock face

Excavating fossils is only a part of what palaeontologists do. They also study the make-up of fossils, and analyse data in laboratories and museums.

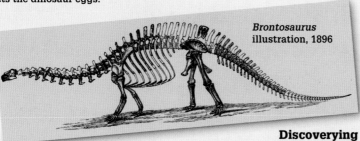

Brontosaurus illustration, 1896

Discoverying *Brontosaurus*

In the late 1800s, more than 130 dinosaur species were found in the USA. Among them was *Brontosaurus* (above), first described in 1879, and later assigned to the *Apatosaurus* species. It is now known to be a separate species to *Apatosaurus*. Although its name means "thunder lizard", it was a plant-eating giant.

Long horn of bone for defence

Bony frill to protect the neck

Triceratops skeleton

Triceratops lived between 75 and 66 million years ago. A plant-eating animal, it inhabited what is now the western USA and Canada when the climate was warmer and wetter than it is today. This *Triceratops* skeleton, and those of other dinosaurs on display in museums, usually contain fossilized bones from several specimens.

Fossilized skeleton of *Triceratops*

1861

The skeleton of *Archaeopteryx*, a feathered dinosaur, was found in Germany. This creature was identified as a missing link between reptiles and birds.

1905

The first specimen of *Tyrannosaurus rex* (king tyrant lizard) was described and named by American palaeontologist Henry Fairfield Osborn.

2014

The largest dinosaur so far discovered was found in Argentina. Belonging to the group of Titanosaurs, it is estimated to have been 40 m (131 ft) long.

Archaeopteryx

117

Pump for extracting blood

Funnel for collecting blood

Blundell's blood-transfusion apparatus

Dandy horse

In 1817, Karl von Drais, a German baron, invented a two-wheeled, human-propelled machine called a dandy horse. It didn't have pedals – the rider pushed it along with their feet.

1818

Blood transfusion

London doctor James Blundell saved a mother from bleeding to death by taking blood from the arm of a donor and injecting it straight into her arm. It was the first successful human to human blood transfusion. Blundell carried out several more, but the procedure would not become safe until the discovery of blood groups.

1815

1815

Safety in mines

Coal miners working deep underground constantly risked death because even the smallest spark from the candles they carried might cause a gas explosion. Humphry Davy solved the problem by containing the flame within a cylinder of fine wire mesh. His miners' safety lamp saved thousands of lives.

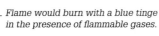

Flame would burn with a blue tinge in the presence of flammable gases.

Wire mesh allows air to pass through but keeps the flame enclosed.

Miners' safety lamp, c 1815

1819

Listening tube

French doctor René Laennec invented the stethoscope to listen to his patients' lungs and heartbeat – he had felt embarrassed pressing his ear against the chests of his female patients. This first stethoscope was a hollow wooden tube. Doctors have used more advanced stethoscopes ever since to diagnose diseases.

Laennec examines a child with his stethoscope

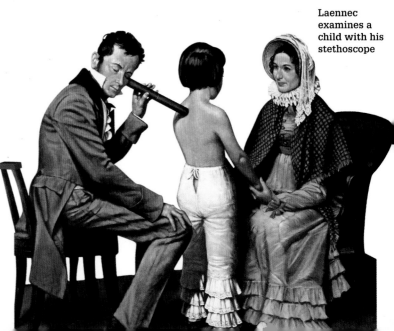

Healing people
See pages 76–77

1820 ELECTROMAGNETISM

Danish physicist Hans Christian Ørsted found that a wire carrying an electric current made a magnetized compass needle move. This inspired French physicist André-Marie Ampère to experiment further with magnets and electricity, and produce a theory of electromagnetism.

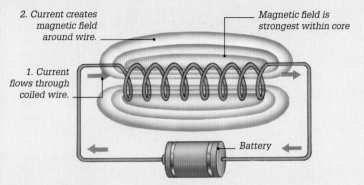

2. Current creates magnetic field around wire.

Magnetic field is strongest within core

1. Current flows through coiled wire.

Battery

Electromagnet

In 1822, Ampère discovered that a coil of wire carrying an electric current produces a magnetic field just like that of a bar magnet. Adding an iron bar inside the coil intensifies the effect, and a switch allows it to be turned on and off. In 1829, US scientist Joseph Henry created some very powerful electromagnets by winding the coils more tightly and adding several layers of coils.

1823

Light at sea

French scientist Augustin-Jean Fresnel invented a special lens to be used in lighthouses. The Fresnel lens, made up of stepped concentric circles, concentrated light into a powerful narrow beam. Ships up to 32 km (20 miles) away could see the light, preventing them from running aground or crashing onto rocks.

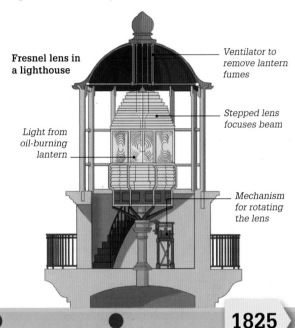

Fresnel lens in a lighthouse

Ventilator to remove lantern fumes

Stepped lens focuses beam

Light from oil-burning lantern

Mechanism for rotating the lens

1825 ▸▸

First steam crossing

The SS *Savannah* was the first ship driven partly by a steam engine to cross the Atlantic Ocean. She left Savannah, Georgia, USA, on 22 May 1819 arriving in Liverpool, England, 18 days later.

Postage stamp showing SS *Savannah*

The story of engines
See pages 130–131

1824

Giant lizard

British naturalist William Buckland identified several fossil bones as those of an extinct reptile. He called it *Megalosaurus* (giant lizard). It was the first scientific description of a dinosaur.

Creature stood 3 m (9 ft) high

Sharp, jagged teeth for eating prey

Reconstructed skeleton of a *Megalosaurus*

1822

Hard to stomach

US Army surgeon William Beaumont studied digestion by dangling pieces of food into the stomach of a patient with an open wound (after a gunshot accident) and then pulling them out to see how the gastric juices were working.

 British geologist Richard Owen invented the word "dinosaur" (terrible lizard) in 1842.

Understanding evolution

From the study of fossils, scientists in the 1800s concluded that life on Earth had changed slowly, or evolved, over billions of years from a single, simple ancestor into the millions of species that exist today. English naturalist Charles Darwin (see pp. 134–135) suggested that this had come about through natural selection. The modern study of genetics has proved him right by explaining the biological mechanisms that drive evolution.

Sexual selection

Rather than passing on a trait that helps an animal survive, sometimes what drives selection is being more attractive to a mate. A peacock, for example, fans out his dazzling tail when he is courting. It seems that peahens choose mates that have a bigger, brighter plumage. As a result, the peacock with the showiest feathers passes on his genes to the greatest number of offspring. This leads, over time, to more colourful birds.

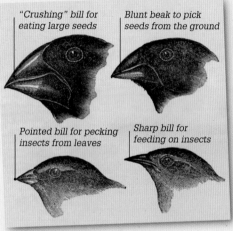

"Crushing" bill for eating large seeds

Blunt beak to pick seeds from the ground

Pointed bill for pecking insects from leaves

Sharp bill for feeding on insects

Darwin's finches

Charles Darwin found different species of finch living on different islands of the Galápagos, (islands off the coast of Ecuador in South America). The finches' bills varied in shape and size. He concluded that they shared a common ancestor, but had evolved into separate species over many generations in order to consume different sources of food available on the islands.

Human evolution

Humans evolved from tree-dwelling apes. We share common ancestors with gorillas, chimpanzees, and orang-utans. Since about four million years ago, all our direct ancestors have walked on two legs. Humans are the only existing member of a group called *Homo*; our species name is *Homo sapiens*.

Proconsul africanus, 23–14 million years ago

Australopithecus afarensis, 3.95–2.95 million years ago

Probable common ancestor of humans and other great apes

Migrated out of Africa and used tools and fire

Walked upright, and had strong arms for climbing trees

Homo erectus, 1.9 million–143,000 years ago

Key events

1809

French naturalist Jean-Baptiste Lamarck argued that living creatures could pass on acquired characteristics to their offspring.

1830

Scottish geologist Charles Lyell showed that Earth had gone through many geological ages over millions of years, paving the way for Darwin's theory of evolution.

1858

English naturalist and explorer Alfred Russel Wallace independently developed similar ideas to Charles Darwin's on natural selection.

1859

Darwin published *On the Origin of Species*, in which he explained in detail his theory of evolution through natural selection.

Alfred Russel Wallace

Natural selection

Individual plants and animals that have a trait which helps them to survive in their particular environment are more likely to pass on that trait in their genes to the next generation. Over time, more and more individuals will come to have the trait.

Shared environment
A population of rabbits share an environment where brown and white individuals are equally likely to survive.

Blending with the scenery
They move into a snowy environment where eagles pick out and kill brown rabbits. The white ones blend with their surroundings and are therefore harder to spot.

New population
More white rabbits survive than brown. After many generations, the gene that determines the white fur colour comes to predominate.

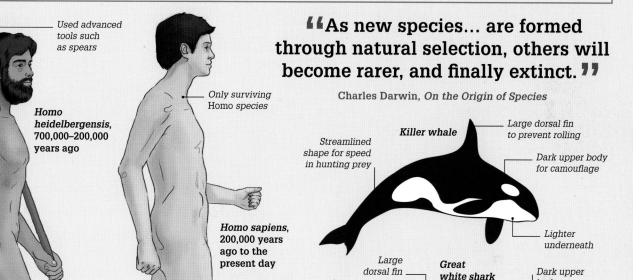

Used advanced tools such as spears

Homo heidelbergensis, 700,000–200,000 years ago

Only surviving Homo species

Homo sapiens, 200,000 years ago to the present day

> **"As new species... are formed through natural selection, others will become rarer, and finally extinct."**
>
> Charles Darwin, *On the Origin of Species*

Killer whale

Streamlined shape for speed in hunting prey

Large dorsal fin to prevent rolling

Dark upper body for camouflage

Lighter underneath

Great white shark

Large dorsal fin

Dark upper body

Streamlined shape

Lighter body underneath

Different but similar
Although killer whales (which are mammals) and great white sharks (which are fish) are completely different species, they have evolved similar characteristics. This is because they fill a similar role in the ocean environment. Biologists call this process "convergent evolution".

1866
Austrian botanist Gregor Mendel published his study of pea plants in which he showed that certain characteristics are passed on from one generation to another.

1909
Danish botanist Wilhelm Johannsen was the first person to use the term "gene" to describe Mendel's basic unit of heredity.

1953
American scientist James Watson and English scientist Francis Crick demonstrated that the structure of DNA, the material that carries genetic information (see pp.198–199), is a double helix (spiral).

2003
The full sequencing of the 3 billion base pairs that make up the human genome (the complete set of genes) was published.

121

1825 ▶ 1835

Continuous roll of paper inside box

Lever presses inked letter against paper.

Replica of Burt's typographer

Dial indicates how many lines have been typed.

1826

First photograph

Joseph Nicéphore Niépce, a French inventor, took the world's oldest surviving photograph. He fixed a metal plate to the back wall of a camera obscura (see p.66) and used it to capture the view from his window. The plate, made of pewter, was thinly coated with bitumen (a light-sensitive, tar-like material). The exposure took several hours.

Niépce's *View from the Window at Le Gras*

"The objects appear with astonishing sharpness... down to the smallest details. "

Niépce describing photography in a letter to his brother

1829

First typewriter

American inventor William Burt patented what is regarded as the world's first typewriter. He called it a typographer. It was quite clumsy to use – writing a letter on it took longer than writing the letter by hand.

1825

1825

Wipe out!

French naturalist Georges Cuvier proposed that Earth had suffered some major catastrophes, which had wiped out large groups of animals. This idea, explaining the existence of fossils that belonged to unknown species, was known as catastrophism.

1828

Animal attractions

The London Zoological Society opened a zoological garden in Regent's Park, London, as a place for the scientific study of animals. Originally only Fellows (members) of the society could make use of it. However, when London Zoo opened its gates to the public in 1847, it became a popular tourist attraction.

Victorian visitors to London Zoo feeding the elephants, 1896

1791–1867   MICHAEL FARADAY

The son of a London blacksmith, Michael Faraday taught himself science before securing a post as assistant to Humphry Davy, an English chemist. Faraday became the greatest scientist of his day. His discovery of electromagnetic induction led to electricity being generated and used in many everyday applications.

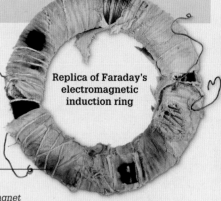

Replica of Faraday's electromagnetic induction ring

Coils of copper wire carrying electric current wrapped in cotton

Man of science
As well as investigating electromagnetism, Faraday discovered benzene, a chemical compound, and established the laws of electrolysis (the chemical reactions that occur when an electric current passes through a liquid).

Driving wheel is cranked to turn copper disc

Horseshoe electromagnet creates magnetic field

Spinning copper disc produces current

Generating electricity
Faraday was able to produce a weak electric current by spinning a copper disc within a magnetic field (electromagnetic induction). In time, his discovery led to the development of machines that could generate large quantities of electricity.

Model of Faraday's disc generator

KEY DATES

1825 Faraday was appointed director of the laboratory at the Royal Institution.

1831 He discovered electromagnetic induction.

1833 Faraday published his laws of electrolysis.

1835

1830

Gradual change
In his book *Principles of Geology*, Scottish geologist Charles Lyell argued that Earth was more than 300 million years old and had gone through many geological ages. This theory of the Earth's history contradicted Cuvier's belief in catastrophes (see p.122).

1831

Voyage of the *Beagle*
HMS *Beagle* left England on a five-year voyage to survey the coast of South America. On board was English naturalist Charles Darwin, who had just graduated from the University of Cambridge, England. He took with him a copy of Lyell's *Principles of Geology*.

HMS *Beagle*

Charles Darwin See pages 134–135

Charles Lyell

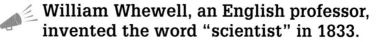

William Whewell, an English professor, invented the word "scientist" in 1833.

Calculating machines

The word "calculate" comes from the Latin word *calculus* meaning "little stone", because pebbles were used in ancient times as a counting aid. Then someone had the idea of putting the stones onto a frame, and the abacus was born. Advances in mathematics and astronomy led to the development of the first calculating machines in the 1700s, which evolved into the tablet computers and smartphones we use today.

Replica of a Roman abacus

Early handheld device

The Romans developed the first portable calculating device – a handheld abacus. Made of bronze, it worked by sliding grooved beads up and down the numbered slots, and was probably used by engineers, merchants, and tax collectors, who needed to make on-the-spot calculations.

Female calculators

Until recently, calculating machines were mostly used in business and finance offices. Humans remained better at some complex mathematical tasks. At a time when female employment was rare, the "Harvard Computers" were a team of women mathematicians employed to analyse astronomical data at the Harvard College Observatory, Cambridge, Massachusetts, USA.

The "Harvard Computers" at work, c 1890

Replica of Schickard's calculating machine

Calculating machine

It is believed that German mathematician and astronomer Wilhelm Schickard built the first calculating machine around 1623. He described it in a letter to fellow German astronomer Johannes Kepler, but it was unfortunately lost in a fire. It seems to have combined Napier's bones (see p.74) with toothed wheels for adding and subtracting.

Babbage's Difference Engine

In the 1820s, English mathematician Charles Babbage developed the first of his calculating machines. Its purpose was to create numerical tables without human error. This is a demonstration model, built in 1832, based on Babbage's designs. He never completed the engine himself. Babbage improved on the calculating machine when he later went on to design the Analytical Engine – an early computer.

Key events

c 2700 BCE

The first abacus was probably invented in Sumer (modern-day Iraq). It was soon adopted everywhere, and remains in use in some parts of the world even today.

1622

English mathematician William Oughtred invented the slide rule. Slide rules are used to multiply, divide, and calculate roots and logarithms. You cannot use them to add or take away.

1642

French philosopher and mathematician Blaise Pascal built the first surviving mechanical calculator to be put to practical use. It is known as a Pascaline.

1820

Charles Xavier Thomas of Colmar, France, built a mechanical calculating machine, the arithmometer, for office use. It was a commercial success.

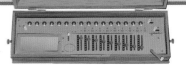

Arithmometer, c 1890

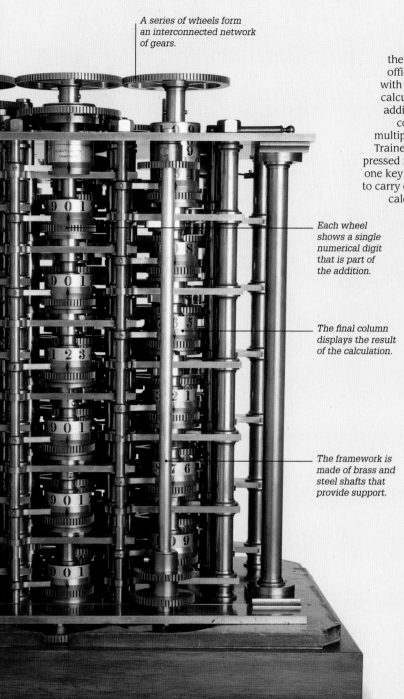

A series of wheels form an interconnected network of gears.

Each wheel shows a single numerical digit that is part of the addition.

The final column displays the result of the calculation.

The framework is made of brass and steel shafts that provide support.

Comptometer

Comptometers were first made in the 1880s and were a main feature of office life until late into the 1970s, with the arrival of the electronic calculator. Primarily used for adding, the comptometer could also subtract, multiply, and divide. Trained operators pressed more than one key at a time to carry out rapid calculations.

Comptometer, c 1920

The keys are arranged in eight columns of nine keys each.

Calculators for all

The development of pocket electronic calculators in the 1970s ended the need for mechanical devices such as slide rules and made it possible for everyone to do calculations at the press of a button. By the 1980s, computers – with their integrated electronic calculators – were becoming widely available. Today, we use our smartphones and smart watches to carry out complex calculations.

Desktop computer, 1980s

1822

English mathematician Charles Babbage began work on the design of his first Difference Engine, a machine capable of performing complex calculations.

1940s

The first electronic programmable calculating machines were developed during World War II to aid in deciphering encoded enemy messages.

1970s

Pocket-sized electronic calculators began to replace other kinds of calculating machines at work, school, and in the home.

1980s

Small, powerful desktop computers with inbuilt electronic calculators became widely available.

Pocket electronic calculator

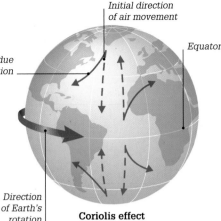

Initial direction of air movement

Equator

Air is deflected east due to Earth's rotation

Direction of Earth's rotation

Coriolis effect

EARLY PHOTOGRAPHY

Two men contributed to the rise of photography after 1835. French artist Louis Daguerre began taking photographs on light-sensitive, silver-plated copper sheets. Named after the inventor, the photographs were called daguerreotypes. British scientist Henry Fox Talbot invented the calotype, a way of producing multiple photographs from a single negative.

Daguerreotype camera

Daguerreotype camera
Alphonse Giroux designed the first commercial camera in 1839. The photographer viewed the object through a focusing screen at the back of the camera before replacing the screen with the light-sensitive plate.

3. The daguerreotype is sealed under glass for protection.

Light-sensitive plate

Sliding the inner box backwards and forwards adjusts focus.

2. Plate is heated with mercury vapour to develop image.

Object being photographed

Lens fitted to outer box

1. Image is captured.

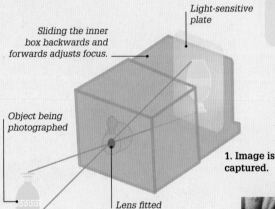

Competing processes
Although the daguerreotype process gave a clear image, it could not be duplicated. On the other hand, Fox Talbot's negatives (on light-sensitive paper), made by the Calotype process he patented in 1841, could be reproduced as positives (black-and-white photographs). So while daguerreotypes were more popular at first, negative photography would prove to be the way of the future.

Paper negative (reversed black-and-white image) by Henry Fox Talbot

1835

Coriolis effect
Gaspard-Gustave Coriolis showed that in the northern hemisphere, because of Earth's rotation, wind that was originally heading towards the Equator will veer west, and wind originally heading away from the Equator will veer east. In the southern hemisphere, the reverse happens. This phenomenon is known as the Coriolis effect.

1835

1836

Fast shooter
American gunsmith Samuel Colt patented the revolver – a handgun that could fire six shots without reloading. The gun's revolving cylinder contained six bullets, and a new bullet moved automatically into the firing position after each shot.

1837

Past ice ages
Geologist and palaeontologist Louis Agassiz was the first person to argue that Earth underwent several ice ages (glacial periods in which a large part of the world is covered with ice) in the past. Agassiz studied glaciers and realized that the movement of ancient glaciers had shaped the landscape we see today, carving out valleys and depositing piled up rock debris (moraines).

1839
Vulcanized rubber
American inventor Charles Goodyear discovered he could make rubber stronger by heating it with sulfur. The process – called vulcanization, after Vulcan, the Roman god of fire – makes rubber less sticky, increasing its practical use. Car tyres are made of vulcanized rubber.

Goodyear experiments with rubber

1815–1852 ADA LOVELACE
Ada Lovelace, the daughter of English poet Lord Byron, was a mathematician who worked with English inventor Charles Babbage on his Analytical Engine, a general-purpose computing machine (see p.124). Lovelace wrote the world's first "computer program" in 1843 and the modern programming language Ada is named after her.

Lovelace predicted that a computer could do more than numerical calculations – perhaps even compose music.

1840

1845

Frog larva cell

Plant cell

Communication
See pages 150–151

Fish cell

Theodor Schwann's drawings of cells

1844
Down the wire
American inventor Samuel Morse sent a long-distance telegraph message down an electric wire from Washington DC to Baltimore, USA. He tapped out a message using Morse code, a system of dots and dashes he had devised to spell out the letters of the alphabet (see p.151).

1839
Cell theory
Theodor Schwann, a German physiologist, published a book called *Microscopical Researches*, in which he showed that all living things – animals and plants – are made from cells, and that the cell is the basic unit of life. He had worked out his ideas in collaboration with German botanist Matthias Schleiden.

When the finger key is pressed, it closes the gap between the upper and lower contact, closing the circuit.

When the upper and lower contacts touch, a dot or dash is sent.

Morse key, 1844

"What hath God wrought?"
First telegraph message, 24 May 1844

Stephenson's locomotive

George Stephenson, an English engineer also known as the "Father of the Railways", built his first locomotive in 1814 to haul wagons at a coal mine in northeast England. He called it *Blücher* after the dynamic Prussian general who would later fight alongside the British at the Battle of Waterloo in 1815. *Blücher* had a top speed of 6.4 km/h (4 mph) and could haul eight loaded coal wagons weighing 30 tonnes up an incline. In 1825, Stephenson oversaw construction of the world's first public railway between the towns of Stockton and Darlington in the north of England. Four years later, Stephenson built his most famous locomotive, the *Rocket*, which reached a record speed of 58 km/h (36 mph).

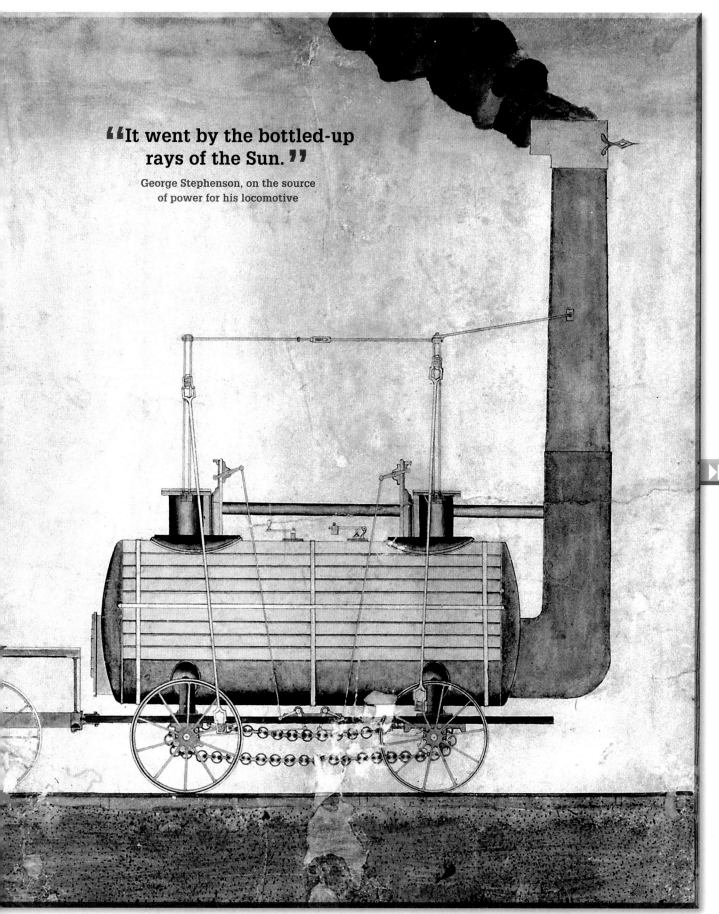

❝It went by the bottled-up rays of the Sun.❞

George Stephenson, on the source
of power for his locomotive

Coloured drawing of George Stephenson's
first locomotive, *Blücher*

129

The story of engines

An engine is a machine with moving parts that converts one form of energy, normally chemical energy from burning fuel, into the energy of motion. The invention of the steam engine, which harnessed the power of steam to operate machinery in mills and factories, gave rise to the Industrial Revolution. By the early 1800s, steam engines were also driving ships and locomotives. The invention of the petrol-fuelled internal combustion engine and the jet plane engine revolutionized transport still further.

Gas engine

In 1860, Belgian engineer Etienne Lenoir designed an engine that generated power by burning gas and air inside a cylinder. It was the first successful internal combustion engine (the type of engine where fuel is ignited inside the engine).

Electric-spark ignition system

Gas and air mix inside the cylinder.

Exhaust gases escape through smokestack.

Flywheel is turned by power from the piston, which drives the crank.

Crank is linked to crosshead by a connecting rod.

Boiler heats water to create steam that moves piston.

Cogwheels are turned by crank, creating forward motion.

Crosshead is linked to flywheel by a connecting rod.

Piston rod connects the piston to the crosshead.

First steam locomotive

British engineer Richard Trevithick's *Penydarren* locomotive made the first successful rail journey of 14 km (9 miles) at an ironworks in South Wales, UK, on 21 February 1804. The boiler sprang a leak on the return journey, and the engine was removed from the locomotive. The engine was later used as a stationary engine to drive a heavy hammer at the same ironworks. This model is based on Trevithick's drawings.

Model of Trevithick's *Penydarren* locomotive

Key events

c 50 CE

Greek inventor Hero of Alexandria designed a device that used steam to spin a sphere. It had no practical purpose.

Hero's device

1712

British inventor Thomas Newcomen built the first practical steam engine for commercial use. It used low-pressure steam inside a large cylinder.

1765

James Watt designed a much more efficient steam engine, which also converted the linear (up-and-down) movement of the pistons into a rotary motion.

1804

Richard Trevithick mounted a compact, high-pressure steam engine on wheels to create the world's first steam locomotive.

Power transmission

Today's motor vehicles have a transmission system that transmits power from the internal combustion engine (see p.148), through the gearbox, to the wheels.

The gearbox controls the speed of the car by adjusting the speed ratios between the engine and the wheels.

5. The differential (a kind of gear mechanism) controls the turning of the wheels.

4. The driveshaft under the car transmits power to the rear axle.

3. Combinations of gears in the gearbox increase the car's speed and force.

2. The rotating crankshaft transmits power to the gearbox.

1. The moving pistons turn the crankshaft, which converts up-and-down motion of the pistons to rotary motion.

"I sell here, Sir, what all the world desires to have – POWER. "

Matthew Boulton, James Watt's business partner, 1776

Horsepower

Traditionally, the power of an engine was measured in horsepower (hp). The term was coined by Scottish engineer James Watt to help sell his steam engines – he boasted that one of his engines could harness the power of 200 horses at once. One hp is equivalent to 746 watts, the standard unit of power, named after James Watt.

This automobile from 1897 had a 10-hp engine.

A steamboat on the Mississippi River, c 1859

Steamships

As well as powering locomotives, steam engines were soon being used on ships. Paddle steamers carrying cargo and passengers on major rivers, such as the Mississippi, opened up new areas of the USA to agriculture and trade in the 19th century. The steam from the boiler turns the paddlewheels, driving the steamer forward.

The electric charging station connects the car safely to the national grid.

A driver recharges her electric car

Greener engines

Petrol and diesel engines burn a lot of fuel and give off heavily polluting exhaust gases. Today, hybrid cars, which combine a petrol engine and an electric motor, and all-electric cars are increasingly popular.

1876

German engineer Nikolaus Otto invented the petrol-driven four-stroke internal combustion engine. It soon led to the development of the automobile.

1897

Rudolf Diesel, a German inventor, built the first diesel engine. Diesel engines produce more power than petrol engines and can be used to pull heavier loads.

1926

American engineer Robert Goddard invented the liquid-fuel rocket engine. Scarcely recognized at the time, he is now regarded as the father of modern rocketry.

1937

English engineer Frank Whittle and German engineer Hans von Ohain independently developed the turbojet engine that increased the speed of aircraft.

Model of Robert Goddard's rocket

1845 ▶ 1855

" ... the effect was soothing, quieting and delightful beyond measure. "

Queen Victoria, after being given chloroform
as an anaesthetic during childbirth, 1853

1846

Painless surgery
When American surgeon William Morton removed a tumour from a patient's neck, he first used ether fumes to put the patient to sleep. During the operation, the patient felt nothing. The fumes were an anaesthetic, a substance that blocks nerve signals to the brain. The discovery of anaesthetics such as ether and chloroform was a major medical breakthrough.

Pipe to connect to patient's face mask

Chloroform holder

Chloroform inhaler, 1848

1847

Hand hygiene
Ignaz Semmelweis, a Hungarian physician, discovered that deaths from puerperal fever (an infectious disease that killed many women in childbirth) fell if doctors washed their hands between treating patients. Doctors were slow to follow his advice.

Ignaz Semmelweis with a patient

1847

Heat studies
German physicist Hermann von Helmholtz stated that energy cannot be created or destroyed, it can only change its form. This is the first law of thermodynamics (the branch of physics concerned with the behaviour of heat).

 In 1848, physicist Lord Kelvin calculated the lowest possible temperature as −273.15°C (−459.67°F), which he called "absolute zero".

1845

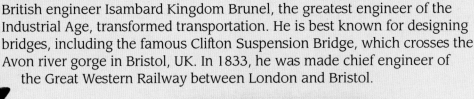

1806–1859   ISAMBARD KINGDOM BRUNEL

British engineer Isambard Kingdom Brunel, the greatest engineer of the Industrial Age, transformed transportation. He is best known for designing bridges, including the famous Clifton Suspension Bridge, which crosses the Avon river gorge in Bristol, UK. In 1833, he was made chief engineer of the Great Western Railway between London and Bristol.

Dangerous apprenticeship
Brunel began work at the age of 16, as his father's assistant on a project to dig a tunnel under the River Thames in London. The hazardous job was abandoned after torrential floods filled the tunnel, almost drowning Brunel.

Ocean liner
In 1845, the SS *Great Britain*, designed by Brunel, sailed from Liverpool, UK, to New York, USA. Revolutionary in design, she was the first steam passenger liner to be built entirely of wrought iron and was driven by a massive propeller instead of paddle wheels. At the time, the *Great Britain* was the longest ship afloat. On her maiden voyage, she crossed the Atlantic in 14 days, breaking previous speed records.

Taking to the skies
See pages
162–163

Henri Giffard
in his airship

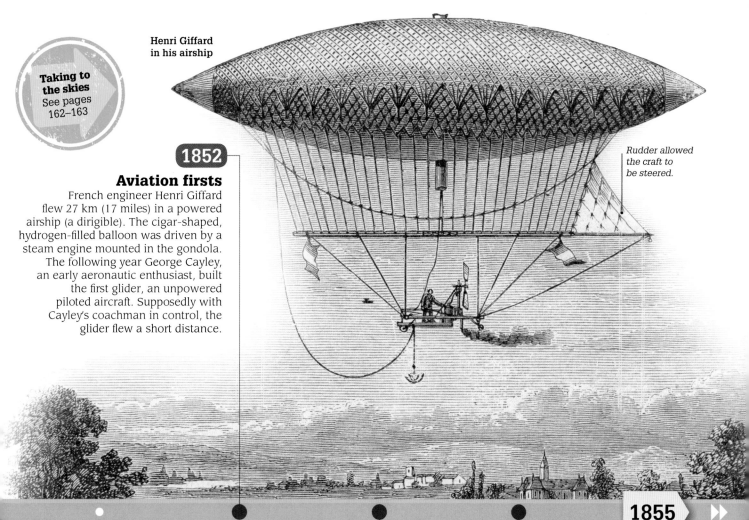

*Rudder allowed
the craft to
be steered.*

1852

Aviation firsts

French engineer Henri Giffard
flew 27 km (17 miles) in a powered
airship (a dirigible). The cigar-shaped,
hydrogen-filled balloon was driven by a
steam engine mounted in the gondola.
The following year George Cayley,
an early aeronautic enthusiast, built
the first glider, an unpowered
piloted aircraft. Supposedly with
Cayley's coachman in control, the
glider flew a short distance.

1855

1853

Cleaner fuel

Canadian geologist Abraham
Gesner invented kerosene – a
light oil refined from coal and
shale. This oil soon replaced
whale oil as the fuel burned in
lamps for lighting houses
and factories, because it
was much cheaper and
did not smell as fishy.

Kerosene lamp, 1853

The Bunsen burner,
a gas burner used
in laboratories, was
invented by German
chemist Robert
Bunsen in 1855.

1854

Death at the water pump

The London doctor John Snow
believed that contaminated
water was responsible for
spreading cholera (a highly
infectious, often fatal disease).
When cholera broke out in
London in 1854, he was able to
trace the source of the disease
to a single water pump. His
detective work brought
about improvements
in sanitation.

**An illustration from
the time shows Death
haunting the water
pump that was the
source of cholera.**

Illustration of Darwin's rhea by John Gould, 1841

Darwin's rhea
Named after the naturalist, this is the smaller of two species of rhea, a flightless bird, which Darwin encountered in South America. Darwin and his team, mistaking this rhea for a more common species, shot and ate the bird. Only after did Darwin realize it was the rarer type and preserved the remaining specimens.

> **"... we are not here concerned with hopes or fears, only with the truth as far as our reason permits us to discover it..."**
>
> Charles Darwin,
> *The Descent of Man*

One of Darwin's notebooks

Darwin's compass

Charles Darwin

English naturalist Charles Darwin (1809–1882) was one of the most influential scientists of all time. His theory of evolution by natural selection explained how life on Earth developed, and is the basic concept upon which the life sciences (the study of living organisms) are built.

Early years

Darwin came from a privileged, intellectual background. His father was a doctor and, on leaving school, Darwin followed in his footsteps and went to Edinburgh University, in Scotland, to study medicine. However, he gave up because he hated the sight of blood and went to the University of Cambridge in England instead, intending to become a clergyman.

The young naturalist

Darwin discovered his love of natural history at Cambridge, where he spent much of his time collecting beetles. He graduated in 1831 and accepted a place as a naturalist on board HMS *Beagle*. The ship's five-year voyage proved to be the most important period in Darwin's life, providing the basis for his future ideas and writings.

Revolutionary idea

On his return to England in 1836, Darwin published an account of his travels, which made him famous. He married, settled at Down House in Kent, and had ten children. Over the years he began to develop his theory of natural selection – the process in which living things with characteristics suited to their environment survive and produce offspring with similar features. He published his revolutionary book *On the Origin of Species* in 1859. This was followed by *The Descent of Man* in 1871, in which he applied his ideas to explaining the evolution of humans.

Round-the-world trip
During his five-year voyage on HMS Beagle, Darwin filled dozens of notebooks with his observations on animals, plants, and geology. He collected thousands of bird specimens, many of which were identified back in England by the ornithologist (someone who studies birds) and illustrator, John Gould. The material Darwin gathered on the Galápagos Islands was very important in shaping his ideas.

Controversial theory
Although many scientists at the time agreed with Darwin's theory of evolution, others were more sceptical. His ideas were violently opposed by traditional Christians, and Darwin was ridiculed for supposedly implying that humans were descended from monkeys. This cartoon appeared in a magazine after the publication of The Descent of Man in 1871.

Man of science
Despite years of ill health, Darwin never gave up studying natural history. He wrote weighty books on many topics including barnacles, orchids, and earthworms. He died in 1882.

"... one general law, leading to the advancement of all organic beings, namely, multiply, vary, let the strongest live and the weakest die."

Charles Darwin,
On the Origin of Species

135

Studying light

The scientific study of light and vision is called optics, and has been a subject of interest for hundreds of years. Several ancient civilizations, including the Ancient Greeks, experimented with light, and early Arab physicians had an advanced understanding of how the eye works. In the 1700s, an argument about whether light was in particle or wave form divided European scientists. We now know that light is a kind of electromagnetic radiation.

Front page of Latin version of the *Book of Optics*

How we see

The *Book of Optics*, written by Arab scholar Ibn al-Haytham (Alhazen) between 1011 and 1021, correctly showed that vision occurs when rays of light enter the eye from outside. Until then, most people thought that visual rays extended from inside the eye outwards.

Spinning colours

English scientist Sir Isaac Newton (see pp.88–89) used a colour wheel to show that white light is made up of bands of colour. When he spun the wheel, the colours – red, orange, yellow, green, blue, and violet – seemed to merge into white. We now know that colours have different wavelengths.

Replica of Newton's colour wheel

> **"... whenever all those Rays with those their Colours are mix'd again, they reproduce the same white Light as before."**
>
> Sir Isaac Newton, *Opticks*, 1704

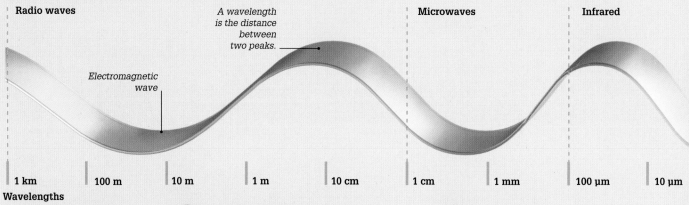

Radio waves

Microwaves

Infrared

A wavelength is the distance between two peaks.

Electromagnetic wave

| 1 km | 100 m | 10 m | 1 m | 10 cm | 1 cm | 1 mm | 100 μm | 10 μm |

Wavelengths

μm – micrometre
nm – nanometre

Radio waves

Radio waves are used to send sound and television signals. Dish telescopes pick up radio waves from space.

Microwaves

Microwaves, or short-wavelength radio waves, are used to heat food and transmit mobile phone signals.

Key events

750 BCE

The oldest known lens, from the Assyrian city of Nimrud (in present-day Iraq), was made of rock crystal and may have been used as a magnifying glass.

1267

Oxford scholar Roger Bacon described the structure of the eye. He made a study of lenses, and said that rainbows were caused by the reflection of sunlight from individual raindrops.

c 1286

The first spectacles, or eyeglasses, were made in Italy. Early spectacles, used by monks and scholars for reading, were balanced on the nose.

1678

Dutch physicist Christiaan Huygens suggested that light is made up of spherical waves that spread out as they travel.

14th-century spectacles

Bending Light

Scientists study the nature of light and also how it can be manipulated. The study of how lenses work is an example of this.

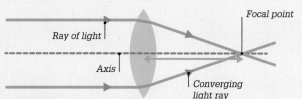

Ray of light
Focal point
Axis
Converging light ray

Axis
Focal point
Diverging light ray
Virtual ray

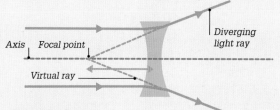

Convex lens

A convex lens bulges in the middle. When parallel rays of light pass through it, they bend inwards (converge), and meet at the focal point just beyond the lens.

Concave lens

A concave lens is hollow in the middle. When parallel rays of light pass through it, they spread out (diverge), and appear to come from a focal point in front of the lens.

Optical illusion

Our eyes can be tricked into seeing things that are not there, with the help of mirrors and reflections. The theatrical device, Pepper's Ghost (named after one of its inventors), uses a large piece of angled glass to bounce the image of a ghostly figure on to the stage.

Pepper's Ghost fools a theatre audience in the 19th century

Electromagnetic waves

Visible light forms a tiny part of the entire range (spectrum) of electromagnetic waves (below) that are travelling through space at extremely high speed, and were first described in the 19th century. The different types of waves have individual uses and functions in our everyday lives.

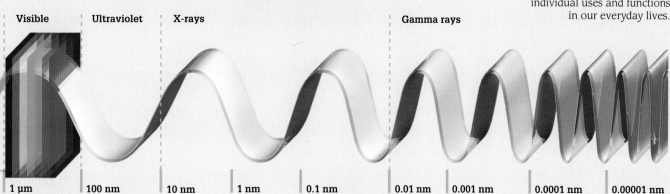

Visible	Ultraviolet	X-rays		Gamma rays				
1 μm	100 nm	10 nm	1 nm	0.1 nm	0.01 nm	0.001 nm	0.0001 nm	0.00001 nm

Visible light

Our eyes are able to see colour within this range of wavelengths. Some animals can see beyond this range.

X-rays

X-rays can be used to see inside our bodies. They penetrate the soft tissue but are blocked by bones and teeth.

1704

Sir Isaac Newton published *Opticks*, in which he opposed Huygens's theory. He described light as a stream of tiny particles (corpuscles) travelling at huge speed in a straight line.

1816

French physicist Augustin-Jean Fresnel carried out a series of experiments that supported the wave theory of light.

Augustin-Jean Fresnel

1864

Scottish mathematician James Clerk Maxwell showed that light is an electromagnetic wave. He went on to predict the existence of other forms of electromagnetic waves.

1905

Physicist Albert Einstein united wave and particle theory by proposing that light is made up of tiny packets of energy called photons that also behave as waves.

1856
Artificial dye
British chemist William Perkin was still a student when he accidentally discovered the first synthetic chemical dye. It was an intense purple colour, which became known as mauve (the French name of the purple mallow flower) and was later given the chemical name mauveine. Perkin set up a factory to produce mauve commercially.

Dress made of silk dyed with Perkin's mauve

1857
Going up
Elisha Otis, an American inventor and businessman, installed the first passenger elevator (lift) at 488 Broadway, New York City. His design included a safety brake that prevented the elevator from falling if the cables broke. Otis safety elevators, installed in tall buildings, helped to trigger New York's skyscraper boom.

Otis gives a public demonstration of his safety elevator

▶▶ **1855**

1856
Steel-making process
British engineer Henry Bessemer patented a furnace for making steel cheaply by blowing air through molten iron to remove the impurities. Steel rails for railways, made by the Bessemer process, lasted ten times longer than iron ones.

1856
Studying pea plants
Austrian monk Gregor Mendel began breeding pea plants. He discovered that inherited characteristics, such as size, are passed on by invisible "factors". We now call them genes. Mendel's work, unrecognized at the time, forms the basis of modern genetics.

1859
Influential book
British naturalist Charles Darwin published a book called *On the Origin of Species*, in which he explained his theory of evolution through natural selection. It is one of the most important books in the history of science.

Charles Darwin See pages 134–135

4. Carbon monoxide gas produced in the process is burned off, and the furnace is tilted to pour out the steel.

3. Slag floats to the surface.

2. Oxygen in the air combines with carbon (to produce carbon monoxide), and with manganese and other impurities, creating slag.

Lining of fire clay bricks preserves heat.

1. Air entering through holes at the bottom of the furnace is blown through molten iron.

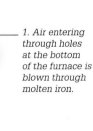

Cross-section through a Bessemer furnace

1858
Transatlantic cable
The first undersea transatlantic telegraph cable, between western Ireland and Newfoundland (off the coast of Canada), came into service, but it failed after three weeks and had to be abandoned. A new, longer-lasting cable was successfully laid between 1865–1866.

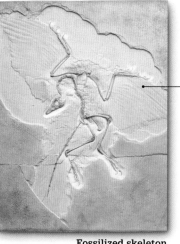

Feathered wing

Fossilized skeleton of *Archaeopteryx*

1865

Making food safe

Asked why beer went sour, French chemist Louis Pasteur found it was due to harmful microbes (tiny organisms) in the air. However, the microbes were destroyed if the beer was heated briefly. Wine and milk could be treated in the same way. The heating process, still used today, is called pasteurization.

Louis Pasteur
See pages 142–143

Milk containers

Heating apparatus

Water bath

19th-century machine for pasteurizing milk

1861

Dinosaur to bird

The almost complete fossil of a creature with wings, feathers, and a toothed beak was found in Germany and given the name of *Archaeopteryx* (ancient wing). These creatures lived almost 150 million years ago, and are thought to have been the evolutionary link between dinosaurs and birds.

1865

1860

Incandescent light bulb

British scientist Joseph Swan developed an incandescent (glowing) light bulb. He passed an electric current through a carbon filament inside a glass bulb, from which most of the air had been removed. This heated the filament until it glowed. The drawback was that the filament burned out quickly. After making improvements to the bulb, Swan patented it in 1878, the year that American inventor Thomas Edison began work on his electric light bulb.

1864

Electromagnetism explained

British physicist James Clerk Maxwell showed that disturbances in electromagnetic fields create waves that radiate outwards. These waves radiate at exactly the same speed as light, proving that light is also an electromagnetic wave. Maxwell summed up his findings in four mathematical equations that laid the foundations of electromagnetic field theory.

Carbon filament

Glass bulb partially emptied of air

Brass support, acting as an electrical conductor

 In 1860, Florence Nightingale established the first school of nursing at St Thomas' Hospital, London.

Replica of Swan's lamp

Thomas Edison
See page 149

Powering our world

Today, electricity powers everything from huge industrial machines to our computers and smartphones, and lights our houses and cities. But people have only been using electricity as a source of energy for less than 150 years. Most of the electricity we use in our homes is made in power plants by huge turbines fuelled by coal, gas, or renewable energy sources.

The dynamo room at Pearl Street station

Early generator

In 1832, French instrument-maker Hippolyte Pixii utilized Michael Faraday's discovery of electromagnetic induction (see p.123) and built an early form of generator, which produced alternating current (AC). It was composed of a spinning horseshoe magnet, its poles pointing upwards, which caused a current to flow in a coil of wire, generating AC electricity. At that time there was little interest in developing AC, and Pixii found a way of converting it to the more popular direct current (DC).

Lighting Manhattan

American inventor Thomas Edison's Electric Lighting Station, on Manhattan's Pearl Street, New York City, USA, was the first permanent station to supply electric lighting on a grand scale. It featured six large dynamos that generated power to light more than 10,000 lamps. The dynamos were driven by steam engines and the steam was then used to heat nearby buildings. Pearl Street station burned down in 1890.

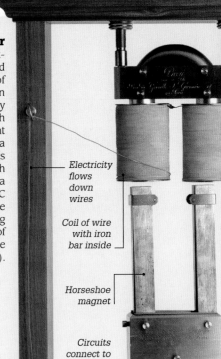

Electricity flows down wires

Coil of wire with iron bar inside

Horseshoe magnet

Circuits connect to the two connection points

Hand-driven crank turns magnet

Pixii generator

AC/DC: Different currents

Edison's power stations delivered direct current (DC) electricity. But DC could only travel a small distance before it decreased in power. In 1887, American engineer George Westinghouse introduced alternating current (AC), which could transmit electricity over longer distances.

- **Direct current**
  DC electricity flows in only one direction. It is used to charge batteries and as a power supply for electronic systems.

- **Alternate current**
  AC electricity changes direction many times every second. Most homes and businesses are wired for AC electricity.

Key events

1752
Future American statesman Benjamin Franklin flew a kite with a key attached to the string into a thunderstorm to prove that lightning is electrical.

1800
Italian scientist Alessandro Volta made the first battery that could continuously provide electric current to a circuit. It was known as a Voltaic pile.

1831
English scientist Michael Faraday discovered electromagnetic induction when he found that he could produce an electric current by moving a magnet in and out of a coil of wire.

1882
Thomas Edison opened the first central power station for generating electricity on Pearl Street in Manhattan, New York City, USA.

Electric street lamp

A horse-drawn vehicle shares the street with an electric streetcar in Chicago, USA, 1906.

Electricity takes over

Energy production increased rapidly in the early years of the 20th century. Power lines, streetlights, and neon signs transformed the urban landscape, while trams and electric railways brought speedier, and cleaner, transport. Electric goods such as refrigerators made life easier at home.

> **"Electricity is doing for the distribution of energy what the railroads have done for the distribution of materials."**
>
> American electrical engineer Charles Proteus Steinmetz, 1922

Rivers of light

From the power stations, electricity flows long distances, through high-voltage power lines to substations that supply homes and businesses with energy. This photo, taken from space, shows the cities of the USA lit up at night.

Renewable energy

At present, most of the world's electricity is made by burning non-renewable fuels, such as coal and natural gas, which contribute to global warming (see pp.220–221). Increasing efforts are being made to develop techniques that exploit renewable energy sources.

Solar power

Energy from the Sun is converted into electricity, usually by photovoltaic panels placed in areas receiving direct sunlight. It is a cheap, silent, and non-polluting source of energy.

Hydroelectricity

The power of falling water is used to turn a turbine to create electricity. It is a reliable energy source, but hydroelectric plants are expensive to build and can affect river flow.

Wind power

Wind is used to turn large turbines to produce electricity. Energy from one turbine can power hundreds of homes.

3. Gear box speeds up the shaft.

2. Low-speed shaft is connected to the turbine blades that turn slowly.

Anemometer measures wind speed and direction.

Controller turns turbine to face the wind.

1. Blades catch the wind and turn.

4. High-speed shaft drives the generator to create electricity.

Modern wind turbine

1884

Charles Parsons, an English engineer, invented the steam turbine, which was used to drive an electric generator, making it possible to produce electricity cheaply and efficiently.

1887

Inventor Nikola Tesla developed an induction motor that ran on AC current, the power delivery system that would later replace the DC system.

1913

The first electric refrigerator for home use came on the market, starting a revolution in domestic appliances.

First electric refrigerator

1954

The world's first nuclear power plant was built to generate electricity for commercial use at Obinsk, Russia.

> **"... knowledge belongs to humanity, and is the torch which illuminates the world. "**
>
> Louis Pasteur

Pasteur in the laboratory
Louis Pasteur is known as the father of microbiology – the scientific study of organisms far too small to be seen with the naked eye, such as bacteria.

GREAT SCIENTISTS

Louis Pasteur

French chemist Louis Pasteur (1822–1895) made several important contributions to science – from introducing pasteurization (the process of briefly heating a substance to kill microbes) to developing vaccines that could fight deadly diseases.

Germ theory

The idea that infectious diseases are spread by germs, or micro-organisms, is known as germ theory. Today, we take it for granted, but this view was highly controversial when Pasteur, then a Professor of Chemistry, began his work in the 1860s. He showed that tiny organisms were responsible for contaminating beer and milk. He also found they caused diseases in silkworms.

Work on vaccines

Pasteur's confirmation of germ theory revolutionized medicine and healthcare by introducing new standards of hygiene. He developed vaccines against two animal diseases – chicken cholera and anthrax – by producing weakened strains of the disease-carrying bacteria in the laboratory. Once injected into animals, these strains produced antibodies (proteins the immune system creates to attack unfamiliar substances) that gave the animals immunity against the disease.

Fight against rabies

Pasteur made a vaccine against rabies, a disease spread to humans by infected animals. In 1886, he used it to successfully cure nine-year-old Joseph Meister, who had been bitten by an infected dog.

Dedication to science

In 1868, Pasteur had a stroke that partially paralyzed the left side of his body. He continued working on his research, with the help of colleagues and assistants. He died in 1895.

Silkworm research
Shown above is the microscope Pasteur used to identify the micro-organisms that were killing silkworms. In front of the microscope are some of the silkworm cocoons he studied. His research saved the silk industry in France.

> **"I am on the edge of mysteries and the veil is getting thinner and thinner."**
>
> Louis Pasteur

The Pasteur Institute
A doctor vaccinates a patient against rabies in the Pasteur Institute, the centre founded by Pasteur in Paris, France, for the study of diseases and vaccines. It still carries out life-saving research in all parts of the world.

Angel of mercy
A cartoon from a French newspaper shows Pasteur as an angel of mercy injecting a mad dog infected with rabies – a deadly killer.

1865 ▶ 1875

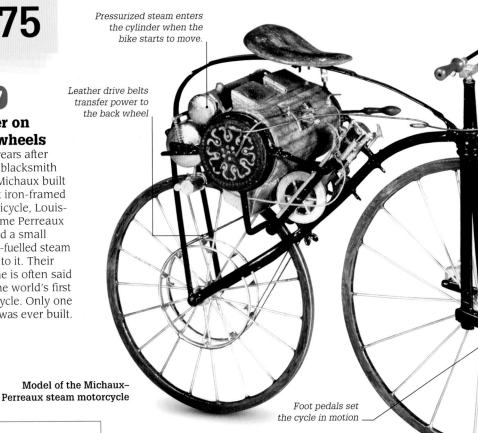

Pressurized steam enters the cylinder when the bike starts to move.

Leather drive belts transfer power to the back wheel

1867
Dynamite!
Alfred Nobel, a Swedish chemist, invented an explosive powder which he called "dynamite". Due to dynamite later being used on the battlefield, Nobel realized his legacy had become associated with death. To change this, in his will Nobel left a large amount of his money to fund the awards that became known as the Nobel Prizes – including one dedicated to those who promote peace.

1867
Power on two wheels
Three years after French blacksmith Pierre Michaux built the first iron-framed pedal bicycle, Louis-Guillaume Perreaux attached a small alcohol-fuelled steam engine to it. Their machine is often said to be the world's first motorcycle. Only one model was ever built.

Model of the Michaux–Perreaux steam motorcycle

Foot pedals set the cycle in motion

1865

1865
Safer surgery
Scottish surgeon Joseph Lister realized patients were dying because their wounds became infected with bacteria. He introduced carbolic acid as an antiseptic to kill bacteria in the operating theatre. It worked and death rates fell, but carbolic acid proved harmful both to patient and surgeon, and Lister later replaced it with boracic acid.

1868
Helium discovered
French astronomer Jules Janssen was watching a total eclipse of the Sun when he spotted a line of yellow light in the Sun's spectrum that did not match the wavelength of any known element. He had discovered helium – the second lightest and second most abundant element in the Universe, after hydrogen.

1869
DNA discovery
Swiss physician Friedrich Miescher discovered a substance inside the nuclei of cells. He called it "nuclein". We now know it to be DNA, the material that carries the genetic instructions for all living organisms.

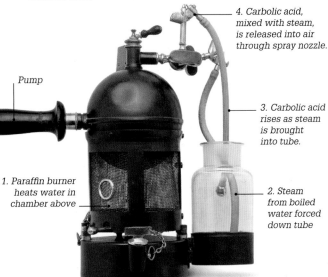

4. Carbolic acid, mixed with steam, is released into air through spray nozzle.

Pump

3. Carbolic acid rises as steam is brought into tube.

1. Paraffin burner heats water in chamber above

2. Steam from boiled water forced down tube

Lister's carbolic steam spray

The code of life
See pages 198–199

Early modern human
A skull discovered in southwestern France was identified as that of an early modern human (Cro-Magnon man), the first example found in Western Europe.

> **"I saw in a dream a table where all the elements fell into place as required."**
>
> Dmitri Mendeleev

Charles Darwin
See pages
134–135

1872

Scientific exploration

HMS *Challenger*, a British ship, set sail on a four-year voyage to explore the world's oceans. It carried a team of scientists, whose many discoveries helped lay the foundations of oceanography (the branch of science that involves the study of seas and oceans).

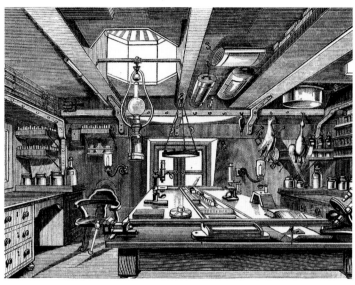

The zoology laboratory on board HMS *Challenger*

1871

Human evolution

Charles Darwin published *The Descent of Man*, a follow-up volume to *On the Origin of Species*. In his new work, he discussed the way in which humans had evolved and his theory of sexual selection. Although Darwin had hesitated before publishing the book, it did not create as much controversy as his first.

1875 ▶▶

1873

Keeping cool

German engineer Carl von Linde designed the first modern refrigeration system, using liquefied gases, for a brewery in Munich, Germany. Refrigeration rapidly transformed the storage of perishable foodstuffs.

The cooling process in Von Linde's invention isn't too different from what is found in modern refrigerators.

1834–1907   DMITRI MENDELEEV

It was as a Professor of Chemistry in St Petersburg, Russia, that Dmitri Mendeleev came up with the concept of a periodic table of elements based on their atomic weight. He later said the idea came to him in a dream while he was preparing a textbook on chemistry. Mendeleev himself called it the Periodic System. The element Mendelevium, discovered in 1955, was named after him, in honour of his discovery.

The periodic table

Mendeleev realized that if he arranged the 63 known elements in ascending order of atomic weight, he could organize them in groups, or "periods", sharing similar properties. Using this, he was then able to predict the existence of three more elements – gallium, scandium, and germanium – all of which were found in the next 16 years (see pp.188–189).

Mendeleev's notes

Von Linde's refrigerator

Learning chemistry

Chemistry is concerned with matter, the stuff that every object in the Universe is made of. It is what many processes key to modern life are based on, from improving the quality of food in the supermarket to the obtaining of petrol for a car. The study of chemistry became popular in Europe in the 1700s when scientists began to investigate substances, such as gases and liquids, and how they change. They carried out experiments to isolate and identify the elements (substances that cannot be broken down into simpler substances), and paved the way for future experiments and discoveries.

Alchemist's laboratory

Medieval alchemists heated and distilled substances in phials and retorts (glass vessels), and mixed and pounded them in mortars, all in the hope of turning lead into gold. They are often regarded as the early pioneers of chemistry.

An alchemist working in a laboratory

Knowledge of metals

This picture comes from *De re metallica* (On the Nature of Metals), an influential early book on chemistry published in 1556 in Germany. It described the extraction of metals by smelting (heating and melting).

1. Guinea pig placed in inner chamber.

Crude oil is heated before reaching the column.

2. Ice, placed in outer chamber, melts from heat of guinea pig's breath.

3. Water from the melting ice collects at the bottom.

Chemistry experiment

In the early 1780s, French chemist Antoine Lavoisier (see p.107) designed the ice calorimeter for an experiment to show that respiration (breathing) is chemically the same process as combustion (burning) – they utilize oxygen and produce heat. The device measured the amount of heat a guinea pig produces when it breathes.

Key events

1661
In his book *The Sceptical Chymist*, Anglo-Irish philosopher Robert Boyle argued that matter is made up of different "corpuscles" (atoms) that are constantly in motion.

1754
Joseph Black, a Scottish chemist, isolated the gas carbon dioxide, which he called "fixed air". He noted it was heavier than air, put out flames, and suffocated animals.

1766
English chemist Henry Cavendish discovered a colourless gas, which he called "inflammable air" – now known as hydrogen.

1789
Antoine Lavoisier published *Traité elementaire de chimie* (Elementary Treatise of Chemistry), the first modern chemistry textbook.

Henry Cavendish

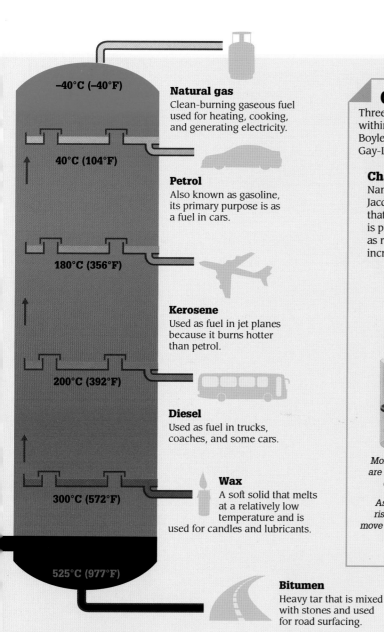

−40°C (−40°F)

Natural gas
Clean-burning gaseous fuel used for heating, cooking, and generating electricity.

40°C (104°F)

Petrol
Also known as gasoline, its primary purpose is as a fuel in cars.

180°C (356°F)

Kerosene
Used as fuel in jet planes because it burns hotter than petrol.

200°C (392°F)

Diesel
Used as fuel in trucks, coaches, and some cars.

300°C (572°F)

Wax
A soft solid that melts at a relatively low temperature and is used for candles and lubricants.

525°C (977°F)

Bitumen
Heavy tar that is mixed with stones and used for road surfacing.

Chemistry in industry
As research into chemical processes progressed, industry began to use the findings to develop the processes we see today. One such process is the distillation of crude oil – a complex mixture of hydrocarbons (compounds of hydrogen and carbon). These are separated inside a fractionating column (above). As the oil boils, the hydrocarbons turn to gas and rise up the tower. They rise, then cool and condense (turn back to liquid) at different temperatures, and are collected and refined into useful products, such as petrol.

Gas laws
Three important laws describing the movements of molecules within gases are named after their discoverers. The first is Boyle's law (see p.83). The other two are Charles' law and Gay-Lussac's law.

Charles' law
Named after French scientist Jacques Charles, this law states that the temperature of a gas is proportional to its volume, as raising the temperature increases the volume.

Gay-Lussac's law
First described by French chemist Joseph Louis Gay-Lussac, this law states that for a fixed volume of gas, the pressure is proportional to its temperature.

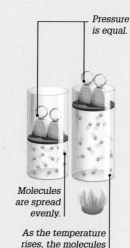

Pressure is equal.

Molecules are spread evenly.

As the temperature rises, the molecules move faster and spread out, increasing the volume.

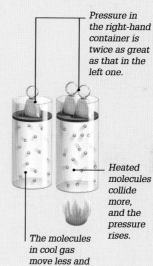

Pressure in the right-hand container is twice as great as that in the left one.

Heated molecules collide more, and the pressure rises.

The molecules in cool gas move less and the pressure remains low.

Synthetic polymers
Plastics were first made in the late 1800s. Produced from organic substances such as wood, coal, or petrol, they are made of polymers – large molecules that are moulded into shape when heated.

Dice made of celluloid, one of the first plastics

1803
English chemist John Dalton presented his atomic theory – the first attempt to describe all matter in terms of atoms and their properties.

1805
Joseph Louis Gay-Lussac discovered that water is made up of two parts hydrogen and one part oxygen.

1811
Italian physicist Amedeo Avogadro realized that simple gases such as hydrogen are made up of molecules of two or more atoms joined together.

1869
Dmitri Mendeleev published the periodic table in which he organized the 66 elements that were known at the time by their atomic weights and properties.

Water molecules

1875 ▶ 1885

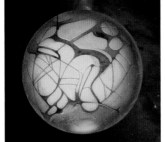

The canals turned out to be optical illusions.

Artist's depiction of Schiaparelli's map of Mars

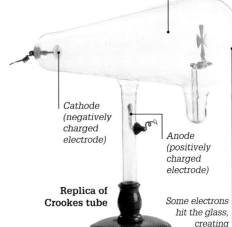

A strong electric field between the two electrodes strips electrons from the atoms in the gas and pushes them away from the cathode.

Cathode (negatively charged electrode)

Anode (positively charged electrode)

Replica of Crookes tube

Some electrons hit the glass, creating a glow.

1876
Invention of the telephone
American inventor Alexander Graham Bell patented the telephone. His device for transmitting and receiving human speech converted sound vibrations into electrical signals, and vice versa.

Communication
See pages 150–151

1876
Bacterial breakthrough
Robert Koch, a German bacteriologist, showed that anthrax – a deadly, infectious disease of sheep and cattle that can spread to humans – is transmitted by a bacterium called *Bacillus anthracis*. His finding confirmed French chemist Louis Pasteur's germ theory (see p.143).

1877
Life on Mars
Italian astronomer Giovanni Schiaparelli reported seeing *canali* on Mars. *Canali* simply means "channels" in Italian, but it was mistakenly translated into English as "canals". This caused a storm of rumours that Mars was inhabited by intelligent beings.

1878
Crookes tube
William Crookes, an English chemist, invented the cathode ray tube (also called Crookes tube). This tube, holding only a miniscule amount of gas, contained a negatively charged electrode (an electrical conductor) called a cathode, as well as a positively charged one, an anode. It would later be used to discover electrons and X-rays (see p.158).

⏵⏵ 1875

1876   FOUR-STROKE ENGINE

German inventor Nikolaus Otto invented the four-stroke internal combustion engine, which ignites fuel inside a cylinder. The Otto engine operates on a four-stroke cycle that moves a piston up and down in the cylinder. German engineer Karl Benz later adapted it as an automobile engine.

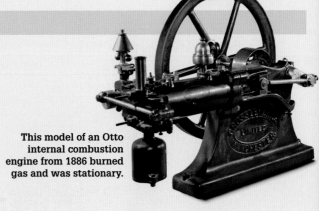

This model of an Otto internal combustion engine from 1886 burned gas and was stationary.

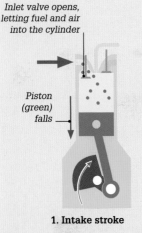

Inlet valve opens, letting fuel and air into the cylinder

Piston (green) falls

1. Intake stroke

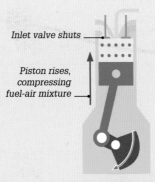

Inlet valve shuts

Piston rises, compressing fuel-air mixture

2. Compression stroke

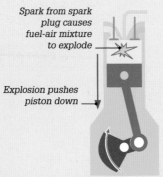

Spark from spark plug causes fuel-air mixture to explode

Explosion pushes piston down

3. Ignition stroke

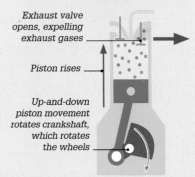

Exhaust valve opens, expelling exhaust gases

Piston rises

Up-and-down piston movement rotates crankshaft, which rotates the wheels

4. Exhaust stroke

1847–1931 THOMAS EDISON

American scientist Thomas Edison began work as a telegraph operator at the age of 15. He went on to become one of the most famous inventors of all time, with more than 1,000 patents to his name. He set up the world's first industrial research laboratory at Menlo Park, New Jersey, USA.

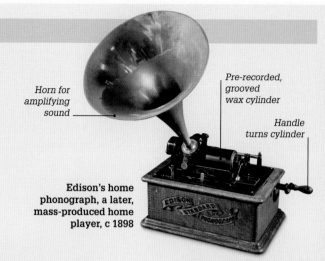

Horn for amplifying sound

Pre-recorded, grooved wax cylinder

Handle turns cylinder

Edison's home phonograph, a later, mass-produced home player, c 1898

Looped carbon filament

Connecting wire

Edison's light bulb

One of Edison's best-known creations is the electric light bulb. He improved on English chemist Joseph Swan's design (see p.139), and produced a pure vacuum inside the glass bulb, while using a longer-burning, carbonized bamboo fibre for the filament.

First sound recording

Edison invented the phonograph in 1877. A needle in the instrument engraved the vibrations of the human voice on a rotating tinfoil cylinder. To play the sound back, the needle retraced the grooves.

1885

1881
First electric tramway

The first electric tramway was opened in Lichterfelde, a suburb of Berlin, Germany. Each car was equipped with an electric motor, with the current supplied via the running rails. People and horses often received electric shocks at railroad crossings before an overhead wire was introduced in 1891.

1881
Brighter cities

Though arc lights (see p.114) had lit up a number of large cities since the 1870s, the small town of Godalming, UK, caught the attention of the world when it became the first place to install electric light bulbs. The electric supply, which also lit houses, was generated by a water-powered dynamo.

Illustration of the first electric tramway

Moving horse

Photographs taken by English photographer Eadweard Muybridge revealed that a trotting horse has all four legs off the ground at the same time.

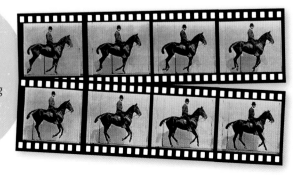

> **"We will make electric light so cheap that only the rich will be able to burn candles."**
>
> Thomas Edison, 1879

Communication

In past centuries, long-distance communication between people was a slow process. Letters, carried on horseback or by ship, could take days or even weeks to reach their destination. Things speeded up with the invention of the telegraph, which sent a message along an electric wire instantaneously. The telephone, radio, and television soon followed. Today, using computers and handheld devices, we can make instant contact with each other almost anywhere in the world.

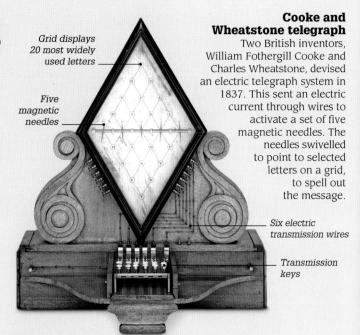

Cooke and Wheatstone telegraph

Two British inventors, William Fothergill Cooke and Charles Wheatstone, devised an electric telegraph system in 1837. This sent an electric current through wires to activate a set of five magnetic needles. The needles swivelled to point to selected letters on a grid, to spell out the message.

Grid displays 20 most widely used letters

Five magnetic needles

Six electric transmission wires

Transmission keys

Pony Express riders carried the mail in leather pouches on their saddlebags.

Carrying the mail

The Pony Express, which began operating in 1860, delivered mail from Missouri in the midwest of the USA to California in the west, a hazardous journey of nearly 3,000 km (2,000 miles). Using a relay system, with lightning changes of horses and riders, the high-speed service cut at least 10 days off the time taken by rival mail companies. The coming of the telegraph saw the end of the Pony Express in 1861.

> **"Mr Watson – come here – I want to see you."**
>
> First words spoken over the telephone, by Alexander Graham Bell to his assistant, 10 March 1876

Electric signals travel along wire

Horseshoe magnet

Wires attach here to take signals to and from the telephone

Bell telephone, 1870s

Key events

1844
American inventor Samuel Morse gave a public demonstration of his telegraph system when he sent a message down a wire from Washington DC to Baltimore, USA.

1858
The first undersea transatlantic cable came into service, linking Europe and North America by telegraph. It ran from Ireland to Newfoundland, Canada.

1876
Alexander Graham Bell designed the first working telephone, which could transmit and receive human speech.

1886
Heinrich Hertz detected the existence of radio waves, first theorized by James Clerk Maxwell. This discovery paved the way for future research into wireless radio communication.

Alexander Graham Bell

Morse telegraph

The electric telegraph sent messages, using Morse code (see p.127), as a series of electrical pulses representing the different letters of the alphabet. The operator pressed a key to transmit the pulses along a wire. At the receiving end, an electromagnet moved a pen that marked out the coded message on a paper tape.

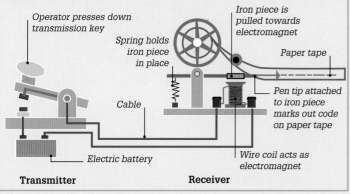

Operator presses down transmission key

Spring holds iron piece in place

Iron piece is pulled towards electromagnet

Paper tape

Cable

Pen tip attached to iron piece marks out code on paper tape

Electric battery

Wire coil acts as electromagnet

Transmitter

Receiver

Early Marconi radio receiver

Radio at sea

Italian physicist Guglielmo Marconi invented the first long-distance radio (or wireless) communication system, which transmitted signals in Morse code. Used by ships at sea to send distress signals, it saved lives. The ocean liner *Titanic,* which sank in 1912, sent its last messages by Marconi radio, raising public awareness of the technology.

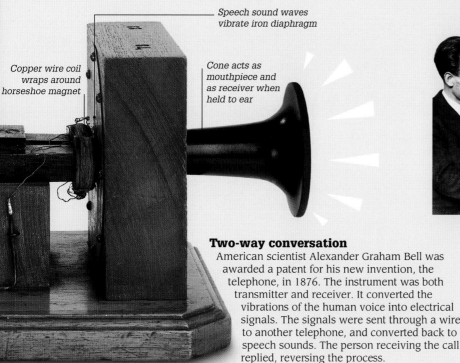

Speech sound waves vibrate iron diaphragm

Copper wire coil wraps around horseshoe magnet

Cone acts as mouthpiece and as receiver when held to ear

Two-way conversation

American scientist Alexander Graham Bell was awarded a patent for his new invention, the telephone, in 1876. The instrument was both transmitter and receiver. It converted the vibrations of the human voice into electrical signals. The signals were sent through a wire to another telephone, and converted back to speech sounds. The person receiving the call replied, reversing the process.

Screen

Farnsworth with a 1935 model of his television

Electronic television

In 1927, two years after John Logie Baird's mechanical television, American inventor Philo T Farnsworth built the first all-electronic television. It used a video camera tube (a type of vacuum tube) to capture images and transmit them as an electrical signal before reassembling them on a screen – a much faster process than Baird's use of a mechanical spinning disc.

1901–1902

A system designed by Irish-Italian physicist Guglielmo Marconi sent and received the first transatlantic radio signals, over a distance of more than 3,300 km (2,000 miles).

1925

Scottish inventor John Logie Baird transmitted the first moving image in a public demonstration of mechanical television.

1962

The first communications satellite, Telstar I, was launched into space from Cape Canaveral, Florida, USA, enabling television programmes to be broadcast across the Atlantic.

1973

The first call was made on a handheld mobile phone. It weighed 1.1 kg (2.4 lb) and was the size of a brick.

First mobile phone

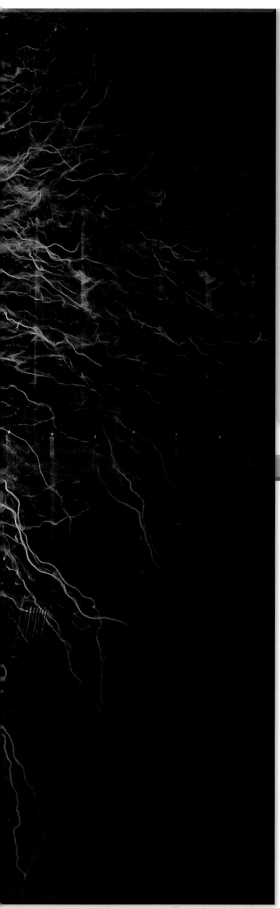

Magnifying Transmitter

Electrical engineering pioneer Nikola Tesla (see p.155) was a visionary and a practical inventor. He believed it was possible to distribute electrical power wirelessly around the world by the transmission of high-voltage, high-frequency alternating currents. In 1899, he moved to Colorado Springs, in Southwest USA, where he built the Magnifying Transmitter, which was capable of generating millions of volts and discharging sparks several metres long. Tesla spent nine months there, keeping a diary of his experiments. He returned to New York to continue his work into wireless transmission, before running out of financial backers. Tesla's dream of transmitting electric current wirelessly around the world is yet to be realized.

"... I feel certain that of all my inventions, the Magnifying Transmitter will prove most important and valuable to future generations. "

Nikola Tesla, *My Inventions*, 1919

Nikola Tesla sits beside his Magnifying Transmitter

1885 ▶ 1895

Dunlop's son on his bicycle with the new tyres

1885

Rabies vaccine

Nine-year-old Joseph Meister became the first person to receive an anti-rabies vaccine after being bitten by a rabid dog (rabies is a fatal disease passed on by animal saliva). It was French chemist Louis Pasteur who prepared the vaccine. Meister did not develop the disease.

Louis Pasteur
See pages 142–143

Meister is given the anti-rabies vaccine under Pasteur's supervision.

1887

Pneumatic rubber tyres

Scottish-born John Dunlop, a veterinary surgeon and inventor, cut up an old garden hose, fitted the pieces to the wheels of his son's tricycle, and filled them with air. It gave a much smoother ride, and Dunlop went on to create the first practical pneumatic (air-filled) tyres for bicycles. As a result, cycling soared in popularity.

▶▶ 1885

1885

First automobile

German engineer Karl Benz built the first automobile. It had three wire wheels and seating for two, and was powered by a four-stroke engine (see p.148). It reached a top speed of 16 km/h (10 mph) on its first outing.

1886

Radio waves

German physicist Heinrich Hertz carried out a series of experiments to confirm the existence of radio waves, a form of electromagnetic radiation, first predicted by Scottish physicist James Clerk Maxwell in 1867. The hertz (Hz) unit of frequency (the number of cycles per second) is named in his honour.

Frames from Le Prince's moving picture of traffic on Leeds Bridge

1888

Moving pictures

While staying in Leeds, UK, French photographer Louis Le Prince shot the first moving pictures on paper film using a single-lens camera. The film was never shown in public. Later, in the 1890s, American inventor Thomas Edison developed the Kinetoscope, an early motion picture viewing device.

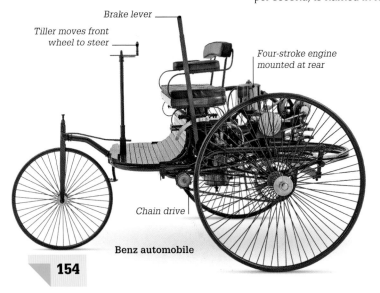

Brake lever

Tiller moves front wheel to steer

Four-stroke engine mounted at rear

Chain drive

Benz automobile

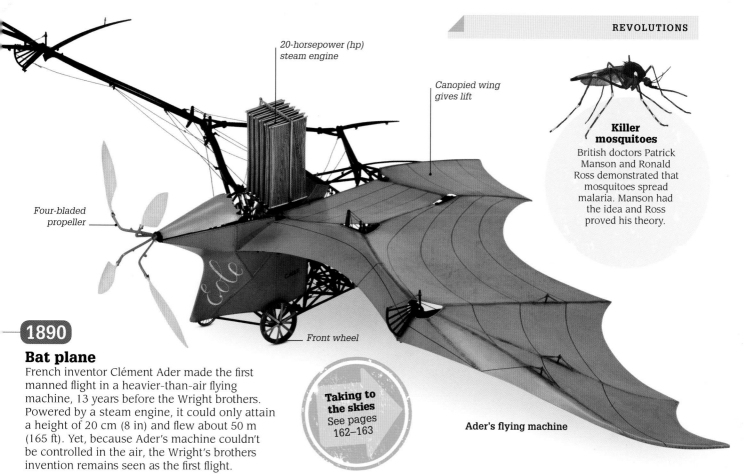

20-horsepower (hp) steam engine

Canopied wing gives lift

Four-bladed propeller

Killer mosquitoes
British doctors Patrick Manson and Ronald Ross demonstrated that mosquitoes spread malaria. Manson had the idea and Ross proved his theory.

Front wheel

1890

Bat plane

French inventor Clément Ader made the first manned flight in a heavier-than-air flying machine, 13 years before the Wright brothers. Powered by a steam engine, it could only attain a height of 20 cm (8 in) and flew about 50 m (165 ft). Yet, because Ader's machine couldn't be controlled in the air, the Wright's brothers invention remains seen as the first flight.

Taking to the skies
See pages 162–163

Ader's flying machine

0   1895 ▶▶

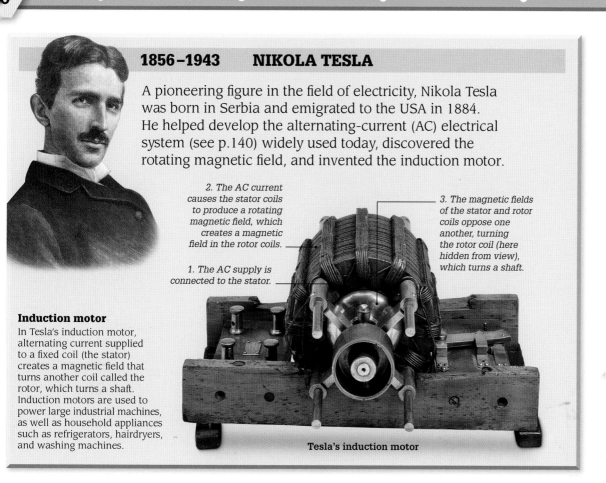

1856–1943   NIKOLA TESLA

A pioneering figure in the field of electricity, Nikola Tesla was born in Serbia and emigrated to the USA in 1884. He helped develop the alternating-current (AC) electrical system (see p.140) widely used today, discovered the rotating magnetic field, and invented the induction motor.

2. The AC current causes the stator coils to produce a rotating magnetic field, which creates a magnetic field in the rotor coils.

3. The magnetic fields of the stator and rotor coils oppose one another, turning the rotor coil (here hidden from view), which turns a shaft.

1. The AC supply is connected to the stator.

Induction motor

In Tesla's induction motor, alternating current supplied to a fixed coil (the stator) creates a magnetic field that turns another coil called the rotor, which turns a shaft. Induction motors are used to power large industrial machines, as well as household appliances such as refrigerators, hairdryers, and washing machines.

Tesla's induction motor

The noble gas argon was first isolated in 1894. It makes up 0.94 per cent of Earth's atmosphere.

1895–1945
The atomic age

An era that experienced two devastating world wars also witnessed the arrival of aircraft, radio, and television, and saw cars and many electrical appliances become everyday items. The period began with the discovery of radioactivity and led to a better understanding of what lies inside atoms, including their vast energy potential. At the other end of the scale, major advances were made in our understanding of the Universe, and how it formed and developed, while astronomers proved that our galaxy was not alone, but one of billions in space.

1895 ▸ 1900

Thomson using his cathode ray tube

1895

Cinema arrives

In Paris, France, 33 people formed the first paying cinema audience as they watched 10 short movies projected onto a screen by a cinématographe. This device, invented by French brothers Auguste and Louis Lumière, projected 16 photographs per second, giving the illusion of movement. The photos were taken on a 35-mm- (1.377-in-) wide film.

Poster advertising the first cinema show that people paid to see

1897

Discovery of electrons

While studying cathode rays (electric light tubes, see p.148), English scientist J J Thomson discovered electrons. These tiny particles orbit the centre of atoms and carry a negative electrical charge. This was the first step towards understanding the structure of atoms. Thomson won the 1906 Nobel Prize in Physics for this discovery.

1897

World's largest telescope

Astronomers began using the world's largest refracting telescope (one that uses a lens rather than a mirror) at the Yerkes Observatory, USA. It has a 102-cm- (40-in-) diameter glass lens to gather in light from distant stars, planets, and galaxies. The telescope was used to discover the spiral shape of the Milky Way in 1951.

▸▸ **1895**

1895   DISCOVERY OF X-RAYS

While experimenting with electric light tubes, German physicist Wilhelm Conrad Röntgen discovered mysterious waves of energy that passed through flesh and paper, but not other materials such as bone and metals. He named them "X-rays" because "X" is used in mathematics to describe an unknown. Röntgen took the first X-ray images.

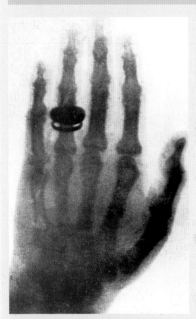

Röntgen's first X-ray image shows the bones and wedding ring on the hand of his wife, Anna.

X-ray radiation

Early X-ray machines were basic and patients had to stand still for a long time for images to be captured. With little understanding of the potential dangers, staff and patients were often harmed by repeated or prolonged overexposure to these rays. With controlled and screened doses of radiation, X-rays have now become vital to detect bone fractures, lung problems, and foreign objects inside the body.

Röntgen using an early X-ray machine on a boy

Main tube is 19.2 m (63 ft) long and holds the giant glass lens, which weighs 225 kg (500 lb).

Refracting telescope at Yerkes Observatory, Wisconsin, USA

Mount supports the main tube and helps point the telescope at different parts of the night sky.

Paths in the sky
See pages 72–73

In 1896, French physicist Henri Becquerel discovered radioactivity by chance while working with uranium salts.

1899
Aspirin goes on sale
The drug acetylsalicylic acid (ASA) was developed in 1897 by the company Bayer in Germany, and was branded and sold as Aspirin from 1899. It reduced pain in the body's nerve endings and was to become the world's most common pain reliever, with more than 100 billion tablets taken every year.

1899
First flashlight
English inventor David Misell created the first tubular flashlight (torch) by enclosing three "D cell" batteries in a fibre paper tube. When the contact switch was pressed, an electrical circuit was completed and the batteries lit up the small bulb, but only for a short time, hence the nickname "flashlight".

1900

1898
First remote control
Austrian-Hungarian inventor Nikola Tesla demonstrated the first use of radio waves to control an object wirelessly when he sailed his 1.2-m- (47-in-) long metal boat in a tank. Tesla sent radio signals to make the boat turn and switch its electric motor on and off.

1898
Discovery of noble gases
British chemists William Ramsay and Morris Travers discovered three chemical elements: krypton, neon, and xenon. All three are noble gases, which have no colour or smell and are mostly inert, which means they rarely react with other substances.

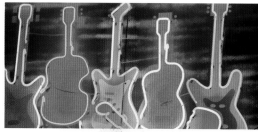

Neon gas glows when electricity passes through it, as in these colourful lights.

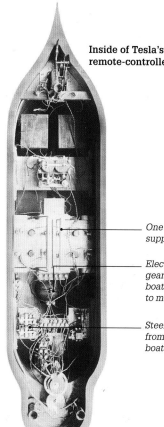

Inside of Tesla's remote-controlled boat

One of four batteries that supplied power to the boat.

Electric motor powered gears, which turned the boat's propeller screw to move the boat forwards.

Steering motor received signals from radio receiver to turn the boat's rudder to steer.

Booth's vacuum cleaner, pulled by horse

1900

Zeppelin airship takes off

The Zeppelin LZ1 made its first flight from Lake Constance, Germany. It was the first airship built around a rigid structure – in this case, a light but strong aluminium frame covered with cotton cloth. Inside, hydrogen gas in 17 rubberized cotton cells provided lift. Two aluminium gondolas hung below the 128-m- (420-ft-) long airship to carry crew and passengers.

First flight of the LZ1

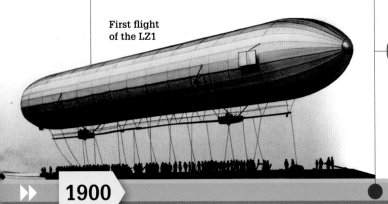

1901

First powered suction vacuum cleaner

Built by English engineer Hubert Cecil Booth, this giant vacuum cleaner was powered by an internal combustion engine. A piston pump inside it drew air through pipes past a cloth filter, which collected dust and dirt. The device was parked outside houses and flexible pipes fed in through doors and windows.

1901

Blood groups

The first major blood groups, or types – A, B, and O – were identified by Austrian biologist Karl Landsteiner. He discovered that mixing blood of two different types caused red blood cells to clump together and stop working, while mixing blood of the same type did not. This enabled doctors to prepare safer, more effective blood transfusions.

1900

> **" ... its size greatly exceeds any carnivorous land animal hitherto described. "**
>
> Henry Fairfield Osborn
> on the *Tyrannosaurus rex*, 1905

1902

Tyrannosaurus rex

American palaeontologist Barnum Brown discovered the fossil remains of a large, two-legged, meat-eating dinosaur in the Hell's Creek rock formation in Montana, USA. The creature was originally named *Dynamosaurus imperiosus*, but later renamed *Tyrannosaurus rex* (*T rex*), meaning "tyrant lizard king".

1902

Layers of the atmosphere

After a decade of research using more than 200 weather balloons, French meteorologist Léon Teisserenc de Bort described and defined accurately the lowest two layers of Earth's atmosphere. The troposphere extends from ground level up to an average altitude of 10 km (6.2 miles) while the stratosphere is found between heights of 10 km (6.2 miles) and 50 km (31 miles).

Temperature decreases with increasing altitude in the troposphere.

The boundary between the two layers is called the tropopause.

Stratosphere

Troposphere

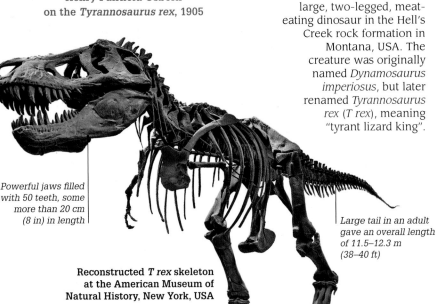

Powerful jaws filled with 50 teeth, some more than 20 cm (8 in) in length

Large tail in an adult gave an overall length of 11.5–12.3 m (38–40 ft)

Reconstructed *T rex* skeleton at the American Museum of Natural History, New York, USA

1903

Electrocardiograph

Dutch doctor Willem Einthoven invented the first accurate electrocardiograph (ECG). This machine measures the tiny electric currents generated by the heart as it beats. ECGs are now widely used to detect heart problems.

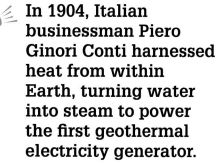

In 1904, Italian businessman Piero Ginori Conti harnessed heat from within Earth, turning water into steam to power the first geothermal electricity generator.

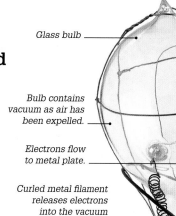

Glass bulb

Bulb contains vacuum as air has been expelled.

Electrons flow to metal plate.

Curled metal filament releases electrons into the vacuum when heated.

Machine reads electric signals from the patient conducted via salt water.

Patient's hands and foot are dipped in salt water.

Patient being scanned by an ECG, 1911

1904

Vacuum diode

English engineer John Ambrose Fleming patented his vacuum diode in 1904. This device converted alternating current (AC) electricity to direct current (DC) by allowing electricity to flow in only one direction (see p.140). Fleming's diode spurred the invention of many early electronic devices, and was used in radios as well as the first computers.

Model of Fleming's diode

1905

THE WRIGHT BROTHERS

American brothers Orville (1871–1948) and Wilbur Wright (1867–1912) ran a bicycle-making business in Dayton, Ohio, USA. Fascinated by flight, the inventors built their own kites, gliders, and a wind tunnel to understand the forces involved in flight. They flew the first heavier-than-air, powered aircraft, the 1903 Wright Flyer (see p.162).

Orville and Wilbur Wright

Wright gliders

The brothers made more than 200 flights in self-built gliders, learning how aircraft could move in one of three axes: pitch (up and down), yaw (side to side), and roll (see p.163). They developed control surfaces such as a steerable rudder to control yaw and wing warping, with wires bending the wing tips to allow the plane to roll while flying.

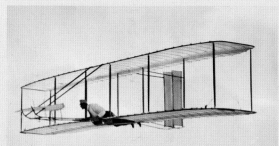

Wilbur Wright glides over Big Kill Devil Hill, North Carolina, USA

Chromatography

In 1903, Russian botanist Mikhail Tsvet developed chromatography, a process that can separate out mixtures of pigments, such as in plants or inks. Today, it has many uses, including in forensics.

Different chemical substances travel up the blotting paper at different speeds, separating from each other.

Blotting paper dipped in ink

Taking to the skies

For centuries, people dreamt of taking to the air with bird-like wings, but attempts at winged flight usually ended in injury or death. Powered, controlled flight took a long time to engineer, and when it arrived, the pace of change was rapid. American brothers Orville and Wilbur Wright played a key role in this. The 1903 Wright Flyer – the first powered aircraft – flew 36 m (118 ft) on its maiden voyage in 1903, but just 11 years later, German aviator Karl Ingold flew a Mercedes Aviatik-Pfeil non-stop across 1,699 km (1,055 miles).

> **"To invent an airplane is nothing. To build one is something. But to fly is everything."**
>
> Otto Lilienthal

Wingspan of 6.7 m (22 ft)

Lilienthal with his glider in the mid-1890s

Avro 504 biplanes being manufactured at a factory in Hampshire, England, during World War I

Gliding ahead

A scientific study of the principles of flight by English engineer George Cayley and German aviation pioneer Otto Lilienthal, among others, heralded the development of unpowered aircraft, which could glide short distances. Lilienthal made more than 2,000 glider flights, some going as far as 250 m (820 ft). His pioneering experiments took place between 1891 and his death in a gliding crash in 1896.

Powered flight

Inspired by Otto Lilienthal, Orville and Wilbur Wright, popularly known as the Wright Brothers, studied all aspects of gliders and flight before constructing the first powered aircraft, the Wright Flyer. It had a 12-horsepower (hp) petrol engine that turned two 2.4-m- (8-ft-) long propellers to deflect air backwards, thrusting the aircraft forwards.

Model of 1903 Wright Flyer

Pilot lay across wing

Key events

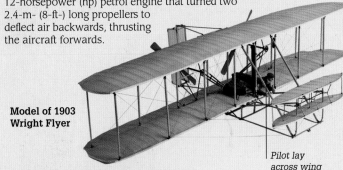

1903

The Wright Flyer made the first controlled flight by a powered aircraft at Kill Devil Hills, North Carolina, USA. The pilot, Orville Wright, lay down on his stomach to reduce drag and the flight lasted 12 seconds.

1909

French aviator Louis Blériot was the first to fly the English Channel in his Blériot XI monoplane, which had a top speed of just 75.6 km/h (47 mph).

1911

The first take-off and landing on a ship were both performed by American aviator Eugene Ely piloting a Curtiss biplane. He took off from and landed on the USS Pennsylvania in San Francisco Bay, USA.

1927

American pilot Charles Lindbergh made the first solo non-stop crossing of the Atlantic in his Spirit of St Louis monoplane. Around 1,700 litres (451 gal) of fuel were crammed into its wings and fuselage.

Plane fever

Wilbur Wright toured Europe in 1908–1909, making more than 200 flights and inspiring aviation fever. Dozens of plane makers sprang up, and innovations led to the first seaplane in 1910 (built by French aviator Henri Fabre) and the first four-engined aircraft in 1913 (the Le Grand, built by Russian-American Igor Sikorsky). World War I (1914–1918) saw aircraft manufactured in large numbers, mostly out of a wooden frame covered in stretched linen or canvas.

How planes fly

The four forces need to be in balance for a steady flight.

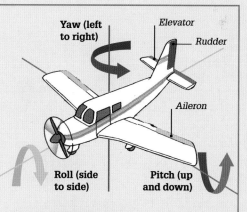

Four forces of flight

As the plane starts moving, air flowing over its wings creates the force of lift. This must exceed the force of gravity for the plane to take-off. Once in the air, the force of thrust from the engine must exceed the force of drag (wind resistance) for the aircraft to move forwards.

Yaw, pitch, and roll

Once in the air, an aircraft can move in one of three axes using hinged panels called control surfaces. Ailerons on the wings roll the plane from side to side. On the tail, a rudder yaws (turns) the plane from left to right and elevators pitch it up and down.

Golden age

Aviation blossomed in the era after World War I with a range of peacetime applications, from spraying of farm fields by cropduster planes to aerial surveying and airmail services. Engines became more powerful and reliable, enabling larger aircraft to be built to carry cargo and passengers. One passenger plane was the Douglas Sleeper Transport (above), launched in 1935, which carried 14 overnight passengers.

Flying science

RADAR

Short for RAdio Detection And Ranging, RADAR transmits radio waves, which bounce back off solid objects in order to detect aircraft and missiles.

World War II RADAR installation, Germany

Ejection seats

An explosive charge or a rocket motor in the seat launches a pilot out of the stricken aircraft (usually military) in an emergency and allows him or her to parachute to safety.

Autopilot

The first autopilot was devised by American aviator Lawrence Sperry in 1912. This device keeps a plane flying on a course by adjusting control surfaces and engine power automatically.

1938

The first airliner with a pressurized cabin, the Boeing 307 Stratoliner, flew 33 passengers. It reached an altitude of 6,000 m (20,000 ft), well above weather disturbances to cruise more smoothly and at higher speeds.

1939

The maiden voyage of the Heinkel He-178 became the first flight of an aircraft powered by a jet engine. It was built by German aircraft designer Ernst Heinkel.

1952

The de Havilland Comet became the first jet airliner to enter service with an airline, BOAC (British Overseas Airways Corporation). Its four jet engines gave it a range of up to 2,400 km (1,490 miles).

1957

The first business jet – the Lockheed JetStar – took flight. It seated ten passengers and two crew. Some 204 JetStars would be built.

1905 ▸ 1910

Bakelite radio

1905

Haber–Bosch process

German chemist Fritz Haber described a process to make a chemical called ammonia – a crucial ingredient in fertilizers – from a chemical reaction involving nitrogen and hydrogen. German chemist Carl Bosch scaled up Haber's laboratory process so that industrial quantities of ammonia could be produced.

Learning chemistry
See pages 146–147

Tractor tows a fertilizer sprayer

1906

Defining allergies

Austrian physician Clemens von Pirquet defined the term "allergy". It is an overreaction in the body triggered by the body's immune system in response to something in the environment, such as dust, pollen, or certain foods it sees as being harmful.

1907

Pioneering plastic

Belgian-American chemist Leo Baekeland developed a pioneering type of plastic (later named Bakelite) using a chemical called phenol, derived from coal tar and formaldehyde, derived from wood alcohol. Bakelite was cheap to produce, set hard, and had high resistance to electricity and heat. It became widely used as an electrical insulator and was moulded into thousands of products – from telephones to jewellery.

1905

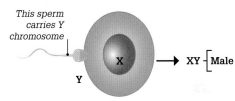

This sperm carries X chromosome

X → XX ⌐ Female

Egg carries X chromosome

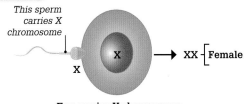

This sperm carries Y chromosome

X → XY ⌐ Male

Y

Egg carries X chromosome

1906

Seismic waves

British geologist Richard Dixon Oldham defined the different types of seismic wave (energetic waves caused by vibrations of moving rocks underground) that occur during earthquakes. "P", or primary, waves travel through solids, liquids, and gas at speeds of 1–14 km/s (0.8–9 miles/s); "S", or secondary, waves can only travel through solids at speeds of 1–8 km/s (0.8–5 miles/s); and surface waves, which are the slowest of all.

S waves force rock to move from side to side, at right angles to the direction of the wave's path.

Types of seismic wave

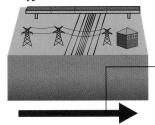

P waves travel horizontally deep below the ground and are often heard but not felt. They stretch rock, sometimes causing it to fracture.

S waves may cause buildings to crack and collapse.

Surface waves can roll and buckle the landscape, causing serious damage.

1905

Sex chromosomes

American geneticists Nettie Stevens and Edmund Beecher Wilson independently described the XX and XY system of sex chromosomes that play a role in reproduction. Sperm cells from males, which fertilize egg cells from females, either carry an X (female) or Y (male) chromosome. This joins with the X chromosome found in the egg cell to form either a male (XY) or female (XX) child.

The code of life
See pages 198–199

1908 MEASURING RADIATION

In 1907, German physicist Hans Geiger worked with physicist Ernest Rutherford of New Zealand to help him refine his theories about atomic nuclei. In 1908, Geiger made a device to detect radiation (see p.168), later refined and known as the Geiger counter.

Geiger (left) and Rutherford (right) in the laboratory

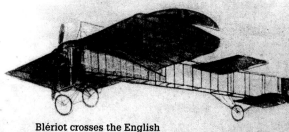

Copper tube with gas inside | **Early Geiger counter, 1932**

Geiger counter
A Geiger counter is a gas-filled tube with a high voltage wire inside. When radiation enters the tube and collides with the gas, it releases electrons that are attracted to the wire. This creates an electric current that produces a clicking sound and interacts with the counter's gauge. The device can detect alpha, beta, and gamma radiation.

Acidity ← | Neutral | → Basicity

0 1 2 3 4 5 6 7 8 9 10 11 12 13 14

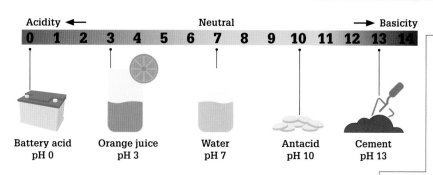

Battery acid pH 0 · Orange juice pH 3 · Water pH 7 · Antacid pH 10 · Cement pH 13

1909

Sørensen's pH scale
Devised by Danish chemist Søren Peder Lauritz Sørensen, the pH scale provides an easy way of judging whether a substance is an acid, neutral, or base. The scale runs from 0 (most acidic) to 14 (most basic), with pH 7 indicating the neutral point. Each whole number on the scale is a jump (by 10 times) in the level of acidity or basicity.

1910

1909

Channel crossing
French aviator Louis Blériot became the first person to fly across the English Channel separating England and France in a heavier-than-air aircraft. His 36-minute, 30-second journey in a 7.6-m- (24.91-ft-) long Blériot XI monoplane helped boost interest in aviation as a practical form of transport.

Fossil site
In 1909, American palaeontologist Charles Walcott discovered the Burgess Shale in the Canadian Rocky Mountains. It is one of the most abundant fossil sites in the world, yielding more than 65,000 fossils since its discovery.

Fossil of a trilobite, a marine animal that lived 526 million years ago

📢 **In 1907, American scientist Bertram Boltwood measured the decay of uranium in rocks to calculate their age – an early example of radiometric dating.**

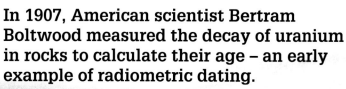

Blériot crosses the English Channel on his historic 1909 flight

1910 ▶ 1915

Object travels away from observer → Light waves from object are stretched.

Redshift

Object looks redder

Object travels towards observer → Light waves from object are squashed.

Blueshift

Object looks bluer

1910

Mapping the brain
German neuroscientist Korbinian Brodmann mapped the outer surface of the brain, called the cerebral cortex. He detailed how different parts of the cortex are responsible for different tasks, such as the primary visual cortex, which analyses signals sent from the eyes.

1910

Halley's Comet photographed
Observed as early as 1066, Halley's Comet was photographed for the first time in 1910. This 15-km-(9-mile-) long, 8-km- (5-mile-) wide comet raced past Earth at a speed of more than 254,000 kph (157,828 mph).

Halley's comet streaks across the night sky, 1910

1912

Redshift and blueshift
American astronomer Vesto Slipher discovered that the Andromeda galaxy was moving towards us by detecting a change to the light reaching Earth from the approaching galaxy, called a blueshift. A redshift occurs when a body in space moves away from the observer.

1912

Piltdown man
The remains of a man and primitive tools were discovered in Piltdown, England. The finds caused much interest as a missing link between apes and early humans, but were proven to be a hoax 41 years later.

1910

1911

Classifying the stars
Danish astronomer Ejnar Hertzsprung and American astronomer Henry Russell devised a star chart that was later named the Hertzsprung–Russell (H–R) diagram. It shows the relationships between a star's temperature and colour and its luminosity (the amount of energy given off by the star). This useful tool helped astronomers to group stars of similar types together.

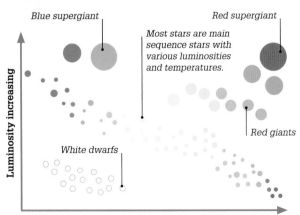

Blue supergiant

Red supergiant

Most stars are main sequence stars with various luminosities and temperatures.

Red giants

White dwarfs

Luminosity increasing

Temperature decreasing

1911

Superconductors
Dutch physicist Heike Kamerlingh Onnes discovered how some metals at ultra-low temperatures conduct electricity with no resistance. These metals, known as superconductors, can carry an electric current without losing any energy and have applications in creating extremely powerful electromagnets and fast electronic circuits.

Amundsen expedition
Norwegian explorer Roald Amundsen led the first successful expedition to the South Pole, reaching it on 14 December 1911. Along their two-month journey, the five-man expedition discovered the Axel Heiberg Glacier.

A member of the Amundsen team with their sled dogs at the South Pole.

1913   FIRST ASSEMBLY LINE

Henry Ford installed the first moving assembly line to produce his Ford Model T car. Before this time, each car was built one by one, which took 12 hours or more. In 1913, the car's 3,000 parts were assembled by workers in 84 separate steps as the partly completed vehicles were pulled by ropes down the assembly line. This speeded things up and cut the time down to 93 minutes. The price of the car more than halved as a result.

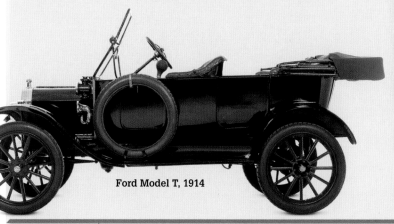

Ford Model T, 1914

Ford's plant at Highland Park
Workers perform their tasks as Model T cars are pulled along the assembly line by ropes at Highland Park, Michigan, USA. Highland Park Ford Plant was the world's biggest manufacturing plant when it opened. At its peak, it saw one completed car leave the assembly line every 10 seconds.

1915

1913
Atomic numbers
English chemist Henry Moseley used X-rays to determine the atomic number of each chemical element. This is the number of protons each atom contains in its nucleus. Oxygen, for example, contains eight protons, while copper contains 29.

Atomic number of gold ——— .79

Au
— Chemical symbol

GOLD

The first ship passes through the Gatun locks of the Panama Canal, 1914.

1914
Panama canal
After two failed attempts, an 80-km- (50-mile-) long canal was built through Panama, connecting the Atlantic and Pacific oceans and slashing thousands of kilometres off voyages. Construction involved more than 45,000 workers, powerful steam shovels, and major schemes to wipe out mosquitoes, which carried malaria and yellow fever. By 2010, one million ships had passed through the canal.

In 1914, Belgian surgeon Albert Hustin discovered substances that stop blood from clotting. This allowed transfusions from stored blood.

The story of the atom

Atoms are the building blocks of matter. These incredibly tiny units typically measure just one tenth of a billionth of a metre. The word "atom" comes from the Greek *atomos*, meaning indivisible. In the 19th century, atoms were considered to be the smallest units of matter, but advances in atomic science have revealed an inner structure made of even smaller particles. Every element has a unique type of atom. So far, 118 different elements have been discovered (see pp.188–189).

Neutrons do not have any charge.

Atomic structure

Atoms are made of particles called protons, neutrons, and electrons. Protons and neutrons form the central part of the atom – the nucleus. Protons carry a positive electrical charge, which attracts the negatively charged electrons and keeps them in orbit around the nucleus.

Protons are found in the nucleus, which is normally stable.

Radioactivity

An atom is radioactive if its nucleus is unstable and breaks apart and decays, emitting energy and particles known as radiation. Decay occurs at a fixed rate and the time it takes for half the mass of a radioactive substance to decay into other elements is called its half-life.

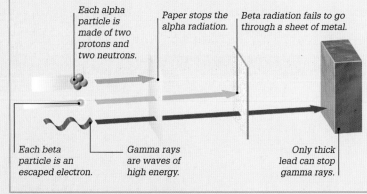

Each alpha particle is made of two protons and two neutrons.

Paper stops the alpha radiation.

Beta radiation fails to go through a sheet of metal.

Each beta particle is an escaped electron.

Gamma rays are waves of high energy.

Only thick lead can stop gamma rays.

Types of radiation

The decay of a radioactive atom involves the emission of three main types of radiation: alpha, beta, and gamma. Alpha radiation (a stream of alpha particles) travels only a few centimetres in air and cannot get through a sheet of paper, while beta radiation can travel further but bounces off thin sheets of metal. Gamma radiation can penetrate many materials.

Key events

c 400 BCE

Ancient Greek philosopher Democritus described how matter is made up of small, indivisible particles, which have different forms and arrangements. He called these particles atoms.

1896

French scientist Henri Becquerel discovered radiation while studying the effects of X-rays on photographic film.

Henri Becquerel

1897

English physicist J J Thompson identified the electron while experimenting with cathode ray tubes. His discovery was the first step in the study of the atom.

1913

Danish scientist Niels Bohr proposed a model of the atom in which electrons occupy shells, or orbits, of differing energy around the nucleus.

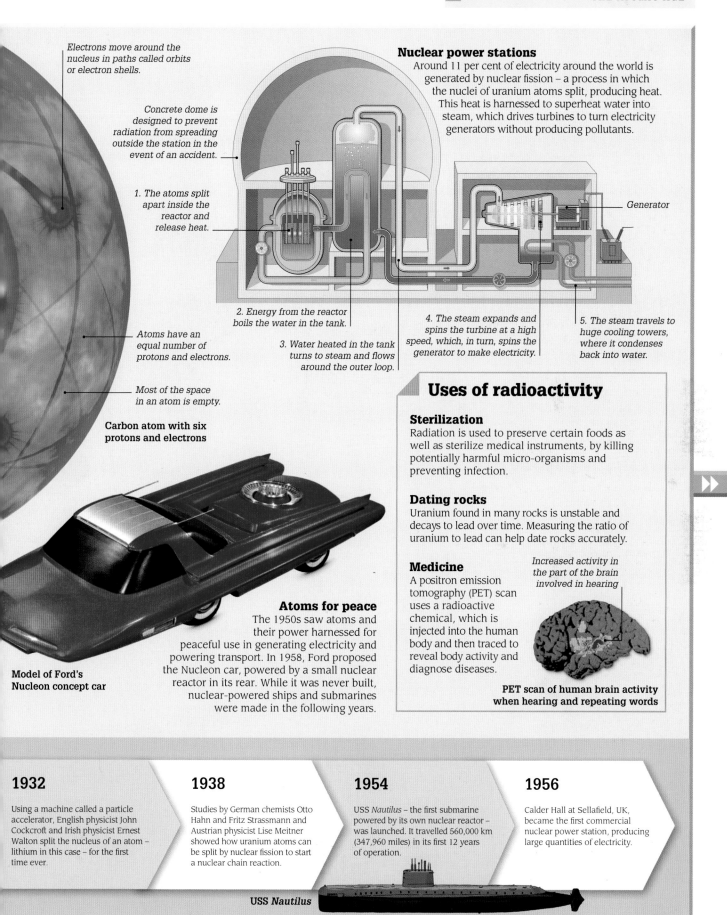

Electrons move around the nucleus in paths called orbits or electron shells.

Concrete dome is designed to prevent radiation from spreading outside the station in the event of an accident.

1. The atoms split apart inside the reactor and release heat.

Atoms have an equal number of protons and electrons.

Most of the space in an atom is empty.

Carbon atom with six protons and electrons

2. Energy from the reactor boils the water in the tank.

3. Water heated in the tank turns to steam and flows around the outer loop.

Nuclear power stations

Around 11 per cent of electricity around the world is generated by nuclear fission – a process in which the nuclei of uranium atoms split, producing heat. This heat is harnessed to superheat water into steam, which drives turbines to turn electricity generators without producing pollutants.

Generator

4. The steam expands and spins the turbine at a high speed, which, in turn, spins the generator to make electricity.

5. The steam travels to huge cooling towers, where it condenses back into water.

Uses of radioactivity

Sterilization
Radiation is used to preserve certain foods as well as sterilize medical instruments, by killing potentially harmful micro-organisms and preventing infection.

Dating rocks
Uranium found in many rocks is unstable and decays to lead over time. Measuring the ratio of uranium to lead can help date rocks accurately.

Medicine
A positron emission tomography (PET) scan uses a radioactive chemical, which is injected into the human body and then traced to reveal body activity and diagnose diseases.

Increased activity in the part of the brain involved in hearing

PET scan of human brain activity when hearing and repeating words

Model of Ford's Nucleon concept car

Atoms for peace
The 1950s saw atoms and their power harnessed for peaceful use in generating electricity and powering transport. In 1958, Ford proposed the Nucleon car, powered by a small nuclear reactor in its rear. While it was never built, nuclear-powered ships and submarines were made in the following years.

1932
Using a machine called a particle accelerator, English physicist John Cockcroft and Irish physicist Ernest Walton split the nucleus of an atom – lithium in this case – for the first time ever.

1938
Studies by German chemists Otto Hahn and Fritz Strassmann and Austrian physicist Lise Meitner showed how uranium atoms can be split by nuclear fission to start a nuclear chain reaction.

1954
USS Nautilus – the first submarine powered by its own nuclear reactor – was launched. It travelled 560,000 km (347,960 miles) in its first 12 years of operation.

1956
Calder Hall at Sellafield, UK, became the first commercial nuclear power station, producing large quantities of electricity.

USS Nautilus

1915 ▶ 1920

A star discovery
Working in a South African observatory, Scottish astronomer Robert Innes discovered the star Proxima Centauri. At a distance of 4.25 light years or 40 trillion km (25 trillion miles), it is the nearest star to Earth after the Sun.

Proxima Centauri as seen by the Hubble Space Telescope

1915 CONTINENTAL DRIFT

In 1915, German geophysicist Alfred Wegener published his theory of how the continents were once joined together, but gradually moved apart over millions of years. Wegener used as proof the fact that the same fossils and similar rock formations could be found in both Africa and South America. His theory was not fully accepted until more was known about Earth's crust (surface) and how it is made up of large plates (see p.211).

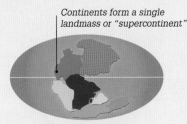

Continents form a single landmass or "supercontinent"

250 million years ago

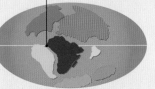

Gap begins to form between South America and Africa

130 million years ago

Atlantic Ocean now lies between South America and Africa

Present day

Moving continents
Around 300 million years ago, all the continents formed one supercontinent called Pangaea. Around 200 million years ago, they began separating, carried by the movement of Earth's plates. The continents are still moving – North America and Eurasia move apart by 2.5 cm (1 in) each year.

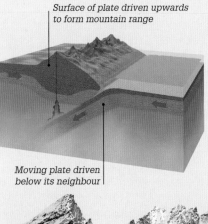

Surface of plate driven upwards to form mountain range

Moving plate driven below its neighbour

Birth of mountains
Alfred Wegener's theory proposed that many mountains formed through the thrusting together of parts of the moving continents, causing them to buckle and fold. Previously, people thought that mountains formed through the cooling and wrinkling of Earth's surface hundreds of millions of years ago.

The Himalayas, in Asia, began forming 40–50 million years ago.

1915

Little Willie
The first prototype tank, called Little Willie, was produced in the UK. It could cross 1.6-m- (5-ft-) wide trenches on its tracks, albeit at a slow top speed of just 3.2 km/h (2 mph). This tank paved the way for the Mark 1, the first tank to serve in battle the following year.

6-mm- (0.2-in-) thick steel body protects crew of 4–6 from gunfire.

Little Willie

Tracks driven by 105 hp engine

The story of the atom
See pages 168–169

1916

Sharing electrons

American chemist Gilbert Lewis suggested that when atoms bond together to form molecules they share their outer electrons. The idea was developed further by another American chemist, Irving Langmuir, in 1919, and is known as the Lewis–Langmuir Theory.

1916

Milky Way location

American astronomer Harlow Shapley established that our Solar System is not at the centre of the Milky Way as many previously thought, but, in fact, thousands of light years away. Shapley came to this conclusion after he studied clusters of distant stars and found that they formed a halo around the centre of the Milky Way.

Everything in its place
In 1917, American zoologist Joseph Grinnell introduced the idea that every creature has its own place or role in its habitat (home), known as an ecological niche.

Chemist Ernest Rutherford changed atoms of nitrogen into oxygen in 1917 by firing particles at the atoms' nuclei – a process called transmutation.

Airship frame measured 196 m (643 ft) long

R34 airship crosses the Atlantic, 1919

Dung beetles eat and bury dung, increasing the amount of nutrients in the soil and making a habitat more liveable for other creatures.

1919

First aerial crossings of the Atlantic

Three different types of aircraft successfully crossed the Atlantic in 1919: the first airship (the R34), the first flying boat (an NC-4), and the first non-stop flight made in a Vickers Vimy plane by British aviators John Alcock and Arthur Brown.

1920 ▶▶

Bacteriophages (in orange) attack a bacterium

Patrol ship uses SONAR to seek out submarines

Sound waves bounce back, reflected off the submarine.

1918

Detecting underwater objects

French physicist Paul Langevin devised the first ASDICS (Aided Sonar Detection Integration and Classification System) for detecting submarines underwater. The system transmitted sound waves in one direction through the water, and measured distances by how long it took signals to reflect back. The ASDICS was the forerunner of modern SONAR (SOund Navigation And Ranging) technology.

Directional sound waves transmitted by ship

1917

Bacteria eaters

While investigating the bacteria that cause the disease dysentery, French-Canadian biologist Félix d'Hérelle discovered and named viruses that attack and destroy bacteria. He called them bacteriophages, meaning bacteria eaters.

Lecturer
Einstein first became a university lecturer in Switzerland in 1908 and a professor in Prague (now in the Czech Republic), four years later. As his fame grew, he was in great demand as a lecturer.

"I believe in intuitions and inspirations... At times I feel certain I am right while not knowing the reason."

Albert Einstein,
The Saturday Evening Post, 1929

Albert Einstein

German-born physicist Albert Einstein (1879–1955) was a clerk working in a Swiss patent office when he published four extraordinary scientific papers in 1905. He continued to do ground-breaking work, all of which confirmed him as one of the greatest thinkers of all time and a scientific genius who changed the way we look at the Universe.

Young Einstein
Born to Jewish parents in Ulm, Germany, Einstein (right) had a younger sister called Maja.

Looking at light

In his first paper, Einstein explained the photoelectric effect, a phenomenon in which electrons are sometimes released when light shines on materials. He rejected the idea that light flows as one continuous stream and argued that it was made up of individual parcels of energy known as photons, or "quanta". His work won him the Nobel Prize in Physics in 1921.

The Special Theory of Relativity

Einstein also showed that the speed of light (299,792 km/s or 186,282 miles/s) is a constant, but time and space are linked and relative. This means that time and space are flexible and can change so that the faster one travels, the slower time passes.

Matter and energy

Einstein altered how science looked at matter and energy in another of his 1905 papers. He introduced his most famous equation: $E = mc^2$ with "E" being energy, "m" being the mass of matter, and "c" being the speed of light. This means that small amounts of matter can contain huge amounts of energy – a principle harnessed both in atomic power and weapons.

Later life

Leaving Europe for the USA in 1933, Einstein took a position at Princeton University where he continued his work and enjoyed life as the world's most brilliant scientist.

School certificate
Einstein's 1896 Swiss exam certificate gave him the grades to study maths and physics at Zürich Polytechnic, Switzerland, at the age of 17. He received top marks in history, physics, algebra, and geometry.

Planet bends space-time (combination of three dimensions of space – length, breadth, and height – with time) creating gravity.

"If I were not a physicist, I would probably be a musician. I often think in music. I live my daydreams in music. I see my life in terms of music."

Albert Einstein,
The Saturday Evening Post, 1929

Leisure time
Einstein enjoyed music and took particular pleasure in playing the violin. He also enjoyed sailing, although he never learned to swim.

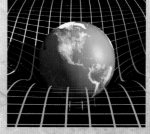

General Theory of Relativity
In 1916, Einstein expanded his special theory of relativity to include gravity. He showed how objects with large mass bend space-time, causing it to curve like a heavy ball bending a rubber sheet. Smaller objects roll towards the heavy ball due to the curve of the sheet. This theory helped explain black holes and why light from distant stars bends.

1920 ► 1925

1920

First sticking plaster

American inventor Earle Dickson developed the first sticking plasters for his wife, Josephine, as small, convenient dressings for minor burns and cuts she suffered while tackling housework. Dickson fixed squares of gauze on sticky surgical tape and reinforced his dressings with strips of crinoline material. The plasters eventually went on sale under the brand name of Band-Aid.

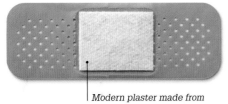

Modern plaster made from gauze fixed to a strip of plastic

Broccoli, spinach, nuts, and seeds are all good sources of Vitamin E.

Cheese, oily fish, and liver are good sources of Vitamin D.

Engine spins propeller at front to provide thrust forwards.

1922

Vitamins D and E

English scientist Sir Edward Mellanby discovered Vitamin D, which helps the body absorb calcium to keep teeth and bones healthy. Later in the same year, Vitamin E was discovered by research physician Herbert Evans and his assistant Katherine Bishop. Vitamin E is believed to play a role in maintaining healthy body cells.

►► 1920

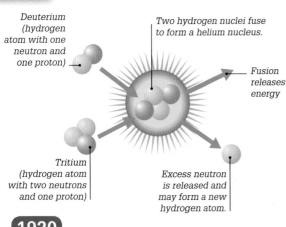

Deuterium (hydrogen atom with one neutron and one proton)

Two hydrogen nuclei fuse to form a helium nucleus.

Fusion releases energy

Tritium (hydrogen atom with two neutrons and one proton)

Excess neutron is released and may form a new hydrogen atom.

1920

How stars work

English astronomer Arthur Eddington suggested that a star gets its energy through a process called nuclear fusion. This involves the nucleus of hydrogen atoms fusing (joining) together at the star's core, forming helium atoms and releasing huge amounts of energy in the process.

 In 1921, the word "robot" was first used in Czech writer Karel Čapek's play *R.U.R.*

1921

Discovery of insulin

After a series of experiments, Canadian scientists Charles Best and Frederick Banting isolated insulin from the pancreas, first of dogs, and then cattle. Insulin is a hormone that helps control sugar levels in the blood and can be used to treat diabetes. A 14-year-old diabetic boy, Leonard Thompson, became the first person to be treated with insulin by Best and Banting the following year.

The 50-year anniversary of the discovery of insulin is celebrated on a Canadian stamp, c 1971.

1921

Vaccine for tuberculosis

The BCG (bacille Calmette–Guérin) vaccine that protects against the infectious disease tuberculosis (TB) was tested for the first time on humans. It helps stimulate the body's immune system to produce substances that fight TB. French scientists took 15 years to develop this vaccine.

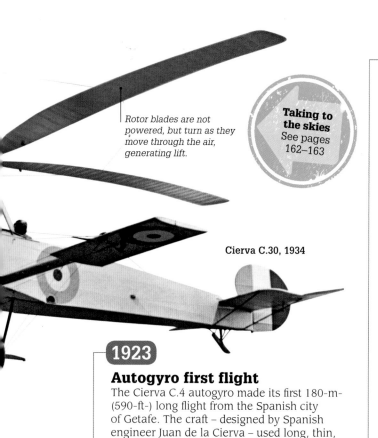

Rotor blades are not powered, but turn as they move through the air, generating lift.

Taking to the skies
See pages 162–163

Cierva C.30, 1934

1924
A new galaxy
American astronomer Edwin Hubble concluded that Andromeda was not a spiral nebula (a large cloud of dust and gas) in the Milky Way galaxy but an entire, separate galaxy. Hubble's discovery came after he measured distances to stars in Andromeda and found them further away than the diameter of the Milky Way. We now know that Andromeda is around 2.54 million light years away and is 220,000 light years across.

The Andromeda Galaxy contains one trillion stars.

1923
Autogyro first flight
The Cierva C.4 autogyro made its first 180-m- (590-ft-) long flight from the Spanish city of Getafe. The craft – designed by Spanish engineer Juan de la Cierva – used long, thin, wing-like rotor blades to provide lift, and helped pave the way for the helicopter.

1925

1923
Dinosaur eggs
The first scientifically proven dinosaur eggs were discovered in Mongolia's Flaming Cliffs region. The expedition, led by American naturalist Roy Chapman Andrews, also discovered *Protoceratops* and *Velociraptor* dinosaur fossils for the first time. At first, the eggs were thought to be from *Protoceratops* but later studies revealed they were eggs of *Oviraptor* – small dinosaurs that lived some 75 million years ago.

Fossilized *Oviraptor* eggs

1888–1946   JOHN LOGIE BAIRD

Scottish inventor John Logie Baird devised shaving razors before constructing his first mechanical television (TV) in 1924 using household objects, such as sewing needles and a biscuit tin. In 1928, he sent the first TV pictures under the Atlantic Ocean from the UK to the USA and also devised a video recorder called Phonovision. The BBC began experimental broadcasts using his mechanical system, which was overtaken by electronic television in the 1930s.

Spinning disc with holes

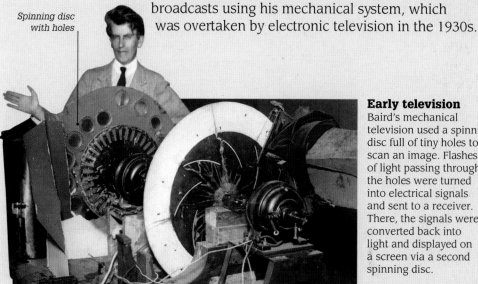

Early television
Baird's mechanical television used a spinning disc full of tiny holes to scan an image. Flashes of light passing through the holes were turned into electrical signals and sent to a receiver. There, the signals were converted back into light and displayed on a screen via a second spinning disc.

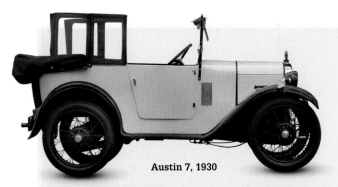
Austin 7, 1930

Driving around

The 20th century saw a phenomenal boom in motor vehicle production as cars and trucks went from being rare novelties to a vital mode of transport used every day. In the United States, for example, there were just four officially registered cars in 1895. By 2016, the number had increased to more than 254 million. Innovations in car design and features – from streamlined body shapes to electric starting and automatic gearboxes – helped spur the phenomenal increase in motor vehicle use.

Cars for everyone

Car production increased greatly in the 1910s and 1920s, as new designs and manufacturing techniques reduced prices and made cars more affordable. The Austin 7, for instance, cost just £165 at its 1922 launch, and 290,000 cars had been built by 1939.

Fender skirts (also known as spats) encase the top half of the rear wheel, helping air to flow smoothly past the wheel.

Evolving designs

Most early cars were boxy, tall, and square before engineers learned how the flow of air around a vehicle could affect its performance. The 1936 Lincoln Zephyr coupe featured a curved and streamlined body that helped ease air around the vehicle, resulting in higher speeds and lower fuel use.

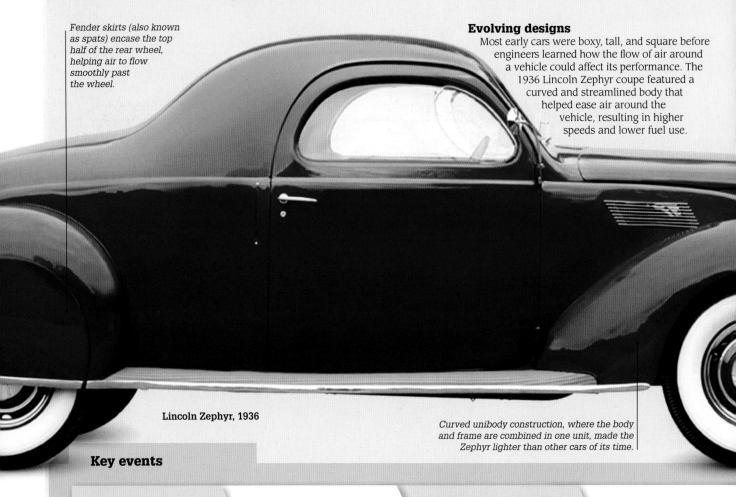
Lincoln Zephyr, 1936

Curved unibody construction, where the body and frame are combined in one unit, made the Zephyr lighter than other cars of its time.

Key events

1894
The Benz Velo was the first car built in significant numbers, with more than 1,200 produced. Its 3 horsepower (hp) engine gave it a top speed of 19 km/h (12 mph).

1896
The first electric starter was installed on a car in London, UK. Electric starters dispensed with the need to turn a crank at the front of the car to start the engine.

1902
The Oldsmobile Curved Dash became the first mass-produced car. More than 19,000 of this two-seater were built on an assembly line using interchangeable parts.

1908
Henry Ford's Model T car ushered in an era of affordable motoring, especially when his efficient new factory opened and the car price dropped.

Ford Model T

Mini Cooper, 1962

Mini cars

As design innovations continued, some cars – usually big, fast, gas-guzzlers – came to be seen as status symbols. Then in 1959, small and economical started to look good when designer Alec Issigonis launched the Mini. This car, the first of many models, had a space-saving transverse (sideways) mounted engine and fuel-saving front-wheel drive.

A plug-in electric car's charge port connects to an electricity supply to recharge batteries.

Going electric

In the 21st century, pollution caused by petrol-burning cars is a serious problem. Major development of all-electric vehicles could mean cleaner air. These cars use rechargeable batteries to drive electric wheel motors. Most models are used over short distances but some, such as the Tesla Roadster, have a range of more than 300 km (185 miles) between recharges.

Headlights sat flush in curved pontoon fairings rather than sticking out and dragging on the passing air.

Road safety

With more than a billion vehicles on the roads worldwide, car designers and manufacturers take safety seriously.

▶ Crash test dummies
These life-like human models are used to test the effects of crash impacts on people. This helps car engineers to work out how to reduce the risk of injuries.

▶ Seatbelts
Seatbelts, devices which save many lives each year, reduce the forward motion of a person's body if a vehicle stops suddenly.

▶ Airbag
Sudden stops trigger airbags, which inflate in less than 0.05 seconds to cushion people inside a vehicle from harmful impact with the car interior.

Airbag and crash test dummy

Batteries store electricity. Fuel tank Generator produces electricity. Internal combustion engine is smaller than in a regular car.

Hybrid cars

Hybrid cars, such as the Toyota Prius launched in 1997, contain more than one form of propulsion. The Prius's electric motor moves the car at low speeds but works together with the car's petrol engine when acceleration and higher speeds are required. Energy from the car's movement drives the generator to recharge the electric motor's battery.

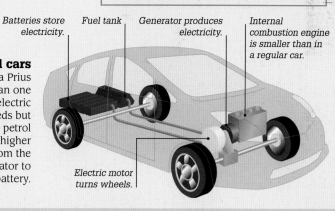

Electric motor turns wheels.

1933
Invented in the 1890s, diesel engines were first used in trucks and buses until the Citroën Rosalie became the first diesel-powered, mass-produced car.

1939
General Motors introduced the Hydra-Matic (a motor transmission that changed gears automatically) for their Cadillac and Oldsmobile ranges. It was the first mass-produced automatic transmission for passenger cars.

1973
The first catalytic converters for production cars were introduced. These convert toxic emissions from the engine into less harmful gases and water vapour.

1997
The Toyota Prius became the first mass-produced hybrid car, with battery-powered electric motors reducing fuel consumption by its petrol engine.

Toyota Prius

Frozen food packed in waxed cartons for storage

Fast-frozen foods

After observing how Inuit peoples in the Arctic froze food rapidly at very low temperatures to preserve its taste and texture, American naturalist Clarence Birdseye invented a double-belt freezer to do the same. His invention kick-started the frozen food industry.

1926

First liquid-fuelled rocket

American engineer Robert Goddard launched the first rocket powered by burning liquid fuel, or gasoline. Although the rocket flew only a short distance over 2.5 seconds, it paved the way for Goddard's L-13 rocket in 1937, which reached an altitude of 2,700 m (8,860 ft).

Stamp shows Goddard near the launch frame of his first rocket, nicknamed Nell

Penicillium fungi

Fleming observed that blue-green *Penicillium* mould on the petri dishes had created a bacteria-free ring around itself. He grew further colonies of this mould and found that it also worked on bacteria that caused diphtheria, pneumonia and scarlet fever.

1925

Mapping the Mid-Atlantic Ridge

A German scientific expedition discovered that the Mid-Atlantic Ridge runs almost the entire length of the Atlantic Ocean, north-to-south. The ridge extends 2–3 km (1.2–1.9 miles) above the ocean floor and marks the boundary of two tectonic plates. The survey took more than 67,000 depth measurements of the Atlantic over a period of two years.

Mid-Atlantic Ridge

South America   *Africa*

Map showing the floor of the Atlantic Ocean

Galaxy classification

In 1926, American astronomer Edwin Hubble grouped galaxies by their shape as they appeared in photographs. Known as the Hubble sequence diagram, it classified galaxies as elliptical, spiral, and barred spiral.

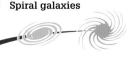

Spiral galaxies

Barred spiral galaxies

Elliptical galaxies

Nurse places a polio patient in an iron lung, 1938

1927

Iron lung

American researchers Philip Drinker and Louis Agassiz Shaw invented a box-like machine called the iron lung – an artificial respirator powered by an electric motor. A patient who could not breathe unaided was placed inside the machine and then air was pumped in and out of it. This changed the air pressure inside it and pulled air into and out of the patient's lungs

1928 DISCOVERY OF PENICILLIN

Scottish scientist Alexander Fleming discovered a mould that could destroy harmful *Staphylococcus* bacteria on unwashed petri dishes in his laboratory. Fleming realized that the mould was producing an anti-bacterial substance, which he named penicillin. It eventually proved a successful antibiotic, able to tackle a range of infections and diseases caused by bacteria. By 1944, chemical plants were mass-producing penicillin to supply armed forces. Today, penicillin is still one of the most widely used antibiotics in the world.

"One sometimes finds what one is not looking for."

Alexander Fleming

Alexander Fleming in his laboratory

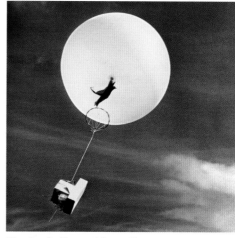

Weather balloon with a radiosonde attached

1929
First radiosonde flight

French scientist Robert Bureau invented a device called a radiosonde – a small, battery-powered pack of scientific instruments, which flies suspended under a weather balloon. As a radiosonde rises through the atmosphere, it signals back useful data on air pressure and temperature. This invention was a key step in our understanding of weather.

1930 ▶▶

In 1928, a newly invented plug-in heart pacemaker (an electronic device to drive the heart) revived a stillborn baby in Sydney, Australia.

1929
Van de Graaff generator

This device was invented by American scientist Robert J Van de Graaff to create high voltages of electricity to power early particle accelerators (machines in which atomic particles are speeded up and collide with one another). Smaller versions of the generator are used to demonstrate static electricity and are used as a teaching aid.

Static electricity makes the person's hair stand on end.

Metal dome collects electric charge and transfers it to the person's hand when touched.

1928
The Cori Cycle

Czech biochemists Carl and Gerty Cori discovered a biological cycle in which glucose breaks down into lactic acid when muscles work hard. This acid is recycled by the liver and returns to the muscles as a substance called glycogen, which is converted to glucose. This became known as the Cori, or Lactic acid, cycle.

Marie Curie

Polish-French physicist and chemist Marie Curie (1867–1934) overcame traditional barriers to women in science to make major contributions to physics, chemistry, and medicine. She discovered new chemical elements, developed scientific understanding of radioactivity, and founded two world-famous research labs – the Curie Institutes – in Paris and Warsaw.

Partnership with Pierre Curie

Born Maria Salomea Skłodowska in Warsaw, Poland, Marie moved to France to study at the University of Paris. There, she met French chemist Pierre Curie. The pair married in 1895 and began working together, studying the newly discovered phenomenon of radioactivity.

Discovering new elements

The Curies discovered that a uranium ore called pitchblende possessed higher levels of radioactivity than pure uranium and concluded it must contain other, more radioactive, substances. In 1898, after much painstaking work refining pitchblende, they discovered two previously unknown chemical elements – polonium and radium.

Winning the Nobel Prize

In 1903, the Curies, along with Henri Becquerel, won the Nobel Prize in Physics. Marie was the first female winner of the award. Pierre Curie died in a road accident in 1906, but despite this tragedy, Marie continued their work, managing to isolate pure radium in 1910. A year later, she received the Nobel Prize in Chemistry – the first person to win two Nobel prizes.

Wartime service

Marie Curie pioneered the use of radium to fight cancer tumours and helped develop the use of X-rays as a vital medical tool. When World War I began, she raised funds, organized, and even drove ambulances equipped with X-ray machines to battlefields. These were used to diagnose bullet and shrapnel injuries, saving thousands of lives.

Marie Curie's early life
The daughter of two schoolteachers, Marie (on the right here with her sister Hela) proved a bright student. She worked as a teacher and then a governess, before moving to France in 1891 to study physics and mathematics at the University of Paris. In 1906, she became the university's first female professor.

❝Be less curious about people and more curious about ideas. ❞

Marie Curie

Mother and daughter
Curie's eldest daughter, Irène (1897–1953) first worked with her mother as a radiographer during World War I. As a scientist in her own right, Irène Joliot-Curie along with her husband Frédéric won the 1935 Nobel Prize for the discovery of artificial radioactivity.

❝Marie Curie is, of all celebrated beings, the only one whom fame has not corrupted. ❞

Albert Einstein, 1934

Atomic number → | 84 | (209) | 88 | (226) | ← Relative atomic mass

Chemical symbol →

Po   Ra

POLONIUM   RADIUM

New elements
Polonium and radium are the two chemical elements that the Curies discovered. Polonium is named after Marie's home country, Poland.

Radioactive flask
A clear, glass flask that Marie used in her work on radium has discoloured and turned violet-blue after repeated exposure to radiation.

In her laboratory
A lifetime of exposure to radiation took its toll on Marie. Despite battling a blood disease caused by radiation, she worked up to her death in France at the age of 66.

"A scientist in his laboratory is not a mere technician: he is also a child confronting natural phenomena that impress him as though they were fairy tales."

Marie Curie quoted in
Madame Curie: A Biography, 1937

1930 ▸ 1935

 The dwarf planet Pluto was discovered by Clyde Tombaugh in 1930 and named by an 11-year-old girl, Venetia Burney.

3. 0.001 second: Further cooling occurs, but after one second, the Universe is still at a temperature of 5.5 billion °C (42 billion °F).

2. 10^{-10} second: The Universe begins to cool rapidly and the first primitive particles form.

1. 10^{-38} second: The Universe suddenly expands enormously, giving off vast amounts of heat and radiation.

Singularity – point from which the Universe expanded

Barton's bathysphere

1930

First bathysphere dive

In 1934, two Americans dived to a record-breaking depth of 923 m (3,028 ft). Designed by engineer Otis Barton in 1930, and later piloted by American naturalist Charles William Beebe, the bathysphere was a deep-sea submersible featuring a strengthened steel body, able to withstand water pressure at great depths.

1931

The Big Bang theory

Belgian priest and astronomer Georges Lemaître proposed a theory for the birth of the Universe, later known as the Big Bang theory. Lemaître thought that as the Universe was expanding, it must have once been far closer together and begun via a giant burst of energy from a single point he called a "primeval atom" or "cosmic egg".

▸▸ 1930

Empire State Building

When completed in 1931, this 443-m- (1,454-ft-) high skyscraper was the tallest building in the world. About 51,700 tonnes of steel columns and beams were used in its construction.

1. Electron gun emits a beam of very fast moving electrons.

Electron beam

2. Special coils make up an electromagnet (magnet where electric current is used to magnetize the iron).

3. Like a lens, the electromagnet bends the beam to focus on the specimen.

1931

Electron microscope

German engineers Ernst Ruska and Max Knoll produced the first transmission electron microscope. It beamed a stream of electrons through a specimen, enabling far higher magnifications than microscopes that used light. Later electron microscopes achieved magnifications of 50,000 times or higher – enough to view individual molecules for the first time. Later in the 1930s, scanning electron microscopes were developed that used electrons to study the surface of a specimen.

Specimen

4. Electrons reflected from the specimen are directed at a screen, where they form an enlarged image of its surface.

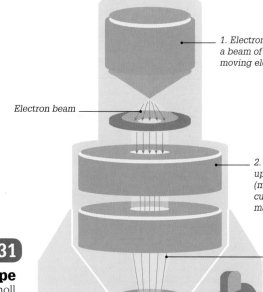

How a scanning electron microscope works

4. *3 minutes:* The first protons and neutrons form and create atomic nuclei of hydrogen and helium.

5. *380,000 years:* The Universe has cooled enough for the first atoms to form. Space becomes transparent and light can shine.

6. *1 billion years:* The earliest stars and galaxies (systems of stars) form.

7. *Present day:* The Universe is thought to be approximately 13.8 billion years old.

The Big Bang theory proposes that the Universe expanded from an individual point, called a singularity.

1935

1934

Catseye
English roadworker Percy Shaw patented a road safety device after noticing how a cat's eyes reflected light. Still used today, the "Catseye" consists of lenses set in a rubber and metal dome that is fitted into the road. The lenses reflect light from a vehicle's headlights to illuminate the middle of the road and sometimes the boundaries between road lanes, without using any power.

1933

Frequency Modulation radio
American engineer Edwin Howard Armstrong invented the first practical FM (Frequency Modulation) radio. Compared to AM (Amplitude Modulation) radios of the time, FM offered a clearer, higher-quality signal with less noise and interference from nearby electrical equipment or storms. The first FM radio stations began broadcasting in the USA in the late 1930s.

The speaker horn broadcasts the signal as sound.

Neutron star glows turquoise in this composite of images taken at different wavelengths.

Tuning dials enable user to switch to the correct frequency to receive a radio signal.

The case contains electric circuits and six vacuum tubes that help to make the radio signal louder.

Armstrong's suitcase FM radio receiver

Remains of a supernova containing a neutron star

1934

Exploded stars
Swiss astronomer Fritz Zwicky and German astronomer Walter Baade proposed that neutron stars (dense, collapsed stars mainly made of neutrons) form from the remains of colossal star explosions, which they called supernovae. A supernova occurs when a giant star exhausts its hydrogen fuel, collapses in on itself, and then rebounds violently to explode. Zwicky went on to discover the remains of 120 supernovae.

The head of this insect, shown at 80 times its original size in this modern-day, SEM image, features two spherical compound eyes made up of 28,000 ommatidia (collections of photoreceptors, or cells that receive light).

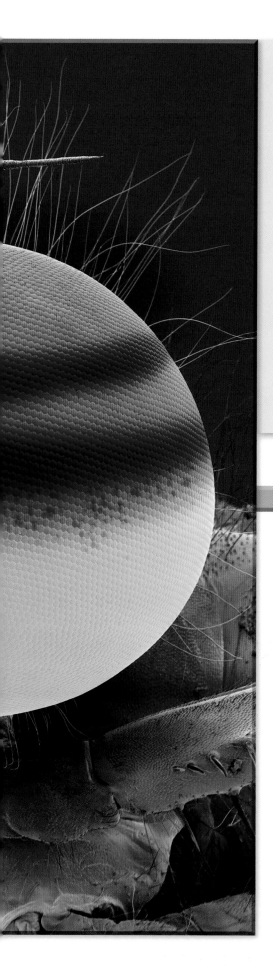

Zooming in on the details

The compound eyes of a large red damselfly loom large in this compelling close-up image. Such images were made possible by the development of the scanning electron microscope (SEM) from the 1930s onwards. SEMs scan a specimen, often held in a vacuum, using an extremely narrow beam of electrons to trace over the object. These microscopes can achieve much higher magnifications (50–100,000 times) and resolutions than optical microscopes, which use light magnified by lenses. Objects measured in nanometres (billionths of a metre) can be imaged clearly by SEMs, making them invaluable for forensics and investigating tiny creatures, new drugs, and materials in incredible detail.

"Our work, it seems to me, can bring us a special bonus of pleasure and satisfaction, through... our ability to peep into the inexhaustible world of the smallest forms of existence. "

Ernst Ruska, inventor of the first electron microscope, 1958

1935 ▶ 1940

Richter scale
American physicist Charles Richter devised a scale for measuring the amount of energy released by earthquakes. Each whole number rise on the scale equals more than 31 times more energy released. Most earthquakes register under 4.0 on the scale. The most powerful measure 9.0 or above.

1935

Ecosystems
The idea of ecosystems was described by British botanist Arthur Tansley. It is a complicated set of relationships between all living things found in a particular habitat. All parts of an ecosystem are interlinked. If one changes, then the whole ecosystem may change.

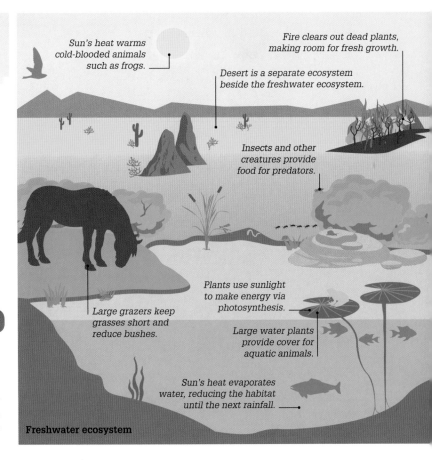

Sun's heat warms cold-blooded animals such as frogs.

Fire clears out dead plants, making room for fresh growth.

Desert is a separate ecosystem beside the freshwater ecosystem.

Insects and other creatures provide food for predators.

Plants use sunlight to make energy via photosynthesis.

Large grazers keep grasses short and reduce bushes.

Large water plants provide cover for aquatic animals.

Sun's heat evaporates water, reducing the habitat until the next rainfall.

Freshwater ecosystem

1935

1935

New fabric
Nylon was made at the American chemicals company DuPont by a team led by Wallace Carothers, who were researching long chains of molecules known as polymers. Tough, light, and hard-wearing, demand for nylon quickly grew for making stockings, toothbrush bristles, and parachute canopies.

1936

Last thylacine
The last known living example of a thylacine, commonly known as the Tasmanian tiger, died in Hobart Zoo, Tasmania. The thylacine was Australia's largest meat-eating marsupial – creatures that carry and nurture their young in a pouch in their bodies. It preyed on wallabies, wombats, and birds.

1937

Radio telescope dish
American astronomer Grote Reber built a 9.4-m- (31-ft-) diameter radio telescope dish in the backyard of his home in Illinois, USA. He was the first to map the night sky for radio waves emitted by stars and galaxies in space, and in 1939, he discovered the galaxy Cygnus A and supernova remnant Cassiopeia A.

1937

First jet engine
Aviation engineer Frank Whittle in the UK and aircraft designer Hans von Ohain in Germany independently developed jet engines, which were both first tested on the ground in 1937. Jet engines take in air, mix it with fuel, and then burn the mixture to generate rapidly expanding gases, which create thrust as they exit the engine.

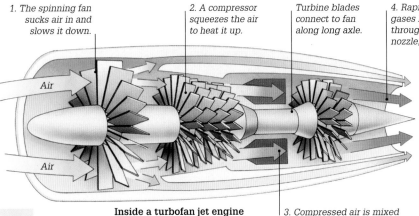

1. The spinning fan sucks air in and slows it down.

2. A compressor squeezes the air to heat it up.

Turbine blades connect to fan along long axle.

4. Rapidly inflating gases leave engine through exhaust nozzle, creating thrust.

Air

Air

Inside a turbofan jet engine

3. Compressed air is mixed with fuel and burned.

Fungi consume dead materials.

In 1939, Albert Einstein wrote to US President Franklin Roosevelt, urging him to make building an atomic weapon a priority.

Rotor blades generate lift.

Igor Sikorsky

Tail rotor allows steering.

VS-300 on its first flight

1938

Discovery of PTFE

American chemist Roy Plunkett discovered polytetrafluoroethylene (better known as PTFE, or by its brand name Teflon) by accident while developing a new fridge coolant. PTFE is unreactive and offers very low friction, making it great for non-stick cookware, and as a lubricant on machine parts such as gears and bearings.

Teflon-coated frying pan

1939

First single-rotor helicopter

The first practical helicopter, VS-300, by Russian-American inventor Igor Sikorsky, made its maiden flight tethered to the ground in Connecticut, USA. It flew freely in 1940. The helicopter's three rotor blades, powered by a 75-hp engine, generated lift. A smaller tail rotor enabled steering and balanced out the turning forces created by the main rotor.

1940

1939

DDT

Swiss chemist Paul Hermann Müller discovered that DDT (dichloro-diphenyl-trichloroethane), first produced in 1874, is a powerful and effective insecticide (a substance that kills insects, which eat crops or carry diseases). It was used widely from 1943 onwards to tackle malaria, typhus, and dengue fever, and later by farmers to rid their crops of pests. Fears about the chemical's harmful effects (see p.202) saw it banned in many countries in the 1970s.

1938

Living fossil discovered

Looking for unusual specimens in a fisherman's catch on South Africa's east coast, museum curator Marjorie Courtenay-Latimer discovered an unusual fish that was later identified as a coelacanth. This fish was thought to have died out 65 million years ago. Coelacanths grow up to 2 m (6.56 ft) long and have four lobed fins that move alternately like a horse trotting.

"The most beautiful fish I had ever seen, five feet long, and a pale mauve blue with iridescent silver markings."

Marjorie Courtenay-Latimer, 1938

Cropdusting aircraft spray DDT at the Congressional Airport, Washington DC, USA, c 1940

Periodic table

In this colour-coded table, chemical elements are arranged in order of their increasing atomic number (the number of protons an atom of an element contains) and in rows, called periods.

All elements in a certain period have the same number of electron shells (the layers of electrons around an atom's nucleus).

In addition, the elements are organized into columns called groups. Each group contains elements with similar chemical properties.

Early attempts

In 1789, French chemist Antoine Lavoisier published his *Elementary Treatise of Chemistry*, in which he grouped 33 chemical elements simply into four types: gases, metals, non-metals, and earths. Some of his elements were later shown to be compounds (made of two or more elements), such as aluminium oxide.

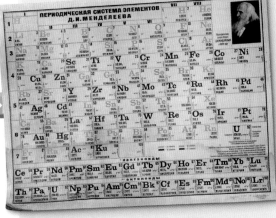

Mendeleev's periodic table

Russian chemist Dmitri Mendeleev ordered the 59 elements known at the time into eight groups (right) based on their relative atomic mass. His periodic table left three gaps for undiscovered elements, which turned out to be gallium (discovered in 1875), scandium (discovered in 1879), and germanium (discovered in 1886).

Periodic table grid

Group 1

1	1.0079
H	
Hydrogen	

Group 2

3	6.941	4	9.0122
Li		**Be**	
Lithium		Beryllium	

11	22.990	12	24.305
Na		**Mg**	
Sodium		Magnesium	

Groups 3–7

19	39.098	20	40.078	21	44.956	22	47.867	23	50.942	24	51.996	25	54.938
K Potassium		**Ca** Calcium		**Sc** Scandium		**Ti** Titanium		**V** Vanadium		**Cr** Chromium		**Mn** Manganese	

37	85.468	38	87.62	39	88.906	40	91.224	41	92.906	42	95.94	43	(96)
Rb Rubidium		**Sr** Strontium		**Y** Yttrium		**Zr** Zirconium		**Nb** Niobium		**Mo** Molybdenum		**Tc** Technetium	

55	132.91	56	137.33	57–71		72	178.49	73	180.95	74	183.84	75	186.21
Cs Caesium		**Ba** Barium		**La–Lu** Lanthanides		**Hf** Hafnium		**Ta** Tantalum		**W** Tungsten		**Re** Rhenium	

87	(223)	88	(226)	89–103		104	(261)	105	(262)	106	(266)	107	(264)
Fr Francium		**Ra** Radium		**Ac–Lr** Actinides		**Rf** Rutherfordium		**Db** Dubnium		**Sg** Seaborgium		**Bh** Bohrium	

Lanthanide and actinide series

57	138.91	58	140.12	59	140.91	60	144.24
La Lanthanum		**Ce** Cerium		**Pr** Praseodymium		**Nd** Neodymium	

89	(227)	90	232.04	91	231.04	92	238.03
Ac Actinium		**Th** Thorium		**Pa** Protactinium		**U** Uranium	

Key

- Hydrogen
- Alkali metals
- Alkaline earth metals
- Transition metals
- Lanthanide series
- Actinide series
- Other metals
- Metalloids
- Other non-metals
- Halogens
- Noble gases

Key events

1669

Phosphorus was isolated from urine by German alchemist Hennig Brand (see p.83). It was the first element to be discovered using chemistry.

Phosphorus match tips

1773

English scientist Joseph Priestley isolated oxygen gas, calling it "dephlogisticated air". German chemist Carl Scheele claimed to have also done so, but in 1772.

1829

German chemist Johann Wolfgang Döbereiner organized elements into groups of three with similar chemical properties (such as chlorine, bromine, and iodine). He called these groups triads.

1869

Russian chemist Dmitri Mendeleev published his pioneering Periodic Table in a Russian journal, which was later translated into German and English.

Symbols for elements

Each element has its own place in the table based on its atomic number and is known by its name, chemical symbol, and its relative atomic mass. This is the average of the mass of all atoms of an element allowing for their proportion of isotopes (atoms of an element with a different number of neutrons than normal).

Atomic number — 11 | 22.990 — Relative atomic mass
Chemical symbol — **Na**
Sodium — Name

Modern periodic table

The table today contains 118 elements, more than 90 of which occur naturally in some form. The rest have been chemically made, often for just fractions of a second, in laboratories. The latest four (115–118) were named in 2016.

					18
					2 4.0026 **He** Helium 1

13	**14**	**15**	**16**	**17**	
5 10.811 **B** Boron	6 12.011 **C** Carbon	7 14.007 **N** Nitrogen	8 15.999 **O** Oxygen	9 18.998 **F** Fluorine	10 20.180 **Ne** Neon 2
13 26.982 **Al** Aluminium	14 28.086 **Si** Silicon	15 30.974 **P** Phosphorus	16 32.065 **S** Sulfur	17 35.453 **Cl** Chlorine	18 39.948 **Ar** Argon 3

8	**9**	**10**	**11**	**12**	**13**	**14**	**15**	**16**	**17**	
26 55.845 **Fe** Iron	27 58.933 **Co** Cobalt	28 58.693 **Ni** Nickel	29 63.546 **Cu** Copper	30 65.39 **Zn** Zinc	31 69.723 **Ga** Gallium	32 72.64 **Ge** Germanium	33 74.922 **As** Arsenic	34 78.96 **Se** Selenium	35 79.904 **Br** Bromine	36 83.80 **Kr** Krypton 4
44 101.07 **Ru** Ruthenium	45 102.91 **Rh** Rhodium	46 106.42 **Pd** Palladium	47 107.87 **Ag** Silver	48 112.41 **Cd** Cadmium	49 114.82 **In** Indium	50 118.71 **Sn** Tin	51 121.76 **Sb** Antimony	52 127.60 **Te** Tellurium	53 126.90 **I** Iodine	54 131.29 **Xe** Xenon 5
76 190.23 **Os** Osmium	77 192.22 **Ir** Iridium	78 195.08 **Pt** Platinum	79 196.97 **Au** Gold	80 200.59 **Hg** Mercury	81 204.38 **Tl** Thallium	82 207.2 **Pb** Lead	83 208.96 **Bi** Bismuth	84 (209) **Po** Polonium	85 (210) **At** Astatine	86 (222) **Rn** Radon 6
108 (277) **Hs** Hassium	109 (268) **Mt** Meitnerium	110 (281) **Ds** Darmstadtium	111 (272) **Rg** Roentgenium	112 285 **Cn** Copernicum	113 284 **Nh** Nihonium	114 289 **Fl** Flerovium	115 288 **Mc** Moscovium	116 293 **Lv** Livermorium	117 294 **Ts** Tennessine	118 294 **Og** Oganesson 7

61 (145) **Pm** Promethium	62 (150.36) **Sm** Samarium	63 151.96 **Eu** Europium	64 157.25 **Gd** Gadolinium	65 158.93 **Tb** Terbium	66 162.50 **Dy** Dysprosium	67 164.93 **Ho** Holmium	68 167.26 **Er** Erbium	69 168.93 **Tm** Thulium	70 173.04 **Yb** Ytterbium	71 174.97 **Lu** Lutetium
93 (237) **Np** Neptunium	94 (244) **Pu** Plutonium	95 (243) **Am** Americium	96 (247) **Cm** Curium	97 (247) **Bk** Berkelium	98 (251) **Cf** Californium	99 (252) **Es** Einsteinium	100 (257) **Fm** Fermium	101 (258) **Md** Mendelevium	102 (259) **No** Nobelium	103 (262) **Lr** Lawrencium

1894

Scottish chemist William Ramsey discovered the element argon. He later discovered three others – neon, krypton, and xenon – and showed how they formed a new group of elements, the noble gases.

1898

Polish–French scientist Marie Curie and French scientist Pierre Curie isolated two new chemical elements, which they named radium and polonium.

Pellet of radium

1913

English physicist Henry Moseley found that the nature of the X-rays an atom emits depends upon the number of protons inside it. This allowed the table to be organized by atomic number not relative atomic mass.

1940

American chemist Glenn Seaborg discovered plutonium and later nine elements that appear after uranium on the table. He proposed the addition of the actinide element series.

1940 ▶ 1945

"The release of atomic energy on a large scale would be only a matter of time."

Enrico Fermi, on the success of Chicago Pile-1

1942
V2 missile
The launch of the world's first missile powered by a liquid-fuelled rocket engine was tested at Peenemünde, Germany. Following three failed launches, the fourth test saw the 14-m- (46-ft-) tall rocket reach a height of more than 85,000 m (278,870 ft). Over 3,000 V2s, each carrying 910 kg (1,785 lb) of explosives, were launched on enemy targets in World War II.

1942
Experimental nuclear reactor
The first nuclear reactor, Chicago Pile-1, ran a nuclear chain reaction for the first time, using uranium as a fuel. Italian physicist Enrico Fermi led the team at the University of Chicago that built the reactor. When the nuclei of uranium atoms were split by nuclear fission (see p.169) in the reactor, they released energy and neutrons, which could then split more nuclei, creating a nuclear chain reaction. This would lead, eventually, to developing nuclear power stations.

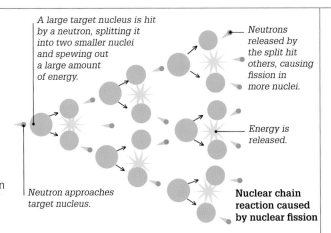

A large target nucleus is hit by a neutron, splitting it into two smaller nuclei and spewing out a large amount of energy.

Neutrons released by the split hit others, causing fission in more nuclei.

Energy is released.

Neutron approaches target nucleus.

Nuclear chain reaction caused by nuclear fission

1940

1940   DISCOVERY OF PLUTONIUM

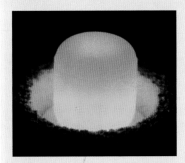

Radioactive plutonium-238 (a form of plutonium) glowing red hot

The element plutonium was discovered by American chemists Glenn Seaborg, Edwin McMillan, Joseph Kennedy, and Arthur Wahl at the University of California in 1940. Named after the dwarf planet, Pluto, this element found use in nuclear weapons – just 100 g (3.5 oz) of plutonium can produce an explosion equal to 2,000 tonnes of TNT. It is also used as a fuel in nuclear power reactors that generate electricity.

Powering Voyager
The two Voyager space probes are each powered by three multi-hundred-watt radioisotope thermoelectric generators (MHW RTGs), which used the heat from the decay of plutonium-238 fuel to generate electricity for power. Voyager 1 is now the most distant artificial object in space from Earth.

Pair of cameras provide high-resolution images.

Voyager 1

Power source containing plutonium fuel mounted on a boom

1943

Aqua-Lung

Frenchmen Jacques Cousteau and Emile Gagnan invented the Aqua-Lung, a self-regulating underwater breathing apparatus. Their portable invention popularized diving. It featured a regulator that adjusted air pressure and managed air supply so that the pressure of air inside a diver's lungs matched with that of the surrounding water.

The diver breathes in air through a tube from the cylinder.

Cylinder contains air

Jacques Cousteau (right) with another diver, wearing Aqua-Lungs

 Work on Colossus – a pioneering early electronic computer used to break German codes and secret messages – began in 1943.

2. Sound waves return to the bat after hitting a moth, the bat's prey.

1. The sound waves from the bat projected in the direction of movement.

Moth

Bat

1944

Echolocation discovered

American biophysicist Donald Griffin coined the term echolocation to describe how bats (as well as some whales, dolphins, and shrews) emit sound waves to navigate and hunt prey. The sound reflects back off objects and is analysed by the animal's brain fast and accurately, helping it detect prey. Some species of bat can catch more than 500 insects per hour using echolocation.

1945

1945

Microwave oven invented

While working on RADAR (RAdio Detection And Ranging) technology at a company called Raytheon, American physicist Percy Spencer discovered how high-powered vacuum tubes called magnetrons gave off microwaves (a type of electromagnetic wave). These waves cause the molecules in food to vibrate and heat up. Spencer and Raytheon developed the first commercial microwave oven, the Radarange.

1943

Antibiotic tackles tuberculosis

The chemical streptomycin was first isolated from bacteria found in soil by staff in the laboratory of American scientist Selman Waksman. It proved to be the first antibiotic to successfully combat the disease tuberculosis. Streptomycin has since been used to treat other diseases such as tularemia, and as a pesticide against certain fungal diseases of fruit crops.

Streptomycin crystals under a microscope

1943

Kidney dialysis

Dutch physician Willem Johan Kolff built the first kidney dialysis machine using materials such as orange juice cans and an old washing machine. The machine worked as an artificial kidney, taking the blood out of a patient whose own kidneys were not working, filtering the blood to remove harmful toxins, and then returning clean blood to the patient.

Hamburger cooked in an original Raytheon Radarange microwave oven

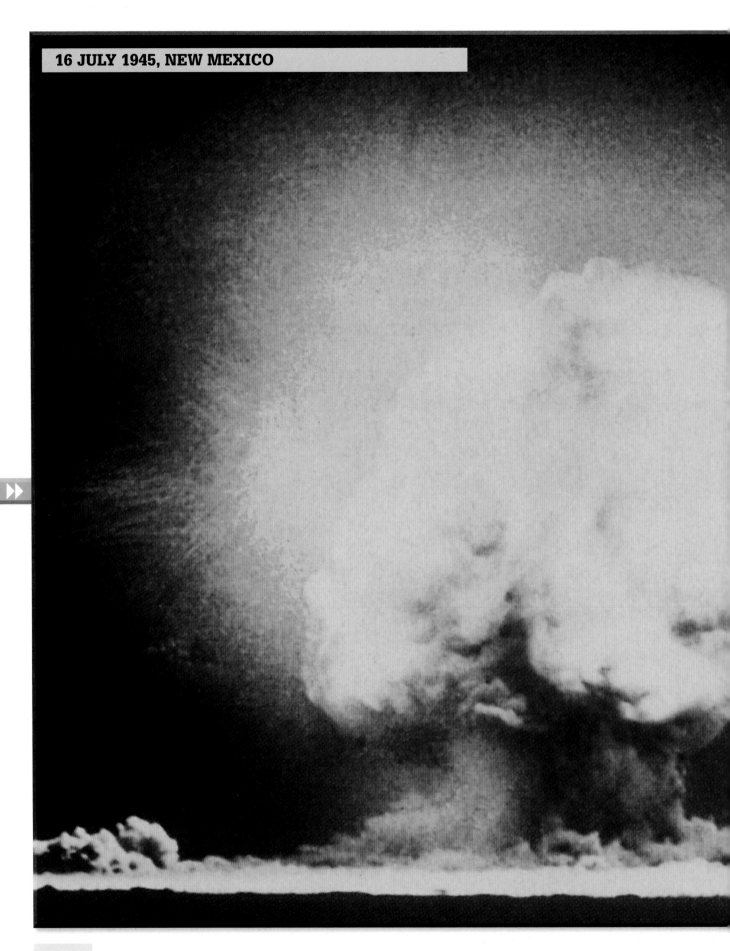

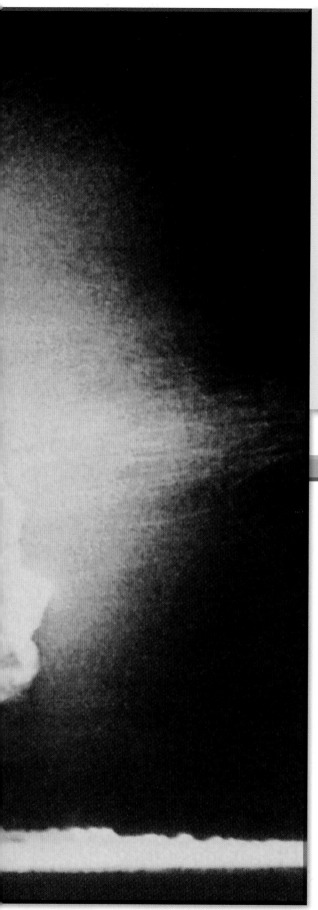

The Trinity Test

On 16 July 1945, the first atomic weapon was detonated in Alamogordo, New Mexico, USA. The test, code-named "Trinity", confirmed the terrifying power of an atomic chain reaction caused by the fission (splitting) of the nuclei of plutonium atoms. Within just 16 thousandths of a second, the mushroom cloud created by the blast had grown almost 200 m (655 ft) tall and would eventually loom up more than 12,600 m (41,340 ft) high. The blast, equivalent to nearly 18,600 tonnes of TNT explosive, generated so much heat that it melted the sand of the desert floor into glass, which became known as trinitite. The atomic bomb dropped on Hiroshima, Japan, followed three weeks later, devastating the city and causing more than 100,000 deaths.

"We knew the world would not be the same. A few people laughed, a few people cried. Most people were silent."

J Robert Oppenheimer, director of the Los Alamos Laboratory (founded during World War II, 1939–1945, to develop nuclear weapons), 1965

The mushroom cloud from the blast of the first atomic weapon rises over Alamogordo Bombing Range in New Mexico.

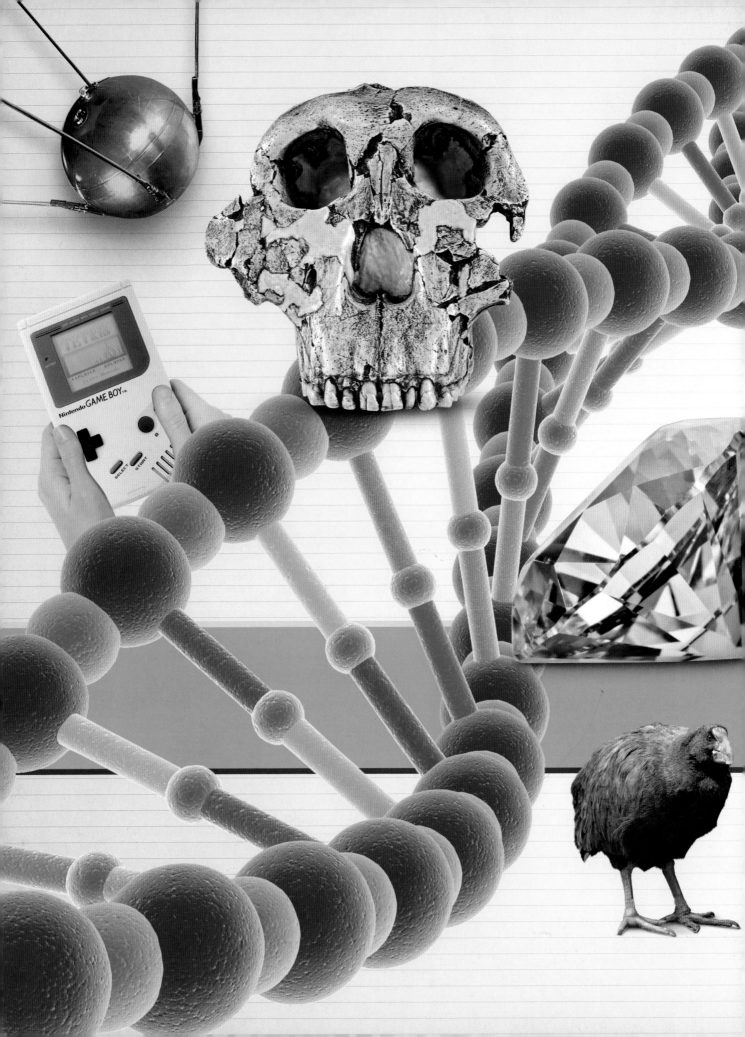

1945–present day
Modern science

This era began with the first computers, some of which were the size of a basketball court, and were very slow and unreliable. The invention of the transistor soon enabled devices to be built that were far smaller and faster, and more powerful and efficient. Further strides in technology saw thousands and later millions of electronic circuits shrunk onto a single silicon chip, spurring the arrival of robots, smartphones, and computer technology in cars and many household appliances. Computing power became available to all, aided by advances in communications and the rise of the Internet.

1945 ▶ 1950

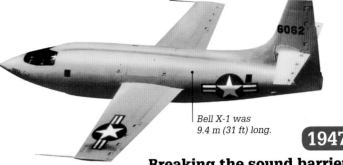

Bell X-1 was 9.4 m (31 ft) long.

1947
Breaking the sound barrier
US Air Force pilot Charles "Chuck" Yeager flew the rocket-powered Bell X-1 aircraft at about 13,000 m (43,000 ft) to become the first human to fly faster than the speed of sound, which is 1,062 km/h (660 mph) at this height. The X-1 has a top speed of 1,130 km/h (700 mph).

1946
ENIAC operational
ENIAC (Electronic Numerical Integrator And Computer), the first electronic, general-purpose computer, started operating at the University of Pennsylvania, USA. This 30-m- (98-ft-) long machine weighed more than 27,000 kg (60,000 lb) and ran different applications, from weather forecasts to calculating the impact of nuclear bomb simulations, until 1955.

1947
Discovery of promethium
A gap in the periodic table (see pp.188–189) was filled with the discovery of the missing element (with atomic number 61) by chemists at Oak Ridge National Laboratory, USA. It was named promethium (Pm).

Programmers reprogram ENIAC using cables plugged into boards

1945

In 1947, British engineer Dennis Gabor invented holography – a system of displaying holograms (three-dimensional images on a two-dimensional surface).

1946
Bouncing off the Moon
The United States Army Signal Corps (USASC) was the first to bounce radio waves off the Moon. Named Diana after the Roman goddess of the Moon, the USASC's project used World War II radar antennae to send the signals and receive them back from the Moon 2.5 seconds later.

Weak electric signal enters via one side of the plastic triangle covered in gold strip, which touches a germanium crystal.

Germanium crystal, on a metal base, amplifies the weak electric signal and makes it stronger.

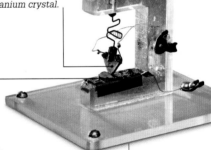

Replica of Bell Labs' original transistor

1947
First transistor
The transistor was invented by American physicists William Bradford Shockley, Walter Houser Brattain, and John Bardeen at Bell Labs in New Jersey, USA. This electronic component could act as a switch in electric circuits, or as an amplifier, increasing the strength of an electric signal. Transistors replaced bulky vacuum tubes and allowed smaller, faster, cheaper, and more reliable electronic goods to be made.

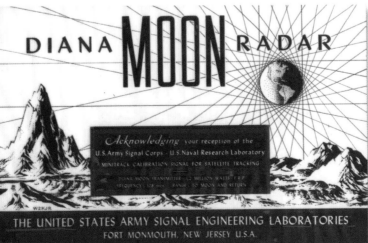

DIANA MOON RADAR

Acknowledging your reception of the
U.S. Army Signal Corps · U.S. Naval Research Laboratory
MINITRACK CALIBRATION SIGNAL FOR SATELLITE TRACKING

THE UNITED STATES ARMY SIGNAL ENGINEERING LABORATORIES
FORT MONMOUTH, NEW JERSEY U.S.A.

Each person who heard the returned Diana signal received this keepsake.

The WHO (World Health Organization) met for the first time in 1948. This UN (United Nations) agency has played a part in promoting healthcare and eradicating diseases.

1949

Positive effects of cortisone

American physician Philip S. Hench discovered how a hormone (chemical in the body) called cortisone could reduce inflammation in patients suffering from the disease rheumatoid arthritis. In the same year, American chemist Percy L. Julian devised a quick and affordable method of making cortisone in laboratories to meet the growing demand for it.

1949

Naming the "Big Bang"

British astronomer Sir Fred Hoyle coined the term "Big Bang" (see pp.182–183) to describe the theory that the Universe began by expanding from a single point. He used the term for the first time on a BBC radio programme.

1949

Structure of penicillin

British chemist Dorothy Crowfoot (later Hodgkin) and her team published the molecular structure of penicillin, a group of antibiotics (medication against bacterial infections). X-ray crystallography (a process in which the patterns cast by reflected X-rays are analysed) was used to make the map of penicillin's atoms and bonds. This helped to develop more successful antibiotics to fight resistant bacteria.

Molecular model of penicillin

1948

Bird rediscovered

Living examples of the flightless takahē bird were discovered near Lake Te Anau, in New Zealand's South Island, by Dr Geoffrey Orbell. The 63-cm- (24.8-in-) long bird was last sighted in 1898 and was thought to be extinct.

1950 ▶▶

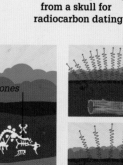

Taking a sample from a skull for radiocarbon dating

1949 RADIOCARBON DATING

American chemists James Arnold and Willard Libby developed radiocarbon dating. Organic materials (made from living things) contain normal carbon, called carbon-12 (C-12), and a radioactive isotope (form) called carbon-14 (C-14). While C-12 levels stay the same, C-14 decays at a known rate (halving in quantity every 5,730 years) – so the ratio of C-14 to C-12 decreases with age. By measuring this ratio, scientists can find out the age of ancient objects made with organic materials, such as wood and cotton.

Rays hit carbon atoms in the atmosphere, making C-14.

Plants absorb C-14 from air.

Animals eat food containing C-14.

Logs   Bones

The amount of C-14 is high in fresh remains.

The amount of C-14 is low in fossils.

1. C-14 is formed
Cosmic rays collide with atoms in the upper atmosphere and produce C-14, which has two more neutrons than regular carbon.

2. Ingesting C-14
Plants absorb C-14 from the air, and animals and humans obtain C-14 through food (plants and animals) that they eat.

3. Death and decay
Following death and burial of an organism, the C-14 in it decays at a constant rate and its amount in the object decreases.

4. Dating samples
Measuring the amount of C-14 in a sample gives an accurate age of objects up to 50,000 years old.

The code of life

Parents pass on traits from themselves to their offspring – from the shape of their nose to the likelihood of them suffering from certain diseases. The instructions for these traits and how the offspring should develop are called genes, which are stored in a chemical called DNA (deoxyribonucleic acid), present in every cell. Genetics is the study of how genes work and are passed down from one generation to another.

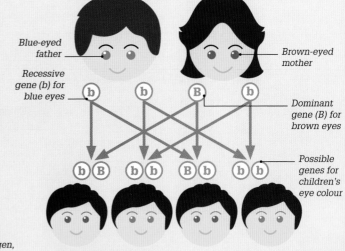

Blue-eyed father

Brown-eyed mother

Recessive gene (b) for blue eyes

Dominant gene (B) for brown eyes

Possible genes for children's eye colour

DNA's "backbone" is made of carbon, hydrogen, oxygen, and phosphorus.

Passing things down

Everyone has two versions of each gene, one from their mother and one from their father. Some of these genes, such as brown eye colour (B) can be dominant, meaning that if you have one brown eye gene and one blue eye gene (b), the dominant gene wins out and you have brown eyes.

DNA

Genes are carried inside cells in DNA. Long ribbons of DNA are formed from two spiralling chains, together called a double helix. Linking the chains together are strands containing pairs of four chemicals, called bases – guanine, cytosine, thymine, and adenine. These base pairs form a four-letter alphabet that acts as a code, telling cells how to make proteins.

Key events

1866

Austrian botanist Gregor Mendel's work on pea plants enabled his discovery of the key laws of inheritance, showing how certain traits are passed on by plants to their offspring.

1911

Through his studies on the chromosomes of fruit flies, American biologist Thomas Hunt Morgan demonstrated that chromosomes carry the genes of a species.

1951

British chemist Rosalind Franklin photographed DNA fibres for the first time in X-ray studies involving her colleagues Maurice Wilkins and Raymond Gosling.

1953

American geneticist James Watson and British biologist Francis Crick published evidence of the double helix structure of the DNA.

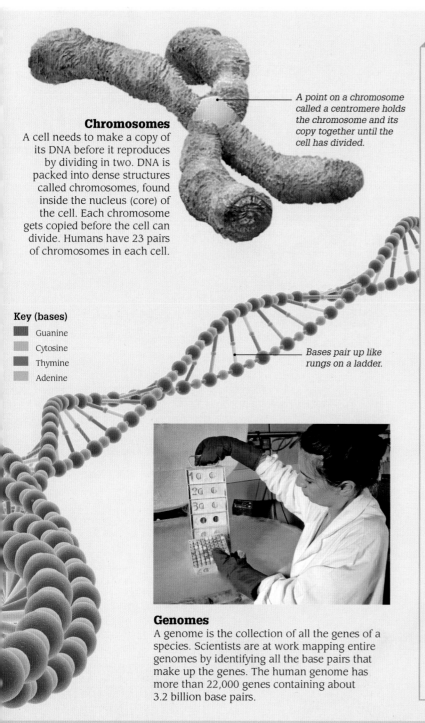

Chromosomes

A cell needs to make a copy of its DNA before it reproduces by dividing in two. DNA is packed into dense structures called chromosomes, found inside the nucleus (core) of the cell. Each chromosome gets copied before the cell can divide. Humans have 23 pairs of chromosomes in each cell.

A point on a chromosome called a centromere holds the chromosome and its copy together until the cell has divided.

Key (bases)
■ Guanine
■ Cytosine
■ Thymine
■ Adenine

Bases pair up like rungs on a ladder.

Genomes

A genome is the collection of all the genes of a species. Scientists are at work mapping entire genomes by identifying all the base pairs that make up the genes. The human genome has more than 22,000 genes containing about 3.2 billion base pairs.

Application of genetics

Genetic engineering

The DNA of organisms can be altered by using enzymes to cut out small pieces of DNA from one species and insert some of its genes into another one. This can give the genetically modified (GM) species useful attributes, such as increasing its nutritional content or making it more resistant to pests.

This GM mouse glows in the dark because of a gene for a fluorescent protein.

Tackling disease

Some diseases, such as cystic fibrosis and colour blindness, are inherited. Genetic screening enables doctors to assess whether a patient may be vulnerable to a disease. Gene therapy is an emerging field of medical treatment. In it, a gene that causes a disease is either removed or replaced with a healthy gene.

DNA fingerprinting

With the exception of identical twins, each person's genes (their genetic fingerprint) are unique. DNA fingerprinting helps to identify relationships between family members. Law enforcement agencies use it to identify people from traces of their DNA left behind in hair, skin cells, or other body samples at crime scenes.

Each row is the DNA fingerprint of different people in a family.

1985

British geneticist Alec Jeffreys and his team at Leicester University, UK, pioneered DNA profiling, a process in which small parts of different people's DNA are compared to identify them.

1999

The first complete human chromosome (Chromosome 22) was mapped as part of the Human Genome Project.

2002

The mouse was the first mammal to have its full genome sequence mapped. It consisted of 3.48 billion bases.

2008

The 1000 Genomes Project was started. Its aim was to map the genomes of more than 1,000 people to learn about the variations in their genes.

1950 ▶ 1955

Solar System, with the Sun at the centre

Orbit of a comet extending to the edge of the Oort Cloud

Comet orbiting close to the Solar System

1950
Oort Cloud
Dutch astronomer Jan Hendrik Oort suggested that some comets come from a cloud of icy bodies that encircles the very edge of the Solar System. This region, now called the Oort Cloud, is believed to lie between 20,000 and 100,000 times further away than Earth's average distance from the Sun.

1951
Ferranti Mark 1
The Ferranti Mark 1 became the first computer to be available for sale, delivered to Manchester University, UK, ahead of Univac 1 computers in the USA. The Mark 1 could perform 600 ten-digit multiplications in three seconds and was used for research. It also ran the first chess-playing program and its "hoot" command made it one of the first computers to play sound.

1950

1950
Treating leukaemia
American pharmacologists Gertrude Elion and George Hitchings developed thioguanine – the first successful drug to help treat leukaemia, a cancer of blood-forming tissues. The pair developed another drug, 6-MP, the following year, which is still used to treat leukaemia today.

1952
First hydrogen bomb
The first hydrogen bomb was tested at Enewetak Atoll in the Marshall Islands (then under US control). The bomb, nicknamed "Ivy Mike", left a crater 50 m (164 ft) deep and 1,900 km (1,180 miles) wide, and sent a 40-km- (25-mile-) high mushroom cloud up into the atmosphere.

1952
Barcodes
American inventors Bernard Silver and Norman Woodland patented the barcode – a series of lines that is scanned and converted into a unique number, which identifies a product. The technology was not introduced until much later, in 1974.

Scanner uses a laser to read the pattern of lines representing a long number

Rising mushroom cloud from the "Ivy Mike" hydrogen bomb test

1953
Flight recorder invented
The modern "black box" flight recorder was created by Australian inventor David Warren. It recorded flight instrument readings as well as voices in the aircraft's cockpit to help experts analyse crashes and air incidents.

The first documented human to be struck by a meteorite was Ann Hodges, who was hit in her home in Alabama, USA, in 1954.

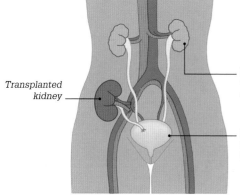

Transplanted kidney

Damaged kidney, which is left in its place

Bladder stores urine sent by the kidney.

Transplanted kidney in a human body

1954

First organ transplant

American surgeon Joseph Murray performed the first successful transplant of a human organ when he transplanted a kidney from one identical twin, Ronald Herrick, into the other, Richard. In this process, a transplanted kidney is implanted into the body and connected to blood vessels so that it can filter excess water and waste chemicals from the blood.

1955

1954

Polio vaccine trials

The largest medical field trial ever began as 1.8 million schoolchildren were vaccinated in the USA. They were given a vaccine that would protect them against the crippling disease of polio. The vaccine had been developed by American virologist Jonas Salk the previous year.

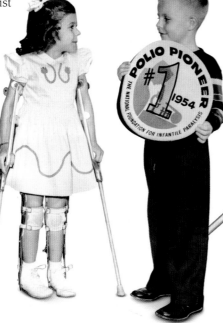

Randy Kerr, the first child to receive the vaccine during the field trial in 1954, stands beside Mary Kosloski who had polio.

1954   SOLAR CELL

A solar cell generates electric current when sunlight falls on it. Solar cells are made of photovoltaic materials. Inside these materials, electrons absorb the energy of the sunlight. This causes them to leave their atoms – and once freed, they flow through the material, creating an electric current. The first practical solar cell was developed at Bell Labs in the USA in 1954. Today, solar cells have become a key source of renewable energy.

First solar cell demonstration
An executive from Bell Labs demonstrated the first practical solar cell in 1954. It generated enough electricity to power a 53-cm- (20.8-in-) high toy Ferris wheel and a small radio transmitter.

Model of Vanguard I satellite, 1958

Vanguard I satellite
Launched in 1958, USA's second successful space satellite was also the first to be powered by solar cells, six of which were fitted to its body. The solar cells ran for almost seven years as the satellite orbited Earth.

Solar cell powering satellite

Artificial diamond
American chemist Howard Tracy Hall created the first artificial diamond by heating carbon to incredibly high temperatures while under intense pressure – more than 100,000 times that of Earth's atmosphere.

Rachel Carson

A lifelong passion for nature and its preservation led American naturalist Rachel Carson (1907–1964) to write several bestselling books. The most notable, *Silent Spring*, had a profound influence on how people viewed conservation and human impact on our planet.

Early life

Born in Springdale, in Pennsylvania, USA, Carson studied English at the Pennsylvania College for Women before switching to biology and gaining a masters degree in zoology in 1932. She began working for the US Bureau of Fisheries in 1935, where she wrote radio scripts and articles on nature and ecosystems, as well as taking part in field trips.

Studying pesticides

Carson's concerns over the effects of artificial pesticides, especially DDT (dichloro-diphenyl-trichloroethane), prompted her to write *Silent Spring*. Published in 1962, this book detailed how the heavy use of chemicals in agriculture and industry polluted streams and soil, damaged animal populations, and posed great risks to health.

Long-term impacts

Carson's research showed how chemicals travel through food chains as they build up in living things that are eaten. She also foresaw how some insects would become resistant to certain pesticides and questioned whether humans had the right to control nature in such ways.

Environmental call to arms

Public interest in the environment was awakened by Carson's extensively researched writings. In 1963, although terminally ill with breast cancer, she testified before committees set up to investigate DDT's impacts. Eight years after her death, DDT was banned in the USA.

Young Rachel
Carson's two passions – writing and nature – began in her childhood in Pennsylvania. She wrote stories for a children's magazine and spent much of her leisure time exploring the insect and plant life in nearby streams or woods, often with her dog Candy.

Normal egg   **DDT-poisoned egg**

DDT damage
A normal peregrine falcon egg (left) contrasts severely with one affected by DDT poisoning. When the birds ate insects and fish contaminated with DDT, it accumulated in their bodies, reducing calcium production. This led to thin, frail eggshells that broke before chicks could hatch, causing a sharp decline in peregrine falcon numbers.

Protecting the environment
The Environmental Protection Agency (EPA) was formed in the USA in 1970, partly in response to Carson's work and the growing conservation movement in the 1960s. One of its stated aims was to make policies that "will encourage productive and enjoyable harmony between man and his environment."

> **The most alarming of all man's assaults upon the environment is the contamination of air, earth, rivers, and sea with dangerous and even lethal materials.**
>
> Rachel Carson, chapter 2
> of *Silent Spring*, 1962

Silent Spring
Carson was criticized and ridiculed by some for her book, and one chemicals company even produced a spoof booklet called The Desolate Year. Today, Silent Spring is considered one of the most influential science books of the 20th century.

Scientist and writer
Carson studies nature under a microscope on the verandah of her home. In 1953, one of her books, The Sea Around Us, was made into an Oscar-winning documentary.

"To understand biology is to understand that all life is linked to the earth from which it came."

Rachel Carson, preface to
Human Biology Projects, 1961

1955►1960

1955
Velcro patented
After studying the tiny hooks of burdock seeds that stuck to his clothes, Swiss engineer George de Mestral invented and patented a new fastening system. Velcro consisted of two strips of material – one with thousands of tiny hooks that catch and latch onto the thousands of loops on the second strip. By 1959, 50 million m (164 million ft) of Velcro was produced each year.

1955
Wireless remote
American electrical engineer Eugene Polley invented the first cable-free TV remote control. Called the Zenith Flash-Matic, it featured a light beam that users directed at one of four corners of their TV set. Photocells on the TV received the light and could change channels, mute the sound, or switch the set on or off.

Controller held a lamp that sent out beam of light.

Pressing trigger operated the controller.

Zenith Flash-matic TV remote control

Sputnik 1
The first artificial satellite was launched by the Soviet Union (now Russia) in 1957. Sputnik 1 was a 58-cm- (23-in-) diameter metal sphere fitted with batteries and a radio transmitter that relayed signals to Earth for 21 days (see p.212).

Spherical body weighed 81 kg (178.5 lb) and contained three silver-zinc batteries.

Four radio antennae broadcast signals to Earth.

1957
Bubble wrap
American inventors Alfred Fielding and Marc Chavannes developed bubble wrap – a plastic material consisting of small pockets filled with air. After use as a 3-D wallpaper, in shower curtains, and as insulation for greenhouses, bubble wrap eventually gained popularity as lightweight packaging.

1955

350 Disk System

1956
First hard disk
The 350 Disk System – the first hard disk drive – was launched by IBM for its 305 RAMAC computer. It stood 1.72 m (5.64 ft) tall, weighed almost a tonne, and stored 3.75 megabytes of data on magnetic platters (rotating disks).

 The National Aeronautics and Space Administration (NASA) agency was established in 1958.

Edmund Hillary

1956
Vitamin B12
British biochemist Dorothy Hodgkin published the structure of Vitamin B12. Found in meat, fish, and dairy products, this vitamin helps the body produce healthy red blood cells. A shortage of B12 in the body can lead to a form of anaemia.

The SR.N1 hovercraft near Calais, France

1959
First working hovercraft
The Saunders-Roe Nautical 1 (SR.N1) hovercraft, invented by English engineer Christopher Cockerell, made its first English Channel crossing from Calais in France to Dover in the UK. Powered by a piston engine, a large fan raised the craft up on a cushion of air, enabling it to travel with low friction over both land and water.

1959
Zoo as a conservation tool
British naturalist Gerald Durrell created a zoological park at Les Augrès manor house on the island of Jersey. The zoo was designed to focus on conservation and breeding of endangered species for reintroducing them into the wild.

Gerald Durrell at Jersey Zoo with a tapir

1959
Human ancestor
British palaeontologist Mary Leakey discovered the skull of an ancestor of modern humans in Tanzania's Olduvai Gorge. Named *Paranthropus boisei* – and also called *Australopithecus boisei* – it was dated as 1.75 million years old and later proposed to be one of the first human ancestors to use stone tools.

1960

1958
Integrated circuits
American inventors Jack Kilby and Robert Noyce independently developed integrated circuits. These small wafers of material such as silicon or germanium contain an entire electronic circuit and all its components.

1958
Overland crossing of Antarctica
The Commonwealth Trans-Antarctic Expedition completed the first overland crossing of Antarctica via the South Pole. The expedition, led by English explorer Vivian Fuchs and featuring New Zealand mountaineer Edmund Hillary – the first man to climb Mount Everest – used modified tractors and other vehicles to travel 3,473 km (2,158 miles) across the continent in 99 days.

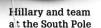

Hillary and team at the South Pole

1906–1992   GRACE HOPPER

This American programming pioneer worked on the Harvard Mark 1 and Univac computers before helping to develop the first practical compiler – a program that converts understandable English commands into code that instructs computers.

COBOL creator
Hopper stands in front of a bank of computer tape drives used for storing data. She played a major part in the creation of the easy-to-use computer language called COBOL-60 (COmmon Business-Oriented Language). Variants of COBOL continue to run thousands of business, traffic management, and banking systems.

1960 ▶ 1965

1960 FIRST WORKING LASER

Using a photographer's flash lamp and a ruby crystal rod, American engineer Theodore H Maiman constructed a device that emitted a concentrated and focused beam of light known as a laser (Light Amplification by Stimulated Emission of Radiation). Lasers emit a single wavelength of light that stays focused and does not spread out, even when travelling long distances.

Dr Theodore H Maiman

Maiman's ruby laser
Atoms within the ruby crystal rod are energized by the energy produced by the flash lamp firing. The atoms generate light that is reflected between the laser's mirrors until a narrow beam of red light shoots out of the laser.

3. Semitransparent mirror reflects back most of the light, but allows some to pass through.

2. Light bounces off the mirror at the back.

1. Flash tube emits white light that provides extra energy to the atoms in the ruby crystal.

4. Red laser beam shines through a hole in the mirror.

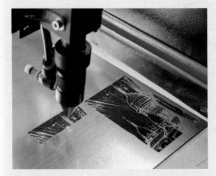

Uses of lasers
Lasers are often used to measure distances in robotics and construction, while surgical lasers can seal blood vessels or destroy diseased cells. Industrial lasers can cut through steel and other tough materials (left) with unerring accuracy.

Trieste **is lowered into the Pacific Ocean**

1960

Deepest spot on Earth
US Navy Lieutenant Don Walsh and Swiss oceanographer Jacques Piccard descended to 10,911 m (35,797 ft) below sea level to Challenger Deep, the deepest part of the Pacific Ocean. Their vessel, a submersible called *Trieste*, had 12.7-cm- (5-in-) thick walls to withstand the immense water pressure at such depths – more than 1,080 times the pressure of Earth's atmosphere at sea level.

 In 1960, *Tiros-1*, the first weather satellite, captured images of clouds and sent them to Earth via radio signals

1960

Unimate 001 handling hot metal castings at a vehicle factory in New Jersey, USA

1961

First industrial robot
A Unimate 001 robot arm was developed by American inventor George Devol and American physicist Joseph Engelberger. This 1.5-tonne hydraulics-powered robotic limb completed 100,000 hours of service by 1971.

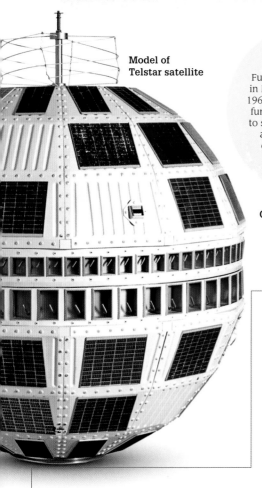

Model of
Telstar satellite

WWF
The World Wildlife
Fund (WWF) was founded
in Morges, Switzerland, in
1961. It was formed to raise
funds and promote action
to stop habitat destruction
and the hunting to
extinction of many
animal species.

Giant panda

1964

Bullet train enters service
The era of high-speed electric trains began
with the Tōkaidō Shinkansen service between
the Japanese cities of Tokyo and Osaka. The
200 km/h (124 mph) trains – later upgraded
to 220 km/h (136 mph) – halved journey
times between the cities.
By July 1967, the trains
had carried an amazing
100 million passengers.

Shinkansen
train runs out
of Tokyo, 1964

1962

Satellite TV
The Telstar 1 satellite was
the first to relay live television
signals across the Atlantic
Ocean. It also transmitted data,
fax (telephonic transmission of
printed material), and telephone
calls. The aluminium satellite
used 3,600 solar cells on its
surface to generate enough
electricity to power its receiver
and transmitter.

1965 ▶▶

1962

Smallest car
Measuring just 137 cm (54 in) long, 100.5 cm
(39.5 in) wide, and 120 cm (47 in) high, the British-
built Peel P50 weighed less than 60 kg (132 lb) and
could be pulled backwards by hand as it possessed
no reverse gear. A small 4.2-horsepower engine
gave it a top speed of 60 km/h (37 mph).

1963

A new island
Approximately 32 km
(19.8 miles) south of Iceland's
coast, a volcanic eruption
began 130 m (426.5 ft) below
sea level. It resulted in a new
island in 1965, which was
named Surtsey after Surtur,
the god of fire in Icelandic
mythology. The eruption
continued until 1967, by which
time the island had reached
171 m (561 ft) in height and
covered an area of 1.4 sq km
(0.5 sq miles). Erosion has
since reduced the island's
height to 154 m (505 ft).

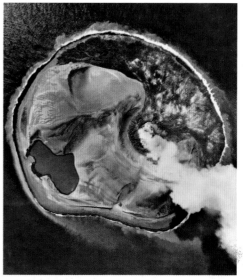

Aerial view of Surtsey island, late 1960s

EME 583B

 The antiviral drug azidothymidine
(AZT) was developed in 1964 to
treat cancer and was later used
for HIV treatment.

207

"When we first heard that inexplicable "hum", we didn't understand its significance, and we never dreamed it would be connected to the origins of the Universe."

Arno Penzias, on his discovery
of the cosmic microwave
background radiation

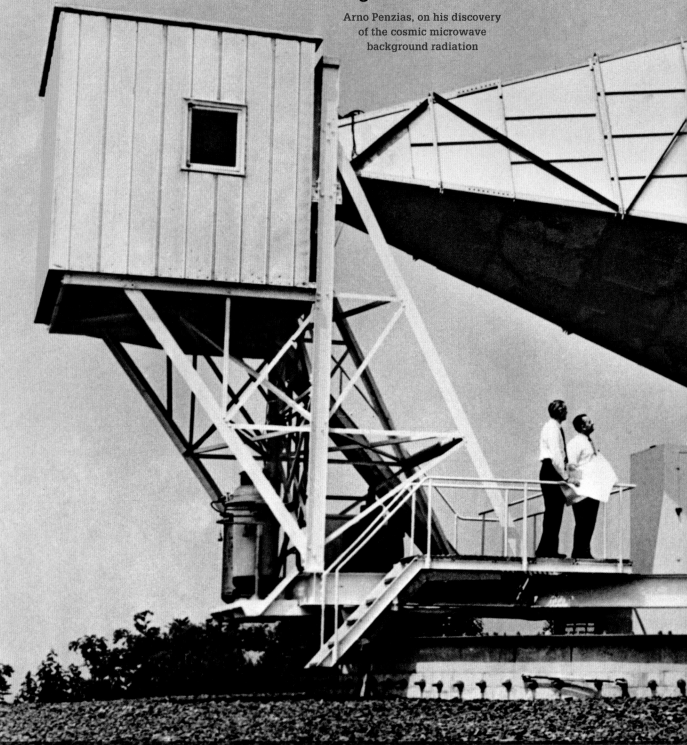

Arno Penzias and Robert Wilson are dwarfed by the 15-m-
(50-ft-) long Holmdel Horn Antenna, New Jersey, USA.

Ear on the Universe

The Holmdel Horn Antenna at Bell Telephone Laboratories in New Jersey, USA, was built in 1959 to monitor radio signals from early NASA satellites. In 1964, two young American astronomers, Arno Penzias and Robert Wilson, puzzled over the low-level background noise the antenna was picking up. They checked everything, from the wiring to removing pigeons and their droppings from inside the aluminium antenna, but the noise continued. Penzias and Wilson concluded that the signals were coming from all directions in space. Penzias and Wilson had discovered cosmic microwave background (CMB) radiation – the radiation left over from when the Universe was just 380,000 years old. This was compelling evidence supporting the Big Bang theory as to how the Universe began.

1965 ▶ 1970

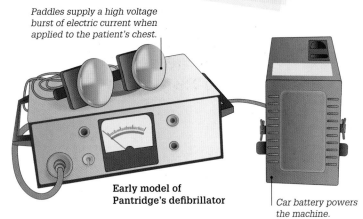

Paddles supply a high voltage burst of electric current when applied to the patient's chest.

Early model of Pantridge's defibrillator

Car battery powers the machine.

1967

Successful heart transplant

South African surgeon Dr Christiaan Barnard transplanted the heart of a young road accident victim into the body of Louis Washkansky, who suffered from incurable heart disease. Although Washkansky survived only a few weeks, the transplant was deemed a success.

Dr Barnard shows the chest X-ray of the first heart transplant patient.

1965

First portable defibrillator

Frank Pantridge, a Northern Irish doctor, built a portable defibrillator powered by car batteries. Found in ambulances and emergency rooms, defibrillators are life-saving devices that can correct a heart's rhythm when it starts beating abnormally or restart it when it stops.

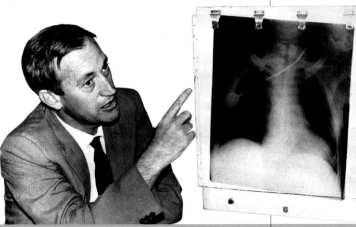

1965

1965

First computer mouse tested

Invented by American engineer Douglas Engelbart and built by his colleague Bill English at the Stanford Research Institute, USA, the first computer mouse had a wooden case, two geared wheels to register vertical and horizontal movement, and one button. Its speed and ease of use won out over joysticks and other input devices when tested.

Kevlar

American chemist Stephanie Kwolek developed Kevlar fibres in 1965. A lightweight material, Kevlar possesses exceptional strength and stiffness, and is used in tyres, bulletproof vests, and undersea cables.

Modern bulletproof Kevlar vest

1967

Video game console

American engineer Ralph Baer developed the Brown Box video games console. It was the first multiplayer home computer game, and was plugged into a television set. The games that could be played included tennis, draughts, and target shooting. In 1972, a revised version of the console went on sale as the Magnavox Odyssey.

Program cards let the user play different games.

Two handheld controllers allowed multiplayer gaming.

Prototype of the first computer mouse

Wheel turns as the mouse moves on the tabletop, sending a signal to move the position of the cursor on the computer screen.

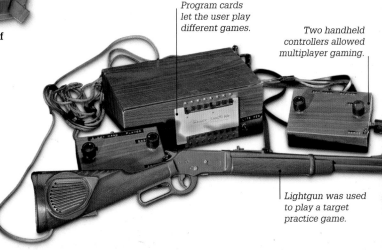

Lightgun was used to play a target practice game.

1967   TECTONIC PLATE MOVEMENTS

British geophysicist Dan McKenzie and American geophysicist W Jason Morgan each described how Earth's surface (crust) is made up of a number of large plates. The movement of the plates causes earthquakes, and creates mountains and new land.

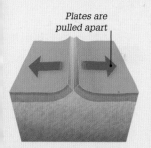

Plates are pulled apart

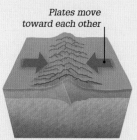

Plates move toward each other

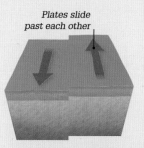

Plates slide past each other

Divergent boundary
Where plates move apart, a ridge, or rift, forms as molten rock from beneath the crust seeps out and makes new seafloor or new land.

Convergent boundary
When plates push together, one may be forced under the other, which may cause volcanoes. The crust may crumple, creating mountains.

Transform boundary
In some places, plates move sideways, sliding past each other. A sudden movement between the plates can lead to earthquakes.

 The US military's ARPANET computer network linked just four computers in 1969, but would herald the coming of the Internet.

1969

Artificial heart transplant
American cardiologist Denton Cooley and Argentinian surgeon Domingo Liotta successfully transplanted a mechanical replacement heart for the first time at the Texas Heart Institute in Houston, USA. The artificial heart was a pneumatic (air-driven) pump, which relied on an external power supply. It was designed as a bridge, or a stop gap, until a donor human heart became available.

1970

1968

Supersonic airliner flight
The Soviet supersonic airliner Tupolev Tu-144 made its first test flight. It was designed to carry up to 140 passengers at twice the speed of sound. A British–French rival, the Concorde, made its maiden supersonic flight less than three months later and entered service in 1976, a year before the Tu-144.

Aérospatiale/BAC Concorde lands at Heathrow Airport, London, UK

Streamlined 3-m- (10-ft-) wide fuselage (main body) carried up to 120 passengers.

Two turbojet engines under each wing gave a top speed of 2,179 km/h (1,354 mph).

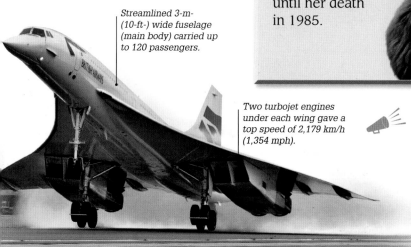

1932–1985   DIAN FOSSEY

American zoologist Dian Fossey encountered the rare mountain gorilla in 1963 on her first visit to Africa. She returned three years later to study this endangered species closely. She documented the gorillas and their behaviour, becoming a world authority on them. Fossey championed their conservation until her death in 1985.

Fossey among the mountain gorillas in Rwanda

 In 1969, American engineer Gary Starkweather invented the laser printer using a laser beam to reproduce text or images via toner powder attracted to a drum.

The space race

The late 1950s and 1960s saw a technological battle for supremacy in space between the planet's two great superpowers, the USA and the Soviet Union (now Russia). The Soviets had made great strides with rocket-powered long-range missiles, which they used to launch objects into space to record a number of milestones, but the USA finally caught up, forming their space agency, NASA (National Aeronautics and Space Administration), in 1958. Both nations enjoyed remarkable achievements during this period.

The race begins
Launched by the Soviet Union in 1957, Sputnik 1 was the first artificial satellite in space. It made some 1,440 orbits of Earth in three months. For its first 21 days in orbit, it sent out beeps via radio waves detectable by radio receivers on Earth.

First travellers in space
Soviet astronaut Yuri Gagarin became the first human in space in 1961 when he orbited Earth in the tiny Vostok 1 spacecraft. His journey lasted 108 minutes and was followed by five longer Vostok missions, including Vostok 6, which made 48 orbits over 2 days, 22 hours as it carried the first woman in space – Valentina Tereshkova.

Yuri Gagarin inside Vostok 1

Hinged panels, which protected the craft during the descent to the Moon, unfolded like petals after landing.

Television antenna transmitted pictures to Earth.

Space probes
Space probes are unmanned machines sent to explore space. The Soviet spacecraft Luna 3 photographed the dark side of the Moon in 1959. Mariner 2, an American space probe, was the first to visit another planet when it reached Venus three years later. In 1966, Luna 9 made the first soft landing on the Moon.

Luna 9 lander

Key events

1958
In response to the Soviet Sputnik 1, the US launched their first space satellite, Explorer 1, which sent back signals to Earth for 105 days.

1962
Astronaut John Glenn, inside a Mercury spacecraft, became the first American to orbit Earth, spending 4 hours, 35 minutes in space.

1965
Soviet astronaut Alexey Leonov left his Voskhod 2 spacecraft to perform the first ever spacewalk. He was tethered to the craft and the walk lasted 12 minutes.

The Apollo missions

The USA made manned exploration of the Moon their major goal. Six of the seven Apollo missions (1969–1972) managed to each place two astronauts on the lunar surface using a lunar module, with a third astronaut in the command module orbiting the Moon and awaiting their return. The missions, followed by millions of people on Earth, returned 382 kg (840 lb) of Moon rock and soil for analysis.

Apollo 11 launches

In 1969, the world's largest, most powerful launch vehicle, the Saturn V, blasted off carrying the Apollo 11 spacecraft. The 110.6-m- (363-ft-) tall rocket weighed 2.9 million kg (6.3 million lb) and featured 11 different rocket engines in three stages, which each fell away when their fuel was exhausted, reducing weight. The first stage's engines used at lift-off generated 3.47 million kg (7.6 million lb) of thrust.

First people on the Moon

American astronauts Neil Armstrong and Edwin "Buzz" Aldrin became the first humans to set foot on the Moon on 20 July 1969 during the Apollo 11 mission. The lunar module in which they descended to the Moon spent 21 hours on the lunar surface.

Lunar rovers

Carried on the Apollo 15, 16, and 17 missions, lunar rovers could transport two astronauts plus equipment over the Moon's surface at a maximum speed of 8 km/h (13 mph). A pair of 36-volt batteries powered an electric motor on each wheel of the rover.

Joint mission

In 1975, the space race ended as the USA and the Soviet Union co-operated to dock a Soviet Soyuz spacecraft with an American Apollo module. A crew of five astronauts performed experiments during the 44 hours of docking.

Apollo 11 launches from the Kennedy Space Center, Cape Canaveral, USA, 1969

1970

The Soviet craft Lunokhod 1 became the first successful space rover. It travelled 10,540 m (34,580 ft) across the Moon's surface.

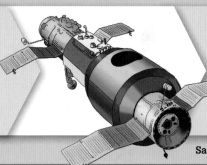

Salyut 1

1971

The first space station, Salyut 1, was launched by the Soviet Union. It orbited Earth for 175 days. Space stations provide long-term bases for astronauts in space.

1972

American astronaut Eugene Cernan, commander of Apollo 17, was the last person to stand on the Moon. No one has visited since.

1970 ▶ 1975

The first space station, Salyut 1, was launched in 1971. A crew of three cosmonauts (Soviet astronauts) spent 23 days on board.

1971
Orbiting Mars
NASA's Mariner 9 became the first spacecraft to orbit another planet when it reached Mars. The unmanned craft sent back 7,329 photos of approximately 85 per cent of the Martian surface, and discovered the Solar System's largest volcano, Olympus Mons.

1971
First CT Scan
A scanner developed by English engineer Godfrey Hounsfield took the first computerized tomography (CT) human brain scan, in London, UK. CT scanners take X-ray images of a part of the body. A computer assembles these to form a complete, sometimes three-dimensional, image.

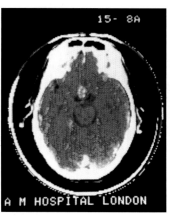

CT scan from a hospital in Wimbledon, UK, 1972

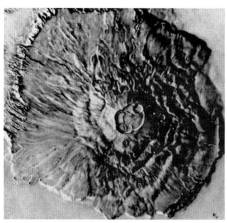

Olympus Mons (as seen by Mariner 9), which is 2.5 times the height of Mount Everest

1970
Earth Day
Communities across the USA came together on 22 April to celebrate Earth Day for the first time. Around 20 million Americans gathered in rallies and events held in more than 12,000 schools and colleges to raise awareness of environmental issues.

1970

1970
Boeing 747 enters service
The Boeing 747 became the first wide-bodied jet airliner to start ferrying passengers. Its 70.6-m- (231-ft-) long fuselage could accommodate up to ten seats in a row plus two aisles (walkways), giving it a maximum capacity of 550 passengers. More than 1,500 Boeing 747 planes would be built.

The first Boeing 747 with its four large turbofan jet engines in Washington, USA.

Taking to the skies
See pages 162–163

1971
Microprocessor
In 1971, a team at the technology company Intel developed the first commercial microprocessor, the Intel 4004. This small chip contained all the functions of a central processing unit of a computer. It went on sale on 15 November 1971.

Intel 4004

1973
Invention of Ethernet

American engineer Robert Metcalfe developed an effective way of linking computers together via cables to form a fast, local network. Called the Ethernet, this technology allowed computers to exchange data easily as well as use the same printers or storage devices. Ethernet-based networks would become popular.

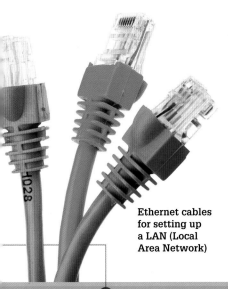

Ethernet cables for setting up a LAN (Local Area Network)

1974   OZONE HOLE

Scientists from the University of California, USA, warned that chlorofluorocarbons (CFCs), chemicals used to make aerosol propellants and coolant liquids in refrigerators, might be depleting the atmosphere's ozone layer. This would allow the Sun's harmful ultraviolet (UV) rays to reach Earth's surface.

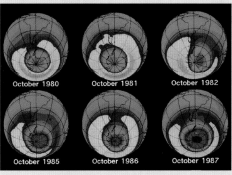

October 1980   October 1981   October 1982
October 1985   October 1986   October 1987

A hole in the ozone layer (purple) grew over a 13-year period, from 1979–1992.

Ozone layer blocks most UV rays 20–30 km (12–18 miles) above Earth's surface.

CFCs deplete ozone layer.

More UV rays reach Earth's surface through a hole in the ozone layer.

Ozone layer

Ozone is pure oxygen. However, its molecules have three atoms each (O_3) rather than two (O_2). A layer of ozone in the atmosphere blocks UV rays, but CFCs destroy ozone molecules. Over-exposure to UV rays can severely harm life on Earth.

1975 ▶▶

1973
First portable mobile phone

Produced by a team from the electronic communication company Motorola and led by American engineer Martin Cooper, the first prototype mobile phone, called the DynaTAC model, was unveiled in 1973. It was 23 cm (9 in) tall, weighed 1.1 kg (2.42 lb), and offered a talk-time of 20 minutes. Cooper made the first call on the phone to his rival Joel Engel at Bell Labs.

Martin Cooper with the original mobile phone, which held 30 electronic circuit boards inside

1974
Early ancestor

American palaeontologist Donald Johanson discovered the fossil remains of a human ancestor – the oldest known relative at the time – that walked upright on two legs. The specimen, nicknamed "Lucy", was found in Ethiopia and stood around 109 cm (42.9 in) tall. Classified as the early human species *Australopithecus afarensis*, she was dated as living around 3.2 million years ago.

Skull of "Lucy"

1973
CGI film

Computer-generated imagery (CGI) was used in a major motion picture for the first time in the science fiction film, *Westworld*, starring Yul Brynner. The graphics showed images as blocky pixels to depict the world as seen by a robot gunfighter inhabiting a Wild West theme park in the film.

Rubik's cube

The popular Rubik's Cube puzzle was invented by Hungarian architect, Erno Rubik in 1974. There are about 43 quintillion (43 followed by 18 zeros) ways that the cube's 54 coloured squares can be rearranged.

Classic Rubik's cube with nine squares on each side

1975 ▶ 1980

Lens sends light to the CCD.

CCD (charge-coupled device) converts light into electric charges, which are then turned into digital data.

1977
First MRI scan
The first full-body Magnetic Resonance Imaging (MRI) scan was carried out on a human patient by American physician Raymond Vahan Damadian. MRI uses powerful magnetic fields and radio waves to produce detailed pictures of the inside of the human body.

1975
First digital camera
American engineer Steve Sasson invented the first digital camera while working at Kodak. Powered by 16 rechargeable batteries, this 3.6 kg (7.9 lb) camera produced grainy black-and-white images with a resolution of 100 × 100 pixels. It took 23 seconds to shoot one image, which was then stored on a digital cassette tape. Digital cameras store images as digital data in memory rather than physically on film.

Steve Sasson's digital camera

1977
Fibre-optic phone calls
The first live telephone calls sent along optical fibres were transmitted by General Telephone and Electronics Corporation in California, USA. Signals travel as light down the optical fibres, which can carry more information and over longer distances than copper wires and without loss of quality.

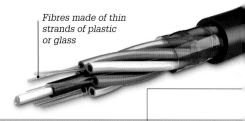

Fibres made of thin strands of plastic or glass

1975

This supercomputer consumed 110 kilowatts of power (as much as used at the time by 8–10 homes).

1976
Supercomputers
The first supercomputer, Cray 1, was designed by American engineer Seymour Cray and sold to Los Alamos National Laboratory, USA, in 1976. This high-performance machine was the world's fastest computer until 1982. Supercomputers are used for complicated data-heavy tasks, such as weather forecasting and code-breaking.

1976
Landing on Mars
NASA's Viking 1 and Viking 2 spacecraft became the first space probes to successfully land on Mars and investigate its surface. The two landers were each equipped with cameras and a robotic arm to take samples of the planet's soil.

Apple 1
The first Apple computer was hand-built by American inventor Steve Wozniak and went on sale in 1976 for US $666.66. Users needed their own case, keyboard, power supply, and video display to enjoy a fully working home computer.

Cray 1 supercomputer

Padded, circular seat concealed large power supply.

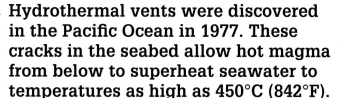

Hydrothermal vents were discovered in the Pacific Ocean in 1977. These cracks in the seabed allow hot magma from below to superheat seawater to temperatures as high as 450°C (842°F).

In 1977, James Elliot, Jessica Mink, and Edward Dunham discover that the planet Uranus has rings just like Saturn.

Louise Brown, aged two, plays at her home in Bristol, UK

1978

First test tube baby

Louise Brown from England became the first baby conceived using IVF (in vitro fertilization). During IVF, an egg cell is removed from a woman's ovaries and fertilized with a male sperm cell in a laboratory. The fertilized egg, known as an embryo, is then returned to the woman's womb to grow and develop. IVF has since helped millions of couples have children.

1979

Reaching Saturn

Launched in 1973, NASA's spacecraft Pioneer 11 became the first space probe to fly past Saturn. Travelling just 21,000 km (13,048 miles) above the planet's atmosphere, the probe discovered two new moons and a new ring around the planet.

Artist's impression of Pioneer 11 passing by Saturn

1980 ▶▶

1978

Early fossil footprints

British archaeologist Mary Leakey reported the discovery of fossilized footprints made by two-legged creatures more than 3.6 million years ago. Found in Laetoli, Tanzania, a trail of some 70 footprints were made in volcanic ash that hardened into rock. They showed how our predecessors walked upright far earlier than previously thought.

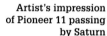

Wingspan of 29.77 m (97.6 ft)

Gossamer Albatross crosses the English Channel

Taking to the skies
See pages 162–163

1979

Channel crossing

The *Gossamer Albatross* aircraft made the first human-powered flight across the English Channel. It was piloted on its 35.7 km (22.1 mile) journey by American cyclist and pilot Bryan Allen, who pedalled to turn a single, large propeller. The plane was made of polystyrene, carbon fibre tubes, and other ultra-light materials, and weighed just 32 kg (70.5 lb).

Part of the 24-m- (78.7-ft-) long trail of footprints found at Laetoli, Tanzania

1980 ▶ 1985

In 1983, scientists defined the metre quite precisely as the distance light travels in a vacuum in $\frac{1}{299792458}$ of a second.

1981
Artificial skin

American scientists John Burke and Ioannis Yanas invented artificial skin to treat burn victims. They made it using collagen from sharks and cows, along with silicone rubber. The material formed a framework known as a scaffold over a burn or wound, onto which the body could regenerate its own new skin cells.

Artificial skin is removed from a culture dish in which it takes around three weeks to grow.

1982
First CD player

Japanese company Sony launched the CDP-101, the first CD (compact disc) player. It used plastic discs encoded with digital audio data that were read by a laser and converted into sound. CDs were later used to store other forms of data, such as computer software.

1980
Smallpox wiped out

In 1980, the World Health Assembly declared that the lethal disease smallpox (see p.110) had been eliminated. Smallpox was contagious and often resulted in death or blindness. Some 50 million cases of the disease occurred each year in the 1950s, but global vaccination campaigns and public health initiatives helped get rid of the disease.

1980

1981
Reusable spacecraft

NASA introduced its first manned, reusable spacecraft with the test launch of the first space shuttle, *Columbia*. Shuttles were launched using rocket engines, but on their return, glided back to Earth and landed like aircraft. Space shuttles made 135 missions into space until the fleet's retirement in 2011.

46.8-m- (153.5-ft-) long external fuel tank was the only non-reusable part

Booster rockets

Space shuttle

1981
IBM PC launched

American technology company IBM introduced the 5150 computer, more commonly known as the IBM PC (personal computer). It sold rapidly to both offices and the general public. Hundreds of other companies produced additional hardware and programs compatible with the PC's central software, the Microsoft Disk Operating System (MS DOS).

1980–1991 ALVAREZ HYPOTHESIS

American scientists Luis Alvarez and his son Walter Alvarez found high levels of iridium – an element common in asteroids but not on Earth – in rocks that were 65 million years old. This led them to propose that dinosaurs died out at that time because of an asteroid impact. This would have produced enough dust to block out the Sun and cause major climate change.

Artist's depiction of the asteroid crashing into Earth

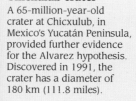

Chicxulub crater
A 65-million-year-old crater at Chicxulub, in Mexico's Yucatán Peninsula, provided further evidence for the Alvarez hypothesis. Discovered in 1991, the crater has a diameter of 180 km (111.8 miles).

Artist's impression of the Chicxulub crater

1984

First untethered space walk
NASA astronauts Bruce McCandless and Robert Stewart left the space shuttle *Challenger* for a space walk – the first untethered space walk for any astronaut – using a Manned Maneuvering Unit (MMU). The MMU was a jet pack containing 11.8 kg (26 lb) of nitrogen fuel, which powered 24 small jet thrusters to move each astronaut through space without a cable tether keeping them attached to the spacecraft.

Astronaut Bruce McCandless on his spacewalk

1985 ▶▶

1983

Handheld cellular phone
More than a decade after a prototype was unveiled (see p.215), the first portable cellular mobile phone – the Motorola DynaTAC 8000X – went on sale. It was priced at US $3995 and weighed 790 g (1.74 lb). It had a 10-hour charge on its battery, and gave its users a talk-time of up to 30 minutes. DynaTAC phones would stay on sale until 1994.

Motorola DynaTAC 8000X

1984

HIV identified
American biomedical researcher Robert Gallo and French virologist Luc Montagnier announced the discovery of HIV (human immunodeficiency virus), which is responsible for the deadly disease AIDS (Acquired Immune Deficiency Syndrome). HIV attacks the body's immune system and weakens a person's ability to fight disease and infections.

1984

Submersible *Nautile* launched
The French deep-sea submersible *Nautile* was launched in 1984. Capable of diving up to 6,000 m (19,685 ft) below sea level, it later filmed the wreckage of the British ship *Titanic* 3,800 m (12,467 ft) underwater, and helped recover more than 1,800 items from the wreck. *Nautile* also salvaged flight recorders of sunken aircraft.

Titanium hull protects passengers.

Cameras and lights

Robot arms move and grip to collect samples.

Changing climate

The blanket of gases that form Earth's atmosphere performs many valuable functions, from containing oxygen for respiration to shielding life from the Sun's harmful ultraviolet (UV) rays. It also traps heat, warming the planet's surface in a process called the greenhouse effect. In the past 200 years, a change to the balance of gases in the atmosphere has resulted in more heat being retained, causing global warming and climate change.

> **"Climate change is no longer some far-off problem... it is happening now."**
>
> US President Barack Obama, 2015

Enhanced greenhouse gases

The enhanced greenhouse effect is caused by an increasing build-up of greenhouse gases in the atmosphere, which trap more heat than in the past, causing temperature rises on Earth. Temperatures will continue to increase if the level of greenhouse gases continues to grow.

Shifting balance

Gases such as methane, carbon dioxide, and sulfur hexafluoride are known as greenhouse gases, and help create the greenhouse effect. Emissions caused by a booming human population and increasing impacts from industry, farming, and environmental damage have led to a rise in the concentrations of these gases in the atmosphere.

Greenhouse gas emissions

Carbon dioxide is the most common greenhouse gas emitted, with some 36 billion tonnes sent into the atmosphere each year. This gas is released from industry, from burning fossil fuels (natural gas, oil, and coal) in vehicle engines, and as part of electricity generation.

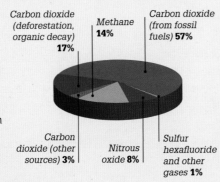

Carbon dioxide (deforestation, organic decay) **17%**

Methane **14%**

Carbon dioxide (from fossil fuels) **57%**

Carbon dioxide (other sources) **3%**

Nitrous oxide **8%**

Sulfur hexafluoride and other gases **1%**

Many causes

The burning of fossil fuels in power stations (left) causes substantial carbon dioxide emissions. Other causes of emissions include cattle, which produce methane, and deforestation, which involves removing large numbers of trees that would normally absorb carbon dioxide.

Greenhouse gases in the atmosphere, showing the effect of increased gases (below, left)

The Sun's energy is absorbed by Earth.

Human activity causes an increase in the level of greenhouse gases.

Enhanced greenhouse gases

More greenhouse gases cause more radiation from Earth's surface to be absorbed and radiated back to Earth.

Key events

1859

Irish physicist John Tyndall discovered how some gases block infrared radiation and suggested that changes in the concentration of atmospheric gases could affect the climate.

1958

American scientist Charles David Keeling began a long-term study of carbon dioxide in the atmosphere. His Keeling Curve graph showed carbon dioxide rising from 310 parts per million (ppm) in 1958 to over 400 in 2015.

1970

The National Oceanic and Atmospheric Administration (NOAA) was founded in the USA. It would become the world's leading funder of climate research.

1978

NASA launched the Scanning Multichannel Microwave Radiometer (SMMR) on the Nimbus satellite, to monitor sea ice in the Arctic and Antarctic.

Nimbus 7 satellite

Warming up

Climate monitoring has revealed evidence of average annual temperature increases, with 15 of the 16 warmest years on record occurring since 2001. The map below shows the average annual temperatures of 2015, which were 0.87°C (1.57°F) above the average for the era 1951–1980.

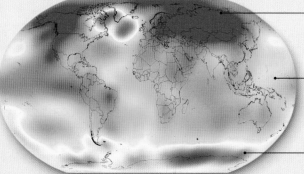

Red: temperature a few degrees above the 1951–1980 average

Orange-yellow: temperature just above the 1951–1980 average

Blue: temperature cooler than the 1951–1980 average

Melting away

Melting ice sheets and glaciers are leading to a loss of habitat for animals that live on the ice, as well as rising sea levels, which are a flood threat to low-lying lands. Arctic sea ice in the summer has dropped from 7.83 million sq km (3.02 million sq miles) in 1980 to 4.63 million sq km (1.78 million sq miles) in 2015.

Some radiation from Earth passes through the atmosphere into space.

Some radiation is absorbed by greenhouse gases and radiated back to Earth.

Natural greenhouse gases

Extreme weather

Global warming is thought to be responsible for an increase in extreme weather events. These include heat waves, heavy rains, and tropical cyclones such as Hurricane Isaac (left), which killed 41 people and caused more than US $2 billion of damage in southern USA, in 2012.

Taking action

Action is being taken at a number of levels to tackle climate change, from international agreements on reducing greenhouse gas emissions to advances in more energy-efficient buildings and technologies, reforestation, and switching away from power generation and vehicles that burn fossil fuels. Individuals can contribute in many ways too, such as:

★ Switch off unnecessary electrical items
★ Reduce dependence on cars by cycling, walking, or using public transport
★ Use green energy options, such as wind or solar power
★ Use energy-saving devices, such as CFL bulbs
★ Plant more trees

1988

American professor James Hansen popularized the term "global warming" when reporting to the US Senate that the average global temperature is rising due to the greenhouse effect.

1997

The Kyoto Protocol (an international treaty to bring countries together to reduce global warming) committed developed nations to reduce emissions of key gases responsible for global warming.

2015

NOAA and other bodies reported that 2015 was the hottest year since climate records began in the 19th century.

2016

The Paris Agreement was signed by 180 nations. It aims to hold back global warming to "well below 2°C or 3.6°F" above pre-industrial levels.

1985 ▶ 1990

📢 **The first version of Microsoft's Windows operating system, called Windows 1.0, was launched on 20 November 1985.**

1985

Buckyball (C₆₀)

Working at Rice University, Houston, USA, British chemist Sir Harold Kroto and American chemists James R Heath, Sean O'Brien, Robert Curl, and Richard Smalley discovered buckminsterfullerene. Better known as C_{60} or buckyball, this football-shaped molecule consists of only carbon atoms. It is an allotrope – a different physical form – of the element carbon.

Computer-generated diagram of a buckyball molecule

1986

Disaster at Chernobyl

The worst nuclear disaster occurred at the Chernobyl nuclear power station in Ukraine when one of the four nuclear reactors at the site exploded. The blast released 400 times more radiation into the atmosphere than the atomic bomb dropped on Hiroshima, Japan, in 1945.

Abandoned school in a contaminated area near the Chernobyl disaster

1986

Challenger disaster

The Space Shuttle *Challenger* exploded just 73 seconds after its launch from the Kennedy Space Center, Florida, USA, killing all seven crew members on board. A faulty seal in one of the solid rocket boosters was responsible for the disaster. Other space shuttles were grounded for 32 months following the tragedy.

▶▶ **1985**

1987

The first statin

After long medical trials, a statin called Lovastatin was approved by the Food and Drug Administration (FDA) in the USA. Statins are drugs that reduce the production of certain fatty substances in the body, including LDLs (low-density lipoproteins) – a type of cholesterol that can clog blood vessels and increase the risk of heart disease.

Lovastatin is found in oyster mushrooms and some other fungi.

1986

Atomic force microscope

German physicist Gerd Binnig, American physicist Calvin Quate, and Swiss professor Christoph Gerber invented the atomic force microscope. This powerful microscope uses an incredibly small probe to measure and make images of a sample's surface down to nanometres (billionths of a metre) in scale.

1986

Mir Space Station

Russian Space Station *Mir* became the first space station to be assembled in Earth's orbit. It was 19 m (62 ft) long and could house three crew members permanently, with larger numbers accommodated for short periods. During its 15 years in orbit, 104 astronauts visited the station, including cosmonaut (Russian astronaut) Valeri Polyakov, who spent a record 437.75 days on board.

 📢 **The world's first laser human eye surgery was performed by German ophthalmologist Theo Seiler in 1987.**

1989

Ivory ban

The Convention on International Trade in Endangered Species (CITES) instituted a worldwide ban on the trade in ivory. The ban came about in response to a rise in poachers killing elephants for their tusks, which halved the African elephant population between 1979 and 1989.

Burning elephant tusks seized by authorities in Nairobi, Kenya, 1995

1989

Arranging atoms

A team of scientists at IBM used a scanning tunnelling microscope (STM) to arrange 35 atoms of the element xenon on a chilled crystal of the element nickel to spell out IBM. Considered a landmark in the field of nanotechnology, this was the first time that individual atoms had been ordered and positioned on a flat surface.

Nanotechnology
See pages
244–245

1988

The Morris Worm

The Morris Worm became the first computer virus to infect computers across the Internet. Written by a university student, Robert Tappan Morris, the virus infected as many as 10 per cent of all Internet-connected computers at the time, causing them to slow down or halt until it was removed.

1989

Game Boy launched

Nintendo's handheld computer gaming machine, the Game Boy, was launched in Japan. Each Game Boy came with the falling blocks puzzle game, *Tetris*. Despite its small 6.6-cm- (3-in-) greyscale screen, more than 118 million units of the Game Boy – and a colour-screen variant called the Game Boy Color – were sold.

1990 ▶▶

1986   3-D PRINTING

Three-dimensional (3-D) printing includes a range of processes in which thin layers of metal, plastic, or some other material are "printed" (laid down) on top of one another until a 3-D object is formed. The directions for the precise shape of each layer are stored in a computer's memory. 3-D printing allows objects to be made quickly and on demand.

Charles W. Hull holding a 3-D printed mask of his face in 2000.

The first 3-D printer

American engineer Charles W Hull received a patent for his 3-D printer, the SLA-1, in 1986. The printer used lasers to build objects from polymer resin according to instructions from a computer.

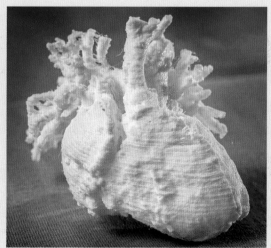

Printing parts

3-D printing is now used in industry to make prototypes and working parts for machines and vehicles. For instance, the Airbus A350 WXB airliner contains more than 1,000 3-D printed parts. Artificial body parts such as dental crowns, bone grafts, and prosthetic limbs can also be 3-D printed.

A model of a 3-D printed heart. Models of organs can be 3-D printed to help doctors plan and explain complicated surgeries.

Stephen Hawking

Born on 8 January 1942, English physicist Stephen Hawking became fascinated by space and theories about its nature and phenomena. Battling through adversity, he has made many brilliant contributions to astronomy and our understanding of the Universe.

A shocking diagnosis

In 1963, while studying at the University of Cambridge, UK, Hawking was diagnosed with a disease called ALS (Amyotrophic Lateral Sclerosis), which destroys nerve cells. Initially given less than three years to live, he survived, although he was confined to a wheelchair from 1969 and lost his voice in 1985. Hawking communicates using a computer linked to a speech synthesizer that produces artificial speech.

Investigating black holes

Hawking began researching the incredibly dense remains of collapsed stars known as black holes. He suggested that they could be viewed as a smaller version of the Big Bang (the way many scientists believe the Universe began from a single point), but working in reverse.

Hawking radiation

Scientists had thought that absolutely nothing could escape the immense gravitational pull of a black hole. However, in 1974, Hawking showed, in theory, how matter in the form of sub-atomic particles could be emitted from a black hole. This emission became known as Hawking radiation. This theory means that black holes do not exist forever but gradually fade as they lose their energy.

A theory of everything

Hawking was the Lucasian Professor of Mathematics at Cambridge University from 1979 to 2009, a post once held by English physicist Isaac Newton. His later research sought a single, unifying theory to explain how the Universe works at both its biggest and smallest levels.

University life
Hawking (waving a handkerchief) with his fellow boat club members at the University of Oxford, UK, in 1961. He studied physics and chemistry at Oxford before moving to Cambridge in 1962 to study cosmology – the study of the origins and development of the Universe.

Event horizon
Hawking's research on black holes enhanced the idea of a boundary (the edge of the "bubble" in the image above) around a black hole called an event horizon. Light or matter (yellow) crossing this boundary from the outside is pulled into the black hole by its incredibly strong gravity.

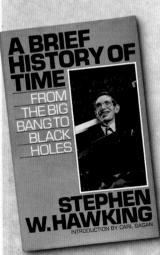

Bestselling author
Hawking has authored hundreds of papers and more than a dozen books, including his 1988 bestseller, A Brief History of Time. This popular science guide to the Universe sold more than 10 million copies and was translated into 40 languages.

> **"My goal is simple. It is a complete understanding of the Universe, why it is as it is and why it exists at all."**
>
> Stephen Hawking, quoted in the book *Stephen Hawking's Universe*, 1985

Zero gravity
In 2007, Hawking experienced zero gravity (weightlessness in space) on board a modified Boeing 727 aircraft that dives and climbs steeply to create a short period of weightlessness. "The zero-G part was wonderful... I could have gone on and on", he exclaimed afterwards.

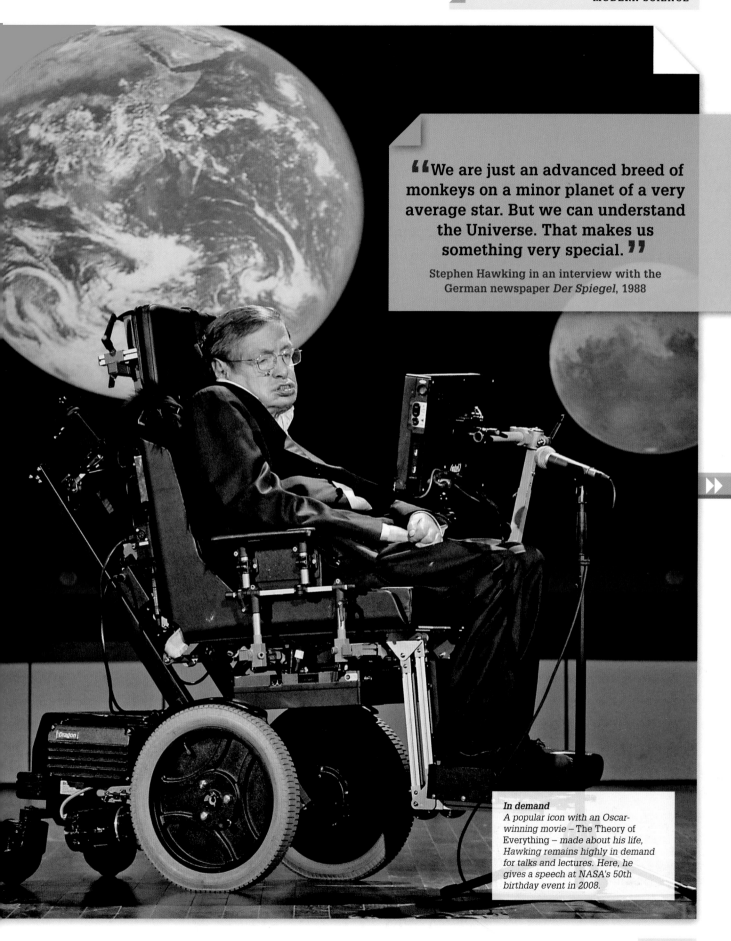

❝We are just an advanced breed of monkeys on a minor planet of a very average star. But we can understand the Universe. That makes us something very special.**❞**

Stephen Hawking in an interview with the German newspaper *Der Spiegel*, 1988

In demand
A popular icon with an Oscar-winning movie – The Theory of Everything – made about his life, Hawking remains highly in demand for talks and lectures. Here, he gives a speech at NASA's 50th birthday event in 2008.

1990 ▶ 1995

Artist's impression of Kepler 22b, an exoplanet, which is around 2.4 times the size of Earth

 In 1992, British engineer Neil Papworth sent the first SMS (short-message service) text, which read "Merry Christmas".

Preserved remains of Ötzi

1991
Frozen mummy
The oldest, frozen, mummified human was discovered in the Ötztal Alps on the Italy-Austria border. Dated as 5,300 years old and later nicknamed Ötzi, the figure was so well-preserved that scientists could study its stomach contents and the 61 tattoos on its body.

1992
Exoplanets
Polish astronomer Aleksander Wolszczan and Canadian astronomer Dale Frail discovered evidence of two planets orbiting a pulsar (a rotating neutron star). These were the first confirmed exoplanets – planets found outside the Solar System. More than 3,300 exoplanets had been discovered by July 2016.

1990

1990

Hubble Space Telescope launched
Taken into space on board the Space Shuttle *Discovery*, the 13.2-m- (43.3-ft-) long Hubble Space Telescope would transform our understanding of space, discovering new stars, galaxies, and moons, and sending back more than 700,000 images (see pp.230–231).

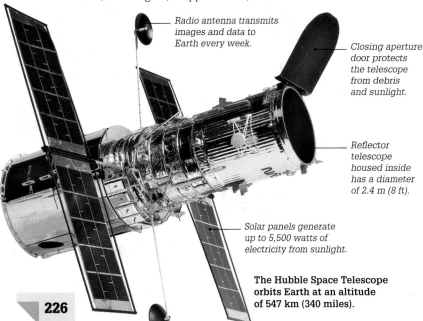

Radio antenna transmits images and data to Earth every week.

Closing aperture door protects the telescope from debris and sunlight.

Reflector telescope housed inside has a diameter of 2.4 m (8 ft).

Solar panels generate up to 5,500 watts of electricity from sunlight.

The Hubble Space Telescope orbits Earth at an altitude of 547 km (340 miles).

1989–1993   WORLD WIDE WEB

In 1989, British computer programmer Sir Tim Berners-Lee founded the World Wide Web (WWW) – a global information system accessed via the Internet. It consists of websites made up of webpages connected by hyperlinks. These enable users to navigate easily between webpages and documents. The WWW is free for anyone to use.

"It was... hard explaining the Web before people just got used to it, because they didn't even have words like click and jump..."

Tim Berners-Lee

1993

Wind-up radio

British inventor Trevor Graham Baylis invented the wind-up radio, the first radio that could run without batteries. This helped people who didn't have access to electricity or batteries to use a radio. When fully wound up, an internal spring stored enough energy to run the radio for about 20 minutes.

BayGen Freeplay wind-up radio, 1995

The handle winds up a spring, whose energy is then converted into electric power.

 In 1994, a team led by American medical researcher Jeffrey Friedman discovered leptin, a hormone (regulatory chemical) that helps control appetite.

1993

First smartphone

IBM Simon was released as the first phone with "smart" functions: applications, email access, and a touchscreen. The 20-cm- (7.87-in-) tall phone weighed 510 g (18 oz) and could be plugged into a regular phone landline. It featured applications for accessing news, seeing maps, and sketching.

A connected world
See pages 228–229

Single-colour LCD display with touch input

Stylus used to navigate the touchscreen

Firm, fresh Flavr Savr tomatoes

1994

First genetically modified food

The Flavr Savr tomato was the first genetically modified (GM) food to go on sale to the public. These tomatoes were modified to slow their ripening process, which delayed softening and rotting.

1995

Early days

Berners-Lee placed the first web server online on 25 December 1990 at CERN, Switzerland. It presented website pages to users who requested them via a web browser program running on their computers. Berners-Lee also developed HTML, a language to encode, or mark up, webpages so that they could be displayed by different computers.

1993

First webcam

In 1991, researchers at the University of Cambridge, UK, rigged up an early digital camera to take photos of the coffee pot outside their computer laboratory, and to display the images on computers connected to their local computer network. In 1993, when web browsers had become capable of displaying images, the camera was connected to the WWW – becoming the first webcam – and remained on the Web until 2001.

1994

Comet crash

The comet Shoemaker–Levy 9 was discovered in 1993, and the following year, it crashed into Jupiter's atmosphere in the first observed collision between Solar System bodies. As it broke apart, some of its fragments reached speeds of 216,000 km/h (134,216 mph). Scientists were able to learn more about comets and Jupiter's atmosphere.

Rediscovered species

The Gilbert's potoroo, thought to be extinct, was rediscovered in southwestern Australia, in 1994. The marsupial's population in the wild numbers under 100 creatures.

A connected world

Giant strides in computing and communications technology have enabled machines to share information, and as a result, billions of people all over the world are connected. Much of this now occurs via computer networks, which link computers and digital devices such as smartphones, allowing people to communicate with one another. Early networks were wired, needing physical connections, but wireless networks are now common.

The Internet

The largest network of linked computers on Earth, the Internet has grown in speed, availability, and number of useful applications, from email and web browsing to social media and live streaming of sound and video. Today, Internet signals are ferried by fibre optic data cables, by satellites, by telephone land lines, and wirelessly. This map shows Internet connections between cities in 2011, with the brightest areas having the most connections.

This smartphone is using an app to display facts about the landmarks being viewed.

Smartphones

These are powerful portable computing platforms that run sophisticated applications (apps). Smartphone apps enable many tasks to be performed on the move, from GPS mapping and video streaming to music editing and foreign language translation.

Going wireless

 WiFi
WiFi enables billions of devices to connect to the Internet wirelessly, within a set range via a computer network, which usually requires a password to access.

 RFID
Radio-frequency identification (RFID) uses radio waves to track objects, reading information stored on tiny RFID tags attached to an item.

 Bluetooth
Bluetooth enables communication over short distances using ultra high frequency (UHF) radio waves. Devices may use bluetooth to connect to wireless printers or headphones.

 NFC
Near field communications (NFC) allows contactless payments and other exchanges of data when digital devices are placed close to each other.

Key events

1969

The first messages were sent between two US computers over ARPANET, a precursor to the Internet. By 1972, 24 hosts (computer systems connected to the network) were on ARPANET, including NASA.

1974

American computer scientist Vinton Cerf and electrical engineer Bob Kahn developed Transmission Control Protocol (TCP), a set of rules that allow computers to send packets of data to each other over the Internet.

1990

The first Internet search engine, called Archie, was created by Canadian computer programmers. It searched through the indexes of FTP (File Transfer Protocol) sites looking for specific files.

1996

The Nokia 9000 Communicator was released. It was one of the first mobile phones with Internet access, enabling web browsing and email.

Nokia 9000 Communicator

Wearable computing

Shrinking digital technology has made it possible to build computers into clothing, jewellery, and lightweight headsets to give convenient access to information, monitor health and fitness, and even create 3-D game experience. Many wearables, such as smartwatches and pendants, usually work together with a smartphone or tablet computer carried by the user.

Google Glass
This innovative, head-worn, voice-controlled display projects information in front of a user's eyes for hands-free computing and communication.

Fitness trackers
Sensors inside this gadget measure the speed, distance, and duration of an exercise undertaken by a person to give feedback on particular fitness targets.

Smartwatches
These wrist-worn devices run apps such as those notifying a user about a message, or pointing out the user's real-time position on a map.

Lights can be programmed, or switched on, off, or dimmed.

Music can be selected and played in any or all rooms.

Electronic locks can be checked, locked, and unlocked.

Security cameras can be made to stream images of house interiors.

Internet of Things
It is not just people who can connect to each other using computers and smartphones. The Internet of Things (IoT) connects many devices – from heating systems to vehicles – over the Internet, allowing them to be accessed remotely. The devices communicate with each other, leading to fully controllable smart homes.

Home heating and cooling can be adjusted.

Using an app to connect to devices remotely

1997
The WiFi standard (a set of specifications) was introduced for wireless network connections. The first WiFi routers (devices that control flow of data) for personal computers appeared two years later.

2008
The first version of the Android operating system for phones and tablet computers was released. By 2016, two-thirds of all mobile devices would be powered by Android.

2013
Amazon and DHL tested their first delivery drones. These unmanned aerial vehicles could quickly deliver essential products to hard-to-reach places.

2015
More than half of all of the 100 billion searches on Google each month were from mobile devices such as smartphones and tablet computers instead of desktop computers.

Delivery drone

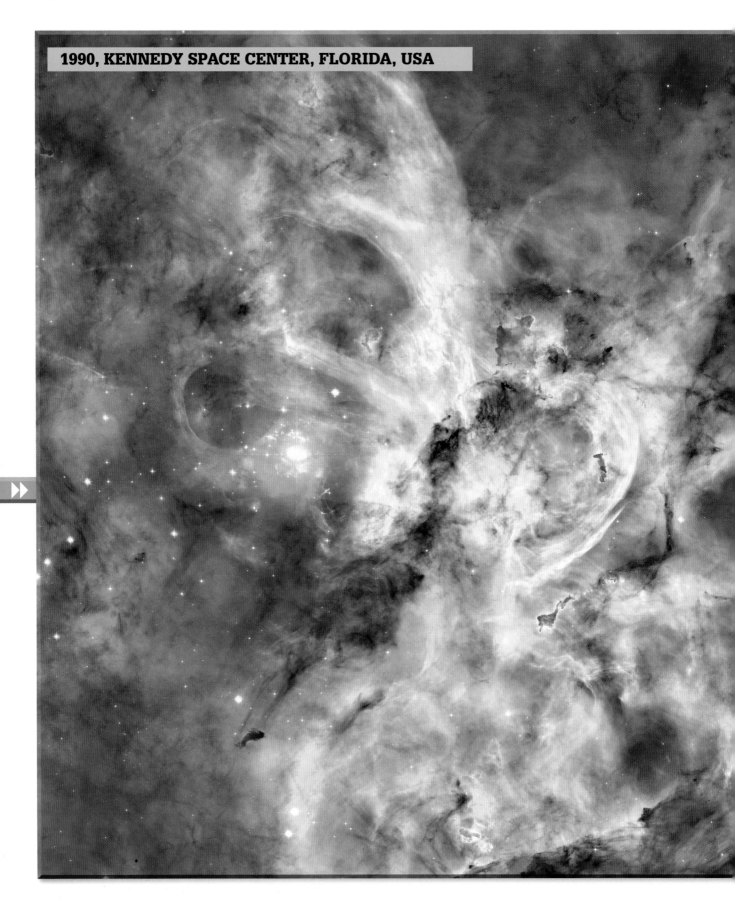

"... with the faintest nebulae that can be detected with the greatest telescopes, we arrive at the frontier of the known universe."

Edwin Hubble, *The Realm of the Nebulae*, 1936

Snaps from space

Hubble, the world's first large space telescope, was launched in 1990 and orbits Earth at an altitude of 547 km (340 miles). Free of the distorting effects of Earth's atmosphere, the images it collects from light gathered in by its mirror are between five and 20 times sharper than those obtained from the ground. This has enabled scientists to detect phenomenally distant nebulae (clouds of hot gas and dust from which stars are made) and galaxies, some as far as 13.4 billion light years away. Hubble has made more than 1.2 million observations since its launch. It sends an average of 140 gigabytes (GB) of data back to Earth each week yet requires just 2,100 watts (W) of power, little more than an electric kettle.

The Carina Nebula's swirling clouds of gas, dust, and young, bright stars is highlighted in this composite of 44 images taken by Hubble. This nebula lies around 7,500 light years from Earth.

1995 ▸ 2000

El Niño phenomenon

El Niño is a warming of the ocean surface that periodically occurs in the tropical regions of the Pacific Ocean. It changes how winds move and, with it, rainfall patterns over much of the planet. In 1997–1998, the strongest El Niño on record resulted in an increase in extreme weather, including severe droughts in Southeast Asia and record rainfalls and flooding in South America.

1995

Galileo orbits Jupiter

NASA's Galileo space probe became the first one to orbit Jupiter. The probe discovered ammonia clouds in Jupiter's atmosphere, measured volcanic activity on Jupiter's moon, Io, and found evidence of saltwater under the surface of three other moons of Jupiter: Callisto, Ganymede, and Europa.

1996

First successful cloning of a mammal

Scientists at the Roslin Institute in Edinburgh, Scotland, created the first healthy mammal by cloning (making an identical copy of) a single cell from an adult sheep. Dolly the sheep was born in July 1996. Later she would give birth to three healthy litters of lambs.

Heavy flooding, caused by El Niño in 1997–1998, destroyed most of the houses in Chato Grande, Peru.

1995

1995   GLOBAL POSITIONING SYSTEM (GPS)

The Global Positioning System (GPS) started as a network of 24 satellites (now expanded to 31) that orbit Earth twice a day at an altitude of 20,200 km (12,552 miles). Groups of four satellites travel on the same orbital plane to provide comprehensive navigation coverage.

Satellite sends signal that includes a precise timestamp provided by its highly accurate on-board atomic clock.

Each satellite's signals take fractionally different times to reach a single receiver.

GPS receiver inside car measures the time it takes signals to arrive from each satellite to calculate precise position.

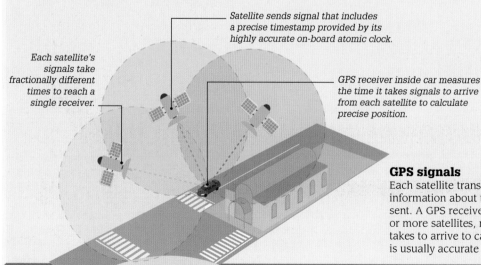

Satellite navigation

An in-car "sat nav" combines a GPS receiver with digital road maps and software to give a constantly updated location and to provide directions to destinations. Since 2000, car drivers and other civilian users have had access to a higher-accuracy GPS signal previously available only to the military.

GPS signals

Each satellite transmits radio signals encoded with information about the precise time the signal was sent. A GPS receiver gathers in the signals from three or more satellites, measuring the time each signal takes to arrive to calculate its precise location. This is usually accurate to within a handful of metres.

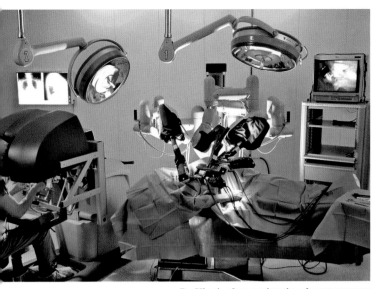

Da Vinci robot assists in a heart surgery

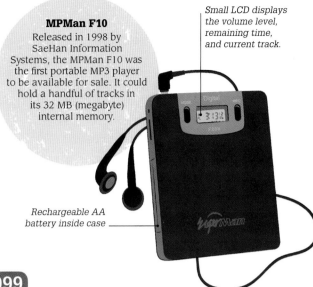

MPMan F10
Released in 1998 by SaeHan Information Systems, the MPMan F10 was the first portable MP3 player to be available for sale. It could hold a handful of tracks in its 32 MB (megabyte) internal memory.

Small LCD displays the volume level, remaining time, and current track.

Rechargeable AA battery inside case

1998

Da Vinci surgical assistant robot
The first heart bypass operation assisted by a surgical robot was performed at the Leipzig Heart Centre in Germany. Dr Friedrich-Wilhelm Mohr controlled a Da Vinci surgical robot and directed its robot arms, which held a camera and wielded surgical instruments with more accuracy than a human hand could manage.

1999

New hormone discovered
The discovery of a hormone called ghrelin was announced in 1999. Secreted by cells mostly in the stomach and the duodenum, but also elsewhere, ghrelin stimulates appetite and also promotes the storage of fat. More ghrelin is produced before meals and when a person is hungry than after meals when they are full.

2000 ▸▸

10.67-m- (35-ft-) long solar arrays convert sunlight into an average of 3 kilowatts of electricity

1999

Breitling Orbiter 3
Swiss aviator Bertrand Piccard and British aviator Brian Jones became the first people to circumnavigate Earth in a hot-air balloon. Their non-stop journey in the Breitling Orbiter 3 began in Switzerland and ended 40,814 km (25,361 miles) later when they landed in Egypt after 19 days and 21 hours. The 55-m- (180-ft-) tall hot-air envelope was maintained by six gas burners and also contained a cell filled with helium for extra lift.

Zarya provided storage and electrical power to other modules of the early space station.

Zarya (left) and Unity (right) unite successfully in space

Breitling Orbiter 3 over the Alps, 1999

1998

International Space Station is born
The first module of the International Space Station (ISS), a 19,000-kg- (41,888-lb-) functional cargo block (FCB) called *Zarya*, was ferried into space on board a Russian Proton-K rocket. In the same year, the first US module, *Unity*, was carried into space on board a space shuttle, before docking with *Zarya*.

 In 1997, Russian world chess champion Garry Kasparov lost to IBM's Deep Blue computer over a six-game contest.

Robotics

A robot is a type of smart, automated machine that can be programmed to perform different tasks, often with little or no supervision. Robots now perform a wide range of tasks, from cleaning skyscraper windows to assisting with surgical operations, sometimes with more accuracy or greater force than humans can manage. Robots are often found performing work that humans find unpleasant, repetitive, or impossible.

Working in factories

The first robot that worked in a factory was a Unimate, which handled red-hot metal castings at an American car-making factory in 1961. There are now more than 1.5 million robots in factories assembling products, welding, picking and packing objects with pinpoint precision, and spray-painting car bodies.

Military robots

Robots can make excellent security guards or roam ahead of human forces as expendable spies or scouts. Some seek out survivors in disaster areas, while others investigate danger zones such as minefields or toxic chemical spills.

Cameras send detailed views to the human bomb disposal team.

A RONS robot, designed by a company called Remotec, disposes of an unexploded bomb.

Robot uses a sensitive gripper to handle an unexploded shell.

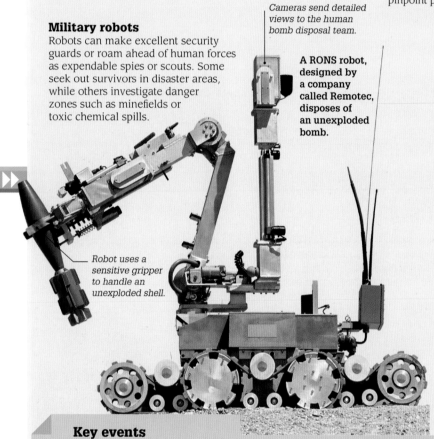

Robots in fiction

Robots emerged in science fiction before they existed in the real world. They are often portrayed as highly intelligent, thinking machines. In reality, robots need to be programmed by humans, although some can learn from their surroundings.

Robot from the science fiction film *Sky Captain and the World of Tomorrow*

Key events

1921
Czech playwright Karel Čapek popularized the term "robot" in a play called *R.U.R.* The term comes from the Czech *robota*, which means drudgery, or forced labour.

1966
Shakey became the first mobile robot able to navigate its way around a series of rooms, using cameras and sensors, in California, USA.

1975
A six-jointed, electric robot arm called Programmable Universal Manipulation Arm (PUMA) was devised by American inventor Victor Scheinman. It proved influential in industrial robot design.

1997
The Sojourner rover was the first robot to move around another planet (Mars) on its electric motor-driven wheels. It sent images from its cameras back to Earth.

Shakey

Eyes change colour to express emotions.

Key robotic components

- **Controller**
  The computer software and hardware that act as the brain of the robot, making decisions and instructing a robot's parts.

- **Sensors**
  Devices such as cameras, distance detectors, and GPS (Global Positioning System), which gather data for the controller.

- **End effectors**
  The parts of a robot that interact with its surroundings. These may include a gripper on an arm, which holds objects.

- **Drive system**
  The system used to power a robot's moving parts. It is usually electrical, pneumatic (operated by compressed gases) or hydraulic (operated by compressed liquid).

Multi-jointed hands with sensors enable robot to grasp small items.

Teaching robots

Robots need advanced hardware and programming to work with people as helpers, assistants, or tutors. The NAO (pronounced "now") robot, developed by Aldebaran Robotics in France, is a humanoid (has a human-like body) robot. It works as a customer assistant at a bank in Japan. The robot is able to link to the Internet by itself to seek out solutions to queries. More than 9,000 NAOs have been sold, mainly in education.

Gears linked to electric motors control limb movements.

NAO robot, 2015

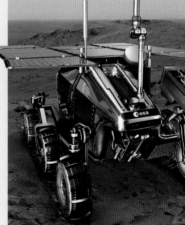

Robotic explorers

Space robots, such as the ExoMars rover (to be launched to Mars as early as 2020), explore places too hostile for humans – such as the Martian surface – and send findings back to Earth using radio signals. Robots explore Earth as well, from inside the narrow shafts of Ancient Egyptian pyramids to the deepest ocean beds.

1999

Sony launched AIBO (Artificial Intelligence Bot). These robotic dogs could be programmed to perform tasks and became popular in education.

2001

An unmanned aerial vehicle (UAV) called Global Hawk plotted its own course as it flew about 13,219 km (8,214 miles) from the USA to Australia.

2011

The Robonaut 2 humanoid robot was sent to the International Space Station. There, the two-armed robot was tested performing repetitive tasks, such as cleaning air filters.

2014

Roomba, a line of robotic vacuum cleaners, became the most common robots in the world. Since their launch in 2002, more than 10.5 million Roombas had been sold.

2000 ▸ 2005

2000

Millennium Seed Bank

This enormous store of seeds, along with partner banks around the world, was launched to conserve seed stocks in the face of any future disasters. The bank aimed to store seeds from 25 per cent of the world's plant species by the year 2020. By 2015, 1.98 billion seeds had already been collected under the scheme.

Seed jars, numbered and barcoded for identification, are stored in dark vaults at –20°C (–4°F)

2001

Segway

Invented by American scientist Dean Kamen, the Segway Personal Transporter (PT) was unveiled on TV. The two-wheeled, self-balancing machine senses shifts of the rider's weight to travel forwards or back. The prototype had a top speed of 20 km/h (12.4 mph) and was driven by two electric motors, which lasted up to 19 km (11.8 miles) on a single battery charge.

Young man rides a Segway PT

2001

First space tourist

American billionaire Dennis Tito became the first space tourist when he travelled to the International Space Station (ISS) in a Russian Soyuz spacecraft. Tito spent almost eight days on board the ISS and paid approximately US$ 20 million for the experience.

2000

Wikipedia, a free, online, user-generated encyclopedia, was launched in 2001 by Jimmy Wales and Larry Sanger.

2001

First tele-operation using robot

While in New York, USA, Canadian surgeon Dr Michel Gagner performed a long-distance medical operation on a female human patient in Strasbourg, France. Gagner controlled a Zeus robot surgical system from more than 6,000 km (3,728 miles) away to successfully remove the patient's gall bladder.

2000

First humanoid robot

Honda's Advanced Step in Innovative Mobility (ASIMO) robot gave its first demonstration in 2000. The 120-cm- (47-in-) tall robot could walk, climb stairs, and recognize and grasp objects. Upgrades in 2003 made it the first two-legged robot to run in controlled fashion, later reaching a speed of 9 km/h (5.6 mph).

2002

Ice water on Mars

NASA found evidence of water ice on Mars on analysing data sent back from the Mars Odyssey space probe in orbit around the planet. The mission mapped the distribution of chemical elements on the planet and led to scientists discovering large amounts of water ice buried beneath the surface of Mars's polar regions.

Robotics
See pages 234–235

Robotics See pages 234–235

Artist's impression of polar ice caps on Mars

In October 2003, Yang Liwei became China's first astronaut, on the *Shenzhou 5* mission.

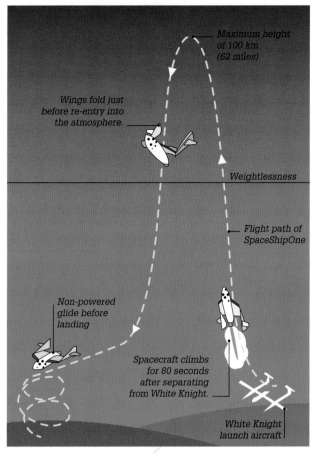

Maximum height of 100 km (62 miles)

Wings fold just before re-entry into the atmosphere.

Weightlessness

Flight path of SpaceShipOne

Non-powered glide before landing

Spacecraft climbs for 80 seconds after separating from White Knight.

White Knight launch aircraft

SpaceShipOne flight path

2004

First private human spaceflight

SpaceShipOne became the first private spacecraft to travel to the border between the atmosphere and space, at an altitude of 100 km (62 miles) above Earth. The spacecraft could hold up to three crew and passengers, and was carried to 15,000 m (49,212 ft) by the White Knight aircraft (a carrier aircraft designed to launch SpaceShipOne) before firing its own rocket motors for 80 seconds. SpaceShipOne made three flights into space and 17 flights in total.

2004

First brain-computer interface

The first patients were fitted with a prototype of the BrainGate interface – a device that detects brain activity from 96 electrodes implanted into a patient's scalp. The signals are translated by computer into instructions to control a cursor on screen, a robot arm, or a wheelchair.

2005

2003

Human Genome Project

The Human Genome Project's completion was announced in 2003. Starting in 1990, this international research effort involved sequencing and mapping the 3.2 billion base pairs (see p.199) that make up all the DNA found in the genes of human beings. Data from the Human Genome Project is used to identify important genes and investigate the genetic causes of certain diseases in order to potentially develop treatments.

The code of life
See pages
198–199

2004

Graphene

Russian-born physicists Andre Geim and Konstantin Novoselov at the University of Manchester, UK, created sheets of graphene from carbon atoms. Graphene is the world's thinnest material, yet is 200 times stronger than steel. The pair won the 2010 Nobel Prize in Physics for their work.

Carbon atoms form a lattice pattern in graphene, just one atom in thickness.

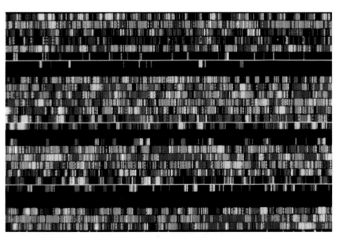

Human DNA sequence displayed as a series of coloured bands

❝With one gram of graphene you can cover several football pitches❞

Andre Geim, on graphene, October 2010

2005 ▶ 2010

📢 Launched in 2006, Blu-ray optical discs could hold up to 10 times the amount of data of a regular DVD.

Artist's impression of Eris

2005

Eris discovered

American astronomers discovered Eris, a rocky body that orbits the Sun beyond Neptune and which was thought to be larger than Pluto. The following year, the International Astronomical Union (IAU) changed Pluto to the status of dwarf planet – a group that includes Eris as well as the asteroid Ceres.

2006

First trials of Argus II prosthetic eye

The prosthetic, or artificial, eye called Argus II features a camera that captures images, which are relayed as signals to tiny electrodes implanted in the retina (light-sensitive layer) at the back of a person's impaired eye. There, the signals stimulate the retinal cells to send signals from the eye down the optic nerve to the brain, enabling sight.

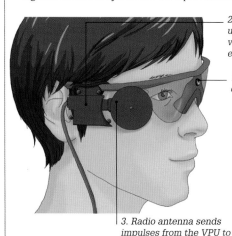

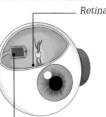

2. Video processor unit (VPU) converts visual data into electrical impulses.

1. Tiny video camera captures the view ahead.

Retina

3. Radio antenna sends impulses from the VPU to an implant inside the eye.

4. Electrode implant receives impulses and stimulates retinal cells.

⏩ **2005**

2005

First partial face transplant

French surgeon Dr Bernard Devauchelle and his team performed the first partial face transplant in Amiens, France, on Isabelle Dinoire, who was attacked and badly disfigured by her dog. The surgical team replaced much of her nose, mouth, and cheeks in a successful and ground-breaking operation.

Cross-section of Airbus 380

Aircraft has a wingspan of 79.8 m (261.6 ft).

2007

Airbus A380-800

The first Airbus A380-800 – the world's biggest airliner – was delivered to Singapore Airlines. The aircraft features two passenger decks that can carry up to 853 passengers in all-economy seating, and has a maximum take-off weight of 575 tonnes.

Approximately 25 per cent of the aircraft's structure is made from carbon-fibre-reinforced plastic.

First-class seats recline into beds.

6.5-m- (21-ft-) wide main deck can hold rows of up to ten economy seats.

Four large turbofan engines give a maximum range of 15,400 km (9,600 miles).

Artist's impression of wave power machines
used in the Aguçadoura wave farm

2009

Kepler space observatory is launched

The Kepler space observatory monitors thousands of stars in the Milky Way for signs of exoplanets (planets that orbit stars other than the Sun). Kepler uses a photometer, a device that measures the intensity of light, to detect variations in a star's brightness caused by an exoplanet passing in front of it while orbiting the star. Within its first seven years, more than 1,280 exoplanets were detected.

2008

First commercial wave farm

The Aguçadoura Wave Farm opened 5 km (3 miles) off the coast of Portugal. It features three wave-power machines – 120-m- (394-ft-) long, hinged cylinders with joints between sections. The up and down movement of the sections caused by waves is harnessed to drive generators, which produce electricity.

2009

Titanoboa fossils discovered

A scientific expedition discovered fossilized remains in La Guajira, Colombia, of 28 giant snakes that lived about 60 million years ago. The species, named *Titanoboa cerrejonensis*, measured as long as 14 m (46 ft), with the biggest individuals estimated to have weighed more than 1,100 kg (2,425 lb). *Titanoboa* had jaws large enough to swallow a whole adult crocodile.

2010

Taking to the skies
See pages 162–163

The first Apple iPhone was launched in 2007 complete with a multi-touch touchscreen.

2008 LARGE HADRON COLLIDER

The Large Hadron Collider (LHC) is a 27-km- (17-mile-) long, artificial underground tunnel on the French-Swiss border. It was completed in 2008. More than 6,000 electromagnets accelerate protons around the LHC at close to the speed of light. These protons collide at four locations within the LHC, and the collisions are analysed by four major instruments: ALICE, CMS, LHC-b, and ATLAS (see pp.240–241).

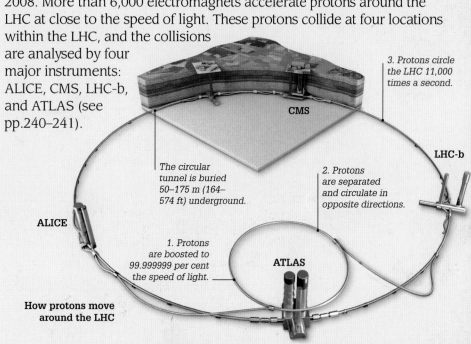

3. Protons circle the LHC 11,000 times a second.

CMS

LHC-b

The circular tunnel is buried 50–175 m (164–574 ft) underground.

2. Protons are separated and circulate in opposite directions.

ALICE

1. Protons are boosted to 99.999999 per cent the speed of light.

ATLAS

How protons move around the LHC

"... there is 95% of the Universe still unknown to us. We have to find out what it is."

Rolf-Dieter Heuer, Director General of CERN

A smashing time

At the heart of the world's most complex set of physics experiments is the ATLAS detector, a part of CERN's Large Hadron Collider (LHC) – a gigantic and powerful machine called a particle accelerator. Huge electromagnets inside the LHC accelerate beams of protons (positively charged particles in atoms) to 99.999999 per cent of the speed of light. The protons smash into one another with unimaginable force, generating more than a billion collisions and interactions per second. ATLAS monitors the results of these collisions, seeking out unknown particles and phenomena. It was instrumental in the 2012 discovery of the Higgs boson particle (see p.243).

The ATLAS detector is 25 m (82 ft) in diameter and weighs nearly 7,000 tonnes, almost as much as the Eiffel Tower.

> **"The structure is so fine that it is 99.99 per cent air."**
>
> Tobias Schaedler (of HRL Laboratories),
> on microlattice, November 2011

2010   *SOLAR IMPULSE*

Taking off from Payerne Air Base in Switzerland, *Solar Impulse* became the first solar-powered aircraft to complete a non-stop flight lasting for more than 24 hours. It travelled 26 hours in total before landing back where it started. The flight was the longest and, at a maximum altitude of 8,700 m (28,543 ft), the highest made by a manned solar aircraft.

Solar Impulse in flight

André Borschberg
In 2015, Borschberg, a co-founder of the Solar Impulse project, made a non-stop flight of 117 hours and 52 minutes in *Solar Impulse 2*, the next craft in the series.

2011

Ultra-light material

An American company called HRL Laboratories produced the world's first metallic microlattice material. An alloy of the metals phosphorus and nickel, it consists of a network of hollow struts that interconnect with each other. It is so light that a 10-cm (4-in) square cube of the material weighs less than 1 g (0.035 oz) and may become a valuable material in aerospace.

2010

2010

iPad launched

Apple's first tablet computer, the iPad, went on sale. The original iPad had no camera, but subsequent models featured front and rear-facing cameras able to take still photos and video footage. More than 300 million iPads have since been sold.

A connected world
See pages 228–229

2010

Jetpack debuts

In 2010, a prototype of Martin Aircraft's Jetpack went on sale. The world's first personal vertical take-off and landing (VTOL) craft, the Jetpack does not use a jet engine. Instead, a petrol-fuelled, 200-horsepower engine spins two ducted fans to lift a person to heights of more than 2,300 m (7,546 ft).

 In 2011, IBM's Watson supercomputer defeated two human contestants on the *Jeopardy!* quiz show.

2012

Deepsea Challenger

Canadian film director James Cameron piloted a submersible called the *Deepsea Challenger* to a depth of 10,908 m (35,787 ft) below sea level. The 7.3-m- (24-ft-) tall craft took two hours and 37 minutes to dive from sea level to the bottom of Challenger Deep – the deepest known point in the Pacific Ocean.

LED panel lights depths up to 30 m (98 ft) away.

Upper structure contains more than 1,000 lithium-ion batteries.

Pilot fits inside sphere made of 6.4-cm- (2.5-in-) thick steel.

Mobile boom carries a powerful spotlight and 3-D cameras.

2012

Higgs Boson

In July, scientists working at the Large Hadron Collider discovered the Higgs boson. This elusive particle proved the existence of the Higgs field, which had been predicted but never proven in the past. The existence of the Higgs field solves the mystery of how individual subatomic particles have mass.

A smashing time
See pages 240–241

2014

Rosetta reaches comet

After a ten-and-a-half year journey from Earth, the European Space Agency's Rosetta space probe went into orbit around Comet 67P/Churyumov–Gerasimenko. The probe launched a lander named Philae, which made the first ever soft landing on a comet and sent back measurements from its surface.

Artist's impression of the Philae lander on the surface of Comet 67P

2015

2012

Curiosity on Mars

NASA's Curiosity rover arrived on Mars after a 563-million-km (350-million-mile) journey. The 899-kg (1,982-lb) rover was 78 times the weight of the Sojourner rover from 1997. Curiosity also included 80 kg (176 lb) of scientific instruments for studying Martian weather, soil, rocks, and radiation, and looking for potential water sources as well as signs of life in the past.

2014

Nanomotor

A team led by American inventor Dr Donglei Fan at the University of Texas, USA, produced the world's smallest motor (see p.245). This nanomotor is about 500 times smaller than a grain of salt. Future models could deliver drugs directly into individual body cells.

 In 2012, after 35 years in space, Voyager 1 became the first space probe to travel beyond the Solar System.

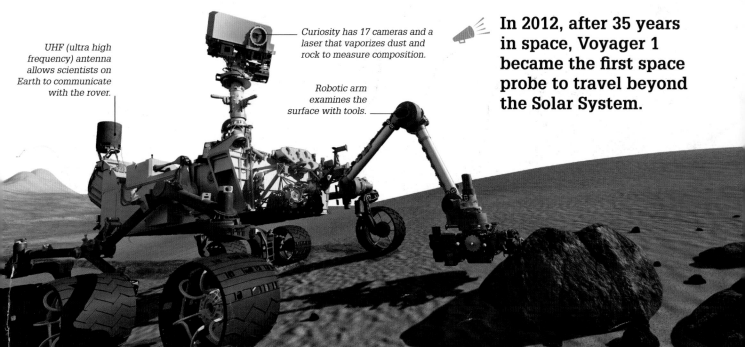

UHF (ultra high frequency) antenna allows scientists on Earth to communicate with the rover.

Curiosity has 17 cameras and a laser that vaporizes dust and rock to measure composition.

Robotic arm examines the surface with tools.

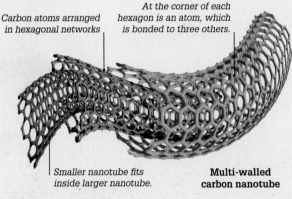

This wood ant measures 4 million nanometres in length.

Nanotechnology

Nanotechnology is the science and engineering of working at a scale utterly invisible to the human eye. A nanometre (nm) is a billionth of a metre – so there are a billion nanometres in one metre. To convey just how tiny nanometres are, this book page is around 100,000 nm thick. Working at such a scale is still in its infancy and mostly at the research stage, but future advances could have enormous impacts on materials science, medicine, robotics, and computing.

Nanoscale

The nanoscale is usually thought of in the range of 1 to 100 nanometres (nm). Objects within the nanoscale include viruses, the width of DNA strands, and many molecules, while a single hydrogen atom is approximately 0.1 nm across.

> **"It is a staggeringly small world that is below."**
>
> Richard Feynman, US physicist in his lecture *There's Plenty of Room at the Bottom*, 1959

Carbon atoms arranged in hexagonal networks

At the corner of each hexagon is an atom, which is bonded to three others.

Smaller nanotube fits inside larger nanotube.

Multi-walled carbon nanotube

Nanomaterials

Materials constructed at the nanoscale can have valuable properties such as great strength, lightness, the ability to repel water or bacteria, or to conduct electricity or heat extremely well. Carbon nanotubes (cylinders of carbon atoms), for example, are much lighter than steel but more than 100 times stronger.

Nanoparticles

Particles at the nanoscale have been added to substances to alter their properties in some way. Titanium dioxide nanoparticles, for example, help to block harmful UV (ultraviolet) rays but do not reflect visible light. They are used in transparent sunscreen lotions.

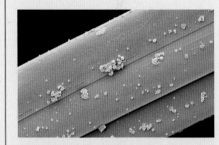

Silver nanoparticles

These nanoparticles can repel and kill bacteria, making them useful in anti-microbial wound dressings (left). They are also used in some sports shoes to kill bacteria that can cause odours.

Titanium dioxide nanoparticles

This air-purifying unit contains nanoparticles of titanium dioxide. When sprayed, they react with UV radiation and water in the air, to break down pollutants.

Key events

1959

American physicist Richard Feynman gave a pioneering early lecture entitled *There's Plenty of Room at the Bottom*. It focused on engineering and technology that could "arrange the atoms the way we want".

1974

The term nanotechnology was used for the first time by Tokyo Science University's Professor Norio Taniguchi to describe working with materials at an atomic scale. It was popularized in the USA by American engineer Eric Drexler.

1989

American scientists Don Eigler and Erhard Schweizer at IBM manipulated 35 atoms of the element xenon using a scanning tunnelling microscope to spell out the IBM logo.

1991

Japanese professor Sumio Iijima publicized carbon nanotubes in a scientific paper. These cylinders are strong, light, and excellent conductors of electricity.

Scanning tunnelling microscope moving atoms

Carbon buckyball acts as a wheel, allowing car to roll across a surface of gold.

Nanomachines

Materials such as graphene (see p.237) and buckyballs (see p.222) can be used to build working machines at the nanoscale. In 2005, researchers at Rice University, Texas, USA, made a nanocar out of polymer and carbon molecules. Measuring under 4 nm, the car moved when the surface it rested on was heated above 200°C (392°F).

Nanopatterning

This process uses a tiny probe around 100,000 times smaller than a pencil point. It is heated to around 1,000°C (1,830°F) to melt a sheet of plastic polymer in order to sculpt a design. In 2014, nanopatterning produced the world's smallest magazine cover (left), small enough for 2,000 copies of the cover to fit on a grain of salt. Future computer parts may be produced using this technique.

National Geographic Kids magazine cover is just 11 micrometres (11,000 nm) wide, magnified to about 4,400 times here

Nanobot carries drug in reservoir, which it injects into cell via a retractable needle.

Infected cells in the bloodstream are found by nanobots using biosensors.

Legs attach to and grip infected cell.

Nanobots

Large numbers of robots constructed at the nanoscale may perform invaluable jobs in the future. Their tasks may range from measuring and repairing materials from the inside or tackling pollution at a molecular level. Medical nanobots may be injected into the human body to combat disease and other health problems, such as scrubbing blood vessels free of fatty deposits.

Artist's impression of medical nanobots providing targeted delivery of drugs directly to cells infected with disease

Nanomotor

2003

The world's smallest guitar was made by scientists at Cornell University, USA. Its strings measure 150–200 nm in width and vibrate at frequencies 130,000 times higher than a real guitar.

Nanoguitar

2008

French physicist Albert Fert and German physicist Peter Grünberg won the Nobel Prize for using metal layers a few atoms thick to discover giant magnetoresistance (GMR). GMR is used to build very high capacity hard disk drives.

2013

Harvard and Illinois University researchers produced batteries smaller than 1 mm (0.04 in) using 3-D printing. Even tinier batteries may be crucial in powering devices such as nanobots.

2014

A nanomotor small enough to fit inside a single human cell was built by a University of Texas team led by American inventor Dr Donglei Fan (see p.243).

2015 onwards

2015

Faster gene editing

The CRISPR-Cas9 tool was developed by US researchers to allow scientists to edit genes of living things and swap parts of a genome (complete set of inherited information stored in each of an organism's cells) in and out faster and more accurately than before. Using CRISPR-Cas9, scientists developed a mosquito that was resistant to catching the parasite that causes the disease malaria.

2015

New human ancestor

A new hominid (early human) species was described and named *Homo naledi*. Extensive fossil remains of this previously unknown human ancestor were found in the dolomite rock of the Rising Star cave system in South Africa in 2013. Around 1,500 fossil fragments of some 15 different individuals were recovered. This human ancestor stood an estimated 150-cm (59-in) tall, walked on two legs, and is thought to have lived about two million years ago.

IVF pups

In 2015, seven puppies became the first "test-tube" dogs to be born as a result of IVF (in vitro fertilization), in which male sperm cells fertilize female egg cells in a laboratory. Other species may be created in the same way.

One of the seven puppies born after IVF research at Cornell University, New York, USA

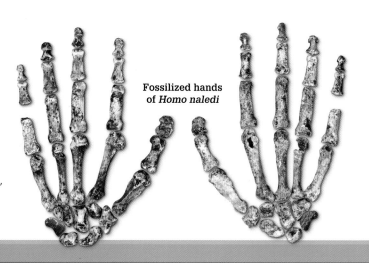

Fossilized hands of *Homo naledi*

2015

2015

First photos of Pluto

After a nine-year journey, NASA's New Horizons space probe finally reached the dwarf planet Pluto. It sent back the first detailed images of Pluto and its moon, Charon. They revealed a more varied landscape than expected, including mountain ranges, ice volcanoes, dunes, and nitrogen ice fields.

Pluto as seen by the New Horizons space probe

2015

Evidence of water on Mars

NASA announced evidence that liquid water may have flowed on Mars under present conditions. This stemmed from findings by NASA's Mars Reconnaissance Orbiter probe that revealed streaks on some slopes on the Martian surface, which may have been made by salty liquid water.

Mars Reconnaissance Orbiter

2015

New antibiotic

Teixobactin, the first new type of antibiotic in more than 20 years, was recovered from soil bacteria. A team at Northeastern University in Boston, USA, used an electronic chip to grow microbes in soil and then isolated their antibiotic chemical compounds.

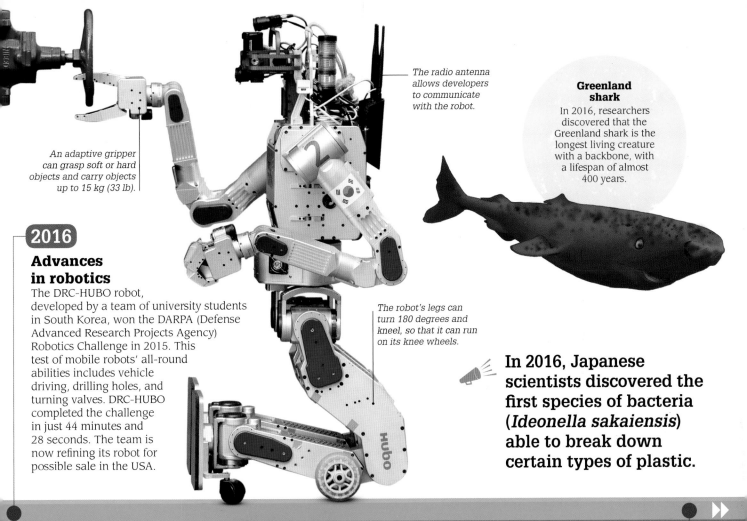

The radio antenna allows developers to communicate with the robot.

An adaptive gripper can grasp soft or hard objects and carry objects up to 15 kg (33 lb).

Greenland shark
In 2016, researchers discovered that the Greenland shark is the longest living creature with a backbone, with a lifespan of almost 400 years.

2016

Advances in robotics

The DRC-HUBO robot, developed by a team of university students in South Korea, won the DARPA (Defense Advanced Research Projects Agency) Robotics Challenge in 2015. This test of mobile robots' all-round abilities includes vehicle driving, drilling holes, and turning valves. DRC-HUBO completed the challenge in just 44 minutes and 28 seconds. The team is now refining its robot for possible sale in the USA.

The robot's legs can turn 180 degrees and kneel, so that it can run on its knee wheels.

In 2016, Japanese scientists discovered the first species of bacteria (*Ideonella sakaiensis*) able to break down certain types of plastic.

2016

Oculus Rift

The Oculus Rift virtual reality headset was released by an American company called Oculus. Designed to offer an immersive experience for gaming, architecture, and design, the headset displays two 1,080 × 1,200 pixel high-resolution images that a set of lenses focus and reshape for each of the user's eyes to create a 3-D picture.

Gamer uses Oculus Rift headset

2018

James Webb Space Telescope

This successor to the Hubble Space Telescope will be launched in 2018. The James Webb Space Telescope (JWST) will feature an infrared instrument that can observe 100 different objects simultaneously. The telescope will possess seven times the light gathering area of the Hubble via its giant 6.5-m- (21.3-ft-) wide primary mirror made up of 18 separate segments that unfold after launch.

This primary mirror is made up of 18 gold-coated, beryllium reflector panels.

2016

Thin solar cell

In 2016, scientists at MIT (Massachusetts Institute of Technology), USA, produced a solar cell about ¹⁄₅₀th the thickness of a human hair. It is light enough to sit on a soap bubble without popping it.

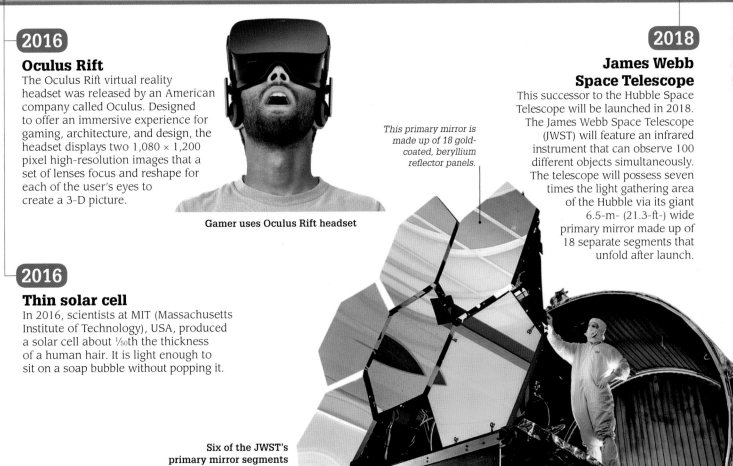

Six of the JWST's primary mirror segments

Glossary
and Index

Glossary

alchemy
An ancient branch of *chemistry*, which aimed to change ordinary metals into gold.

alloy
A material made by mixing a metal with small amounts of other metals or nonmetals.

antibiotic
A medical drug that kills or slows down the growth of *bacteria*.

antiseptic
A medical drug that kills disease-causing *microbes*. Antiseptics may be applied to the skin to prevent infection.

astronomy
The study of objects in space. An astronomer is a scientist who studies objects in space.

atom
The smallest part of an *element* that has the characteristics of that *element*.

bacteria
A group of single-celled *microbes*, some of which cause disease.

battery
A portable *electricity* supply that stores electric charge using *chemicals*.

biology
A branch of science concerned with living organisms. A biologist is a scientist who studies living things.

black hole
An object in space with a *gravity* so strong that no *matter* or light can escape it.

boiling point
The temperature at which a liquid changes into gas.

bonds
The attraction between *atoms* or groups of *atoms* that holds them together in a *molecule*.

breeding
The mating of two animals to produce offspring.

buoyancy
The upward *force* on an object in a liquid, caused by the water pressure underneath it.

carbohydrate
A *chemical compound*, found in starchy foods such as rice and bread, which gives us *energy*.

cell
The basic unit from which all living organisms are made.

chemical
A substance made from *elements* or *compounds*.

chemistry
A branch of science concerned with the composition of *chemicals* and how they react with each other. A chemist is a scientist who studies *chemicals* and their reactions.

circuit
A path along which *electricity* flows around. All electrical and electronic things have circuits inside them.

climate change
Long-term changes in Earth's weather patterns, resulting from global environmental variations or human activity.

cloning
The process of creating an organism from a body cell of another organism, so they are genetically identical.

combustion
A *chemical* reaction in which a fuel, such as wood or coal, burns with oxygen from the air to release heat *energy*.

compound
A *chemical* made by combining the *atoms* or *molecules* of two or more different *elements*.

condensation
The change of gas or vapour into a liquid.

conservation
The preservation of any process, object, or life.

continent
One of Earth's large land masses, such as Africa.

crankshaft
A rod in a car's *engine* that changes the up and down motion of a *piston* into a rotating motion that turns the car's wheels.

diode
An electronic component that allows an electric current to flow through a *circuit* in only one direction.

dissection
Cutting open of a dead body to study its internal structure.

DNA
Deoxyribonucleic acid. The *chemical* inside chromosomes that lets parents pass genetic information on to their offspring.

electricity
A type of *energy* caused by *electrons* inside *atoms*. Static electricity is made by *electrons* building up in one place, while current electricity happens when *electrons* move around.

electrode
An electrical contact, made from a conductor, that connects the main part of a *circuit* to something outside it, such as the *chemicals* in a *battery*.

electromagnet
A magnet that produces a *magnetic field* because of *electricity*.

electron
A subatomic particle with a negative charge found in an *atom's nucleus*.

element
A basic building block of *matter* made from identical *atoms*.

endangered
A *species* of plant or animal that is at risk of getting *extinct*.

energy
A property of an object that allows it to do something now or in the future. Types of energy include kinetic energy (movement energy) and potential energy (stored energy).

engine
A mechanical device that provides power.

enzyme
A substance that living things use to speed up *chemical* reactions inside them.

evaporation
The change of a liquid into a gas or vapour.

evolution
The process by which *species* change over many generations.

extinct
A *species* that has completely died out.

filament
The part of a light bulb that glows when an electric current flows through it.

food chain
A series of organisms, each of which are consumed by the next.

force
A pushing or pulling action that changes an object's speed, direction of movement, or shape.

fossil
Remains of plants and animals that have been preserved in Earth's crust, or outer layer.

freezing point
The temperature at which a liquid turns into a solid.

frequency
A measurement of how often a wave of *energy* moves up and down.

friction
The rubbing *force* between two things that move past one another. Friction slows things down and generates heat.

galaxy
A large group of *stars*, dust, and gas held together by the *force* of *gravity*.

gear
One of a pair of wheels of different sizes, with teeth cut into their edges, that turn together to increase the speed or *force* of a machine.

genetics
The study of genes – the parts of a *cell* that control the growth and appearance of living things.

geophysicist
A physicist who studies Earth and its environment.

global warming
The rise in Earth's temperature that is affecting the world's weather, causing droughts and severe storms.

gravity
The *force* that attracts all objects. On Earth, it is responsible for making objects fall downwards and for giving things weight.

habitat
The place where a plant or an animal normally lives.

heredity
The passing of characteristics through generations.

hormone
A *chemical* in the bloodstream that controls a function of the body.

insulator
A substance that reduces the flow of heat.

Internet
A network that allows computers across the world to exchange information.

latitude
Measurement of how far north or south an object is from the Equator. The Equator is an imaginary line that runs horizontally around the middle of Earth.

lens
A curved, transparent piece of plastic or glass that can bend light rays to make something look bigger, smaller, closer, or further away.

lever
A rod balanced on a pivot that can increase the size of a pushing, pulling, or turning *force*.

light year
The distance light travels in a year. One light year is about 9.5 trillion km (6 trillion miles).

longitude
Measurement of how far east or west of the Prime Meridian an object is. The Prime Meridian is an imaginary line that runs from the North Pole, via Greenwich, England, to the South Pole. Longitude lines run from north to south.

magnetic field
The invisible patterns of *force* that stretch around a magnet.

magnetism
A *force* that can attract or repel certain metals.

mammals
Warm-blooded vertebrates that give birth to young who feed on their mother's milk.

mass
The amount of *matter* that an object contains.

matter
The material which everything around us is made of.

melting point
The temperature at which a solid changes into a liquid.

microbe
A living thing that can be seen only through a microscope. *Bacteria* are the most common type of microbe. Also called micro-organism.

molecule
The smallest amount of a *compound*, consisting of two or more *atoms* bonded together.

motor
A machine that uses *electricity* and *magnetism* to produce spinning movement or movement in a straight line.

neutron
A subatomic particle with no electric charge found in an *atom*'s *nucleus*.

nucleus
The central part of an *atom*, made of *protons* and *neutrons*.

observatory
A building from where astronomers study space.

patent
A government document that grants sole rights to a person to make, use, and/or sell an invention.

pesticide
A substance used to destroy insects and other pests of crop.

philosophy
The study of ideas such as knowledge, reality, nature and existence of life, and mind.

photocell
An electronic device that generates *electricity* using light.

physics
The study of science relating primarily to *energy* and *matter*. A physicist is a scientist who studies the relation between *matter* and *energy*.

piston
A round metal part that fits tightly inside a cylinder and moves back and forwards.

pollution
Damage caused to the environment by dirty or poisonous substances or *chemicals*.

protein
A vital nutrient that helps the body build new *cells*.

proton
A subatomic particle with a positive charge found in an *atom*'s *nucleus*.

radiometric dating
Measuring the amount of radioactive substances in an object to find out its age.

radio waves
A type of *energy* that travels in waves, and can be used to send information, especially sound.

reproduction
The process of creating offspring.

Solar System
The region of space that includes the Sun, the planets and their moons, and other bodies in space whose movements are affected by the Sun's *gravity*.

species
A group of organisms that look alike and can breed mainly with one another.

star
A celestial body that releases *energy* from the nuclear reactions in its core.

theory
An explanation of facts or phenomena based on observation or experiments.

vaccine
Precautionary medical treatment that stops an individual from contracting a disease.

vacuum
An empty space from where air and all other substances have been removed.

viruses
Microbes that multiply by infecting living *cells*, often causing disease.

vitamin
A *chemical compound* that the body needs for growth and development.

►►Index

Acknowledgements

Dorling Kindersley would like to thank: Helen Peters for the index; Polly Goodman for proofreading; Rupa Rao, Esha Banerjee, and Priyaneet Singh for editorial assistance; Mansi Agrawal, Nidhi Rastogi, Roshni Kapur, and Meenal Goel for design assistance; Arun Pottirayil for assistance with illustrations; Vishal Bhatia for technical assistance; and Ashwin Adimari, Subhadeep Biswas, Deepak Negi, and Nishwan Rasool for picture research assistance.

The publisher would like to thank the following for their kind permission to reproduce their photographs:

(Key: a-above; b-below/bottom; c-centre; f-far; l-left; r-right; t-top)

1 Dorling Kindersley: The Science Museum, London (c). **Dreamstime.com:** Andreykuzmin (t). **2 Alamy Stock Photo:** Zev Radovan/BibleLandPictures (crb). **The Trustees of the British Museum:** (cr). **3 Dorling Kindersley:** The Science Museum, London (c). **Dreamstime.com:** Andreykuzmin (ca); Alexei Sysoev (fcr); Olha Rohulya (clb). **Getty Images:** Krzysztof Kwiatkowski/E+ (crb, crb/plugs). **iStockphoto.com:** Benjamin Albiach GalA'n (cb). **6 Alamy Stock Photo:** Werner Forman Archive/Heritage Image Partnership Ltd (clb); Peter Horree (tl). **Dorling Kindersley:** The University of Aberdeen (cb). **Dreamstime.com:** Nickolayv (c). **6–7 akg-images:** Erich Lessing (c). **Dreamstime.com:** Rhombur (Background). **7 Alamy Stock Photo:** View Stock China (cra). **Getty Images:** De Agostini Picture Library (b). **8 Alamy Stock Photo:** Werner Forman Archive/Heritage Image Partnership Ltd (bc). **9 123RF.com:** Peter Vrabel (tr). **Alamy Stock Photo:** Peter Horree (c); The Natural History Museum (clb). **Getty Images:** Danita Delimont (b). **10 Press Association Images:** Martin Mejia/AP (cb). **10–11 123RF.com:** antonel (t/Aged Paper). **11 Rex by Shutterstock:** Universal History Archive / UIG (crb). **12 The Trustees of the British Museum:** (tr). **Getty Images:** Egyptian/Deir el-Medina, Thebes, Egypt (bl). **13 Alamy Stock Photo:** hwo/imageBROKER (bl). **Dorling Kindersley:** The University of Aberdeen (tl). **Getty Images:** Dea Picture Library (bc). **14–15 Science Photo Library:** Javier Trueba/Msf. **16 Alamy Stock Photo:** dpa picture alliance archive (tr). **Getty Images:** Peter Hayman/The Trustees of the British Museum (cra). **Dreamstime.com:** Witr (bc). **Getty Images:** Universal History Archive (clb). **17 Alamy Stock Photo:** Gianni Dagli Orti/The Art Archive (bl). **18–19 akg-images:** Erich Lessing (cb). **Alamy Stock Photo:** Liu Xiaofeng/TAO Images Limited (b). **18 Getty Images:** Dea/A. Dagli Orti (bl). **19 Alamy Stock Photo:** Dea/A. Dagli Orti (tl). **Getty Images:** Leemage (br); Zev Radovan/BibleLandPictures (tc). **Dorling Kindersley:** Peter Hayman/The Trustees of the British Museum (tr). **20 Alamy Stock Photo:** Werner Forman Archive/Heritage Image Partnership Ltd (bl). **Getty Images:** Dea Picture Library (cla). **Wellcome Images http://creativecommons.org/licenses/by/4.0/:** (crb). **20–21 Getty Images:** Dea/G. Dagli Orti (c). **21 Alamy Stock Photo:** andrew parker. **22–23 Getty Images:** Science & Society Picture Library (c). **23 Alamy Stock Photo:** Interfoto (cb). **Courtesy of University Archives, Columbia University in the City of New York:** Rare Book & Manuscript Library (clb). **Dorling Kindersley:** National Maritime Museum, London (cr). **34 akg-images:** Roland and Sabrina Michaud (cla). **Photoshot:** Mel Longhurst (bc). **34–35 Alamy Stock Photo:** Granger Historical Picture Archive (tr). **Wellcome Images http://creativecommons.org/licenses/by/4.0/.** **36 Alamy Stock Photo:** Sheila Terry (cr). **Wellcome Images http://creativecommons.org/licenses/by/4.0/:** (cl). **Getty Images:** Dennis Hallinan (cb). **Getty Images:** De Agostini Picture Library (cl). **SuperStock:** Interfoto (tc). **36–37 Alamy Stock Photo:** Peter Horree (c). **37 Alamy Stock Photo:** 914 collection (b). **Rex by Shutterstock:** Universal History Archive (cla). **Dorling Kindersley:** Stephen Oliver (bl). **Roshdi Rashed: Geometry and Dioptrics in Classical Islam, London, al-Furqān, 2005.:** (cr). **Wellcome Images http://creativecommons.org/licenses/by/4.0/:** Asian Collection (cla). **39 Alamy Stock Photo:** World History Archive (tl). **Getty Images:** Photo Researchers, Inc (cla). **40–41 Alamy Stock Photo:** Bettmann (bl). **Getty Images:** Walter Rawlings/robertharding (ca). **Reproduced by kind permission of the Syndics of Cambridge University Library:** (clb). **NASA:** CXC/SAO (bc). **Wellcome Images http://creativecommons.org/licenses/by/4.0/.** **43 Courtesy of University Archives, Columbia University in the City of New York:** Rare Book & Manuscript Library (crb). **Getty Images:** Bettmann (cr). **44 Alamy Stock Photo:** Prisma Archivo (clb). **Getty Images:** Cem Canbay (cla). **NASA:** Reto Stockli/Alan Nelson/Fritz Hasler (bc). **44–45 Alamy Stock Photo:** Photo Researchers. **45 Alamy Stock Photo:** Granger Historical Picture Archive (clb). **Getty Images:** Hulton Archive (cr); Science & Society Picture Library (tc). **NASA.** **46–47 Getty Images:** Universal Images Group (tc). **46**